ATTORNEY FOR THE SITUATION

Leland Hazard making a point in his Pittsburgh office.

ATTORNEY

FOR THE SITUATION

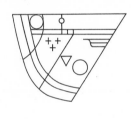

Leland Hazard

Library of Congress Catalog Card Number 74-83549
ISBN Number 0-231-03898

Published by
Carnegie-Mellon University Press

Distributed by Columbia University Press
New York—London

For Mary

Acknowledgments

Acknowledgments to the many people who have touched and made my life are in the book. What I relate of these people, including my wife Mary, in considerable part makes the book.

In the final editing for the printing Professor Joel A. Tarr made many suggestions which I gratefully accepted. His position as Professor of History and Urban Affairs at Carnegie-Mellon University gives him special competence for that contribution.

During the 10 years of the writing of this book, as in many of my other writings, Grace Couchman has been my editorial assistant, searching, verifying, and correcting the text for errors and improvement. Few men write books without such invaluable assistance.

Contents

List of Illustrations

as they follow in sequence the page indicated

Three Score and Ten

Preface

My sentient life has endured for longer than the Biblical time allotted to man. In the beginning I thought all was for the best. This was the Victorian concept: "God's in his heaven—All's right with the world." At age five in 1898 I judged that we Americans were right and the Spaniards were wrong; that Dewey was a hero at Manila Bay; and that Admiral Sampson was the real hero at Santiago because he had the same name as the strong man in Holy Writ. (The difference in spelling of the names eluded me.) In the ensuing three quarters of a century I have formed many judgments, many of them as ill-founded, I suspect, as those about the Spanish-American War.

In any case the rules of chance save me from invariable error. Furthermore, what is error in the judgment of affairs as complex and amoral as those of mankind? Finally, one who makes the pretense of autobiography should pay the penalty of judging whether his efforts and his world were worthwhile.

We men of the 20th Century have a great deal to be modest about. Two of four mighty blows which have grievously wounded our egos have fallen within my lifetime. But it was Copernicus who delivered the first blow—a long time ago (1543). Since we have never recovered from that hurt, it must be mentioned first. We are not the center of the universe; there is no up or down —no heaven or hell; no throne for God or burning place for Satan. We occupy a speck in a complex of bodies inconceivably vast— infinite—and there may be other men. We can no longer be the children—through Adam—of a God who knows only the earth. Our home is no longer special.

Darwin delivered the second blow. We are only one of many, many species of life which have evolved through time only to

xvii

die or to adapt, as we have adapted so far successfully, to an environment subject to devastating cosmic changes.

Sigmund Freud, seeking to cure our illnesses, found that none of us is free of a dark side of our natures which mocks our vaunted rationality. We can't think as straight as we thought we could.

Albert Einstein deprived us of the conviction of certainty. A yardstick, projected in motion, is not a yard in length. Seeing is no longer believing. Man must understand as well as observe. Understanding comes from unwonted thought experiments and finally from mathematical analysis beyond the grasp of all but a few men.

Just now another assault on man's ego is forming. There is no single name yet. It could be Lorenz, or Storr, or Ardrey, the interpreter. The science is biology. The field is the behavior of living things. Aggression is an ineradicable characteristic of all animals—including man. This basic aggressiveness is neutralized in animals including, probably, man, only by an external threat. No external threat, internal enmity. Ardrey's formulation is $A = E + h$, where A is amity; E is enmity, and h is hazard—external threat. The amity which an animal expresses for others of its kind will be equal to the sum of the forces of enmity and hazard which are arrayed against it.

The formula is one of the gloomiest ever proposed to man. Under it world government could not occur because in a secure world men would vent their innate aggression on each other. In secure Sweden the rate of suicide (an inverted form of aggression) is four times that of insecure Israel.

A corollary follows: man is the only animal which enjoys killing. Hitler killed nine million people in organized murder camps — six million Jews. The point is not that they were Jews but that such massive procedures of killing could be mounted with human beings as the agents. It is not enough to say that it was Hitler or Germans. He and they were human beings. No semantics will blur the naked truth. If suddenly I were on some other planet and men there asked me, "What are earth-men like?" I would have to say that in the early 1940's we killed nine million of ourselves without even the excuse of a battle front. Would they be shocked, or would they say, "Oh, we too do that."

Finally, in mid-twentieth century the computer confronts us

with the truth that it (he or she is the pronoun employed by those who associate closely with computers) can recall on the spot vastly more relevant data than even a very bright man can recall. Herbert A. Simon points cheerfully to the fact of other important human aids; writing and numbers among many, and man has happily used them all. But computer science leads in the end to the discovery—a first—of the very processes of thought, which, once discovered, can be modified, for better or for worse, by the instrument of discovery—the computer, not man.

It is no more comfort that we ourselves made the computer than that we ourselves made the "bomb." Our tools are more nearly perfect than we are; now they can act on their own initiative, and we shrink in fear.

But *do* we shrink in fear? It is popular to say so—particularly about the prospect of nuclear incineration. Yet I am one of mankind and I do not shrink in fear. My feeling is that if the bomb wipes out much of civilization — well! civilizations have been wiped out before. There were nine cities of Troy—all tumbled, lying each on top of its vanished predecessor. It was probably the seventh city from whose proud towers of Ilium Priam watched his hero son, Hector, dragged by Achilles' chariot around the walls. Do we think that our canyoned New York City will suffer a happier fate than that of Troy? Of course we do, but for no good reason. Much of California is awaiting the subterranean signal which will slip it into the Pacific. Disneyland will not be exempt.

I have known all this, or much of it, for a long time. Yet I have done my work, and more work than I needed to do to live. This book tells the story—my successes and failures. It has been over 10 years in the writing. Meanwhile much happened in my life. Hence in some cases I have updated the text and in others parenthetically inserted dates. Time flies.

PART I
In the Beginning

Work and Enterprise

My father wore sideburns, and once he owned a Prince Albert—
gained in barter with a tailor whose daughter needed tuition in
our secretarial school, known in those days as a business college.
Father was a proprietor of the school. Another fruit of his enterprise with Sir Isaac Pitman's stenography was our household help
— sometimes a young man, sometimes a young woman, usually
from a Missouri or Kansas farm, trading us work for tuition at the
"College." This was at the turn of our century.

The chores were considerable—a horse and surrey to tend, cow
to milk, and garden to work—all after Father's school hours. The
horse and surrey and the Prince Albert were for going to the
Michigan Avenue Baptist Church, where Father was a deacon
and Chairman of the Finance Committee. The cow was for milk
and butter, the latter by my doing with a wooden plunger in a
wooden churn. This device consisted of a barrel about twenty-
eight inches high bound with brass hoops, quite beautiful when
they were polished. One end of the barrel was fitted with a removable top. The plunger was a wooden rod with a Maltese cross
affixed to its lower end. One filled the churn about one-third full
of whole milk, inserted the plunger, and passed the upper end of
the rod through a hole in the removable top. After about forty-five
minutes of manual churning (up-down, up-down) my part was finished. The agitation had driven the butter fat out of the milk.
Mother would skim the floating globules out of the buttermilk,
knead out the remaining fluid, and then press the butter into a
wooden mold, which left a pattern of rosettes on the pat when it
came to the table in a covered dish of figured glass. When someone said, "Pass the butter, please," I was always sorry to see the
ruin of the handsome structure begin.

Our doctor was a dapper little homeopathist named Mark Edgerton. He looked at our tongues, thumped our chests—left hand spread over the lungs, fingers apart, thumb and middle finger of the right hand tightly joined for hammering on his own fingers—to evoke sounds, whether good or bad I could never tell, from our chests. The stethoscope had been invented years before by the French physician Laennec, who died in 1826. But. Dr. Edgerton did not seem to have one.

The doctor never failed to inveigh against the "old school." *"Similia similibus curantur"* (like cures like), he would affirm, showing himself a disciple of the German Hahnemann, the founder of homeopathy, who almost anticipated Pasteur's discovery that inoculation with a weakened virus of the disease would produce immunity. Their lives overlapped in the 19th Century.

To be sick was no problem. The doctor's little black folding case was fitted, section after section, with slender bottles each with an indistinguishable white powder. He would seem to enter into a half trance, drumming his fingers lightly on the case, trying to decide, I always thought, which bottle was like my disease. Then his hand would land on one bottle to bring it out from its dozens of fellows in the case. White papers about the size of those used for rolling cigarettes were produced from a pack and a half dozen portions of the powder were encased in clever separate self-securing folds of the papers. One powder in a half glass of water, one or two teaspoons every one, two, three hours, as the case might be—such was the delicacy of the tasteless homeopathic dose. We always got well, except my Aunt Virginia Hazard. She died of tuberculosis—a disease we then thought incurable.

Before Automation

There were plenty of vacant lots on our unpaved street, and Father knew an honest carpenter named R. R. Fisher. I was impressed with Mister Fisher (we always used the title) because he looked like the Sunday School picture of the Apostle John and because both of his initials were of the same letter.

Men, horses, plows, and hand-scoopers came to dig the basements for the houses Father would build to rent. A big plow pulled by a horse, sometimes by two horses, would break the ground. Then the hand-scoop. This was of metal shaped like a hand snow shovel with sides but about five times larger in each dimension. There were two wooden handles projecting to the rear from the sides of the shovel. Long leather straps, called tugs, were attached to rings on the sides of the shovel and to a collar around the neck of the horse. Other long straps, called reins, were attached to the bit of the bridle on the horse's head and these extended back to the hands of the man who must operate the shovel.

The man must hold the reins and also keep his hands on the handles of the shovel. Sometimes he would knot the reins together and hang them around his neck. (This was dangerous.) His first command to the horse was "git-up", meaning *go!* As the horse went the man bore down on the handles, thus causing the shovel to bite into the earth, previously loosened by the plow, and so to fill itself. The man would then bear down quickly and quite hard on the handles and the shovel would come out of the earth and, as the horse pulled, slide along the ground to some part of the premises where the earth from the basement was to be used for a fill. The emptying was simple. The man just lifted the handles high, the shovel up-ended to spill its content, which was spread out somewhat as the horse dragged the shovel over it on the way back to repeat the performance.

The horse-drawn-man-assisted scoop was our power shovel around the turn of the Century. Men seemed enough for all the great tasks. They had tools, like the pick, the shovel, the scoop. They had the horse for power. But the power shovels of today, which will take a slice of a mountain or pick up a lead pencil, were beyond our imagination.

After a while men came and put down wooden sidewalks on our street. Another day men came and dug a deep trench, and we had gas lights in our street and in our house. Then one evening, before we had pavements, our neighbor, Ettwein, a prosperous contractor in bumptious Kansas City, Missouri, came home managing the mysterious levers of a horseless carriage.

The world seemed friendly. Even Burney, our horse, was cooperative when, having climbed to a sufficient height on the manger, I put the bridle bit to his soft lips and saw how willingly he opened his huge teeth. Previously he had stood quietly while I curried him. This was done with a metal device composed of rows of shallow teeth on a backing affixed to a handle. Scraping strokes in the direction the hair lay cleaned his coat. Then the brush: it was an oval structure about eight inches long and four inches wide with stiff bristles. There was a transverse strap through which one slipped his hand. The brushing gave the coat a fine gloss. Then there were the mane and the tail to treat the same way. (Some rich people who lived on Armour Boulevard, some blocks away, docked the tails of their horses. By so removing about two-thirds of the tail, they caused the remainder to toss in the air for a spirited effect. We thought this was wrong—not nature.)

Prohibition on the Way

Our surrey had a top with fringe. We used it mostly for going on Sundays to hear the Misses Lida and Lucy Smoot tell Sunday School stories from the Bible. Miss Lida was tall, handsome, and patrician. Both she and Miss Lucy were teachers in the public school system of our town. Miss Lida taught the Sunday School kindergarten—and well enough, I am sure. It is equally certain, I now know, that we young scholars did not get a rounded picture of Old Testament characters—Jacob and Lot, for example. But how else would you do it—disclose Jacob's philandering or Lot's incest with his daughters? Yes, probably, because the glory of the Old Testament is its candor. Yet the skill for such teaching was rare in the late 19th Century—for that matter in any century yet known in our Christian civilization.

Miss Lucy was small and not pretty. One can see her type in the vigorous women of French peasant villages. How incongruously the genes dispose themselves within a single family. Miss Lucy kept the Sunday School attendance records and stood up in the general assembly after the classes to tell us how many were there and the amount of the collection and how the figures compared with the week, month, and year before. I got my first indistinct impression of the difference between the intellectual and the executive, confirmed a little later when it was Miss Lucy who became a school principal. I thought to myself, "But Miss Lida is so much the nicer of the two."

At eleven every Sunday we sat while Brother S. M. Brown preached. It was usual among Baptist folk in Western Missouri to address the minister as "brother." He was usually, as with Brother Brown, untrained—one who emphasized the sacred nature of "the call to the ministry," as compared, invidiously, with professional education. It was godly to be natural so long as we could define nature. Brother Brown inveighed against trained singing voices; sometimes he punctuated an evangelical point with a sweet tenor song—right from the pulpit. In our church we did not believe in card playing, alcoholic beverages, or dancing. One young lady was expelled for dancing. I thought this was going rather far. But, of course, others knew better.

To be saved in our church one must be baptized. On the Sunday on which the ceremony was to be performed the candidate would retire to the pastor's study there to be robed in white. Narrow steps led up and then down into a tank of water up to the chest of the sinner standing with hands crossed over the heart and at right angles to the audience on one side and Brother Brown on the other. The tank just at the rear of the pulpit platform was concealed by velvet curtains. As they were drawn back for the little drama, Brother Brown would deftly grasp the nape with his left hand and pinch the nose with his thumb and index finger while covering the mouth with the palm of his right hand. Then the neophite was tilted backward, fully immersed, body and head, then raised upright—reborn—as the curtains closed.

Immediately thereafter Brother Brown would appear at the church door—dry as a bone, a miracle, I thought, until his young son, my dear childhood friend, showed me the chest-high fishing boots which his father wore at the ducking. We thought that sprinkling or any other substitute for a complete wetting would be ineffectual, but the fishing boots were a bit of a disillusionment for me.

Father belonged to the Prohibition Party. When he was leaving us for the "College" on the morning of election day (this was in the year 1900) half way down the walk to the street he turned and said to my mother, "We (the Prohibition Party) would win today if the women could vote." It seemed to me that my mother —a buxom, handsome woman, taller than father—assented with spousely, but unconvinced, acquiesence. That night we got the election returns by flares in the sky—red for Mr. McKinley, green for Mr. Bryan. We had no telephone, nor did our neighbors. Radio was around the corner but unsuspected by us. The Kansas City *Times* for November 6, 1900, boasted that it would "give the public the election returns in an up-to-date manner . . . if the weather permits *The Times* will send up a number of balloons on election night from different parts of the two Kansas Citys. These balloons will be sent up every hour. If the returns at the hour of ascension indicate that Bryan is in the lead the balloons will carry Green signal lights. If the returns indicate that McKinley is in the lead Red signal lights will be shown. The balloons may be seen at a great distance."

We preferred Mr. Bryan, if Prohibition (John G. Woolley, 209,469 votes) could not win. The red flares for McKinley sent us to bed unhappy.

Although we were prohibitionists, we did not think well of the antics of Carry A. Nation. She began her hatchet wrecking of liquor joints in Wichita (Kansas, neighbor state to our Missouri, was "dry"). The saloons were iniquitous, we knew that. But to go after them with a hatchet—and by a lady at that—well, we were ambivalent. I began to wonder: Why could not everyone who was right be like us?

Things Change

At the Century's turn no one thought life could get any way but better. The words "social security" would have mystified us. If anyone had told Mister Fisher, Father's carpenter, that he should have unemployment compensation or get his wages guaranteed for a year, he would have delivered an incredulous snort. He expected to be "out of work" from time to time. But the world was changing. It was not just Ettwein's automobile. Queen Victoria died. Father looked solemn the evening he brought us the news. I knew that some mooring of our time had been carried away.

Mr. Barnes, whose greenhouse was only a block away, got a telephone. The last of the horse-drawn street car lines had given up in favor of the cable cars. This innovation in public transportation scotched my ambition to get a horse job for Burney and the driver's job for me on a street car. But the prospect of becoming gripman on a cable car remained open.

The gripman was a magnificent figure. He can still be seen in romantic San Francisco. But nothing in that city ever matched the precipitous open trestle which carried the cars from the top

The house that father built, Kansas City, Missouri. 1874.

Mother.

Father.

of the Missouri River bluff, known as Kansas City's Quality Hill, to the union station in the river valley below. If one had a favored seat near the gripman in the leading grip car he could see the moving continuous cable below in the open trestle work, the great claws, known as "the grip", which the gripman could attach to or detach from the swift moving cable by great lever thrusts forward or backward, and the brakeman at the rear furiously grinding the wheel which set the screaming brakes as the open car and its open trailers paused for the passengers to take a deep breath before the dizzy descent.

Even the cable cars were giving way to electric cars. Edwin Ruthven Weeks, Managing Director of the Electric Light Company, pressed Edison's inventions hard in our "cow-town", a nickname given to us because cattle slaughtering, butchering, and meat packing were so important to Kansas City. A strong west wind always reminded the city of its then most important industry.

Edwin Ruthven Weeks, pioneer that he was in urban electrification, believed that man should never attempt to fly. "It's against nature," he said. And he was opposed to electrocution as a means of capital punishment. In his old age he told me that in the electric chair the victim's motor nerves are instantly killed but that his sensory nerves register a million agonies—against which the sufferer cannot cry out—before total death comes. In 1899 Weeks received the award of Doctor of Mercy from a World Convention.

The Persistent Village

Harrisburg was a wide place in the road at the close of the 19th Century. So it is today—1970 population, less than 200. But it was the entirely adequate metropolis which served my grandmother's farm one mile south in Boone County, Missouri. The trip from Kansas City was for men only. Father and I would leave by train in the afternoon and arrive about one the next morning at Higbee or Sturgeon, where a livery team and driver were waiting in the dark to take us the twenty miles or so to Harrisburg, which, for reasons never satisfactorily explained to me, the railroads had missed. Then the last mile of the long night drive, south to breakfast.

The night passage—it is remarkable how much can be seen in the dark out of doors—carried us through dirt roads, sometimes muddy, sometimes thick with dust, and sometimes firm but with a resilience which seemed to give the eight trotting hoofs extra speed. The sense of speed was due in part to the nearness of the dense woods of scrub oak tightly bordering the narrow, winding road. That oak, more properly known as black jack oak, grows only 20 to 30 feet high and is the mark of poor soil. We passed few farm houses but the whippoorwills accompanied our nocturnal venture.

There was conversation on the drive. What happens when an irresistible force meets an immovable body? If a tree crashes to earth in the forest but no man is present to hear, is there a sound? But as Robert Louis Stevenson said in an essay all such questions are to be answered with a good meal and a bottle of wine. Of course we did not have the wine but there is a ham, special to this day to Boone County and the adjoining Cole County, product of the smoke house and age, wine dark, its meat compact as a nut —pungent ambrosia. This and enough eggs and buttered hot biscuits to supply cholesterol for life were the reward for the night journey.

For a small boy the jobs on the farm were not of equal interest. The wheat cradle was a frame of wood attached to a scythe and holding above the scythe wooden fingers running parallel to the curved blade of the scythe. The gleaming sharp edge on its long handle, cradle fingers flashing the sheen of many seasons' cuttings, must be foregone by me. It was for a man. And the man, as he bit the blade into the russet grain, was a sight of beauty. As the blade cut the grain it would fall in perfect order onto the fingers of the cradle. Then on his backswing the man would deposit the stalks in a neat swath on the ground, meanwhile stepping forward for the next stroke—again and again from morning to sunset.

My job was simpler: to gather each swath into a bundle, then with the bundle in the left arm, to select a dozen or so of the longest stalks and tie them in a simple knot around the bundle, giving it a tight, small waist, causing the root stems to spread and the rich grain heads to nestle together. The result was called a sheaf—exactly the kind which bowed to Joseph in his dream and got him into trouble with his brothers.

To make a shock of the sheaves was also my job. Following the cradler, one would carry his sheaves forward to an estimated point, then plant one firmly upright, leaning the others against it —tent-like. It remained then to tie the bundles ahead, carry them back to complete the shock of a dozen or so sheaves. The final operation gave a pleasure such as the architects of the Parthenon or the Pantheon must have experienced. The final sheaf in hand, one would place it across the left elevated thigh, break the stalks with a sharp blow of the right arm, and then place this right-angled sheaf across the top of the shock. This was called the cap. Its function was to keep the shock dry—a rain hood.

Inexorable Mechanization

But the McCormick reaper was driving the cradle to the museum. This machine consisted of two iron wheels, an axle with gear mechanism to activate a sickle bar extending to the right, and a tongue for the horses. The reaper was drawn by two horses or mules, driven by a man who sat in an iron bucket seat mounted on a single leaf of gently bouncing spring. The swath now became, instead of the amount cut at one stroke of the cradle, the space of the bite of the sickle bar into the grain as the man guided the machine along the four sides of the ever diminishing stand of wheat. Now the swath was continuous.

Gathering of the wheat behind the reaper involved *hands and feet*. Moving at right angles to the stalks, one shuffled his feet under them, pushing them forward into a bunch by a series of abbreviated foot movements. Once the feet had made the bunch, the tying, carrying, and shocking were as with the cradle.

It took two boys (my cousin, Roscoe Hazard, and me) to keep up with the reaper. And there was a psychological difference. We felt a hostility to the machine which was absent when the cradler mowed. When the machine broke down, that was no more than our due for rest.

The gathering and shocking, despite all the work, were only for intermediate storage. Before summer passed, the steam-driven threshing machine, owned by an enterprising member of the community, would arrive. Then the shocks, so carefully architectured, would be pitched onto wagons, hauled to the thresher, and pitched into the thresher mow to emerge, grains of wheat rolling into sacks from a spout on one side, stalks blown up and out from the other side to make a mountainous stack of straw. I felt about the shocks as I did about the butter pat so carefully made in our kitchen. It seemed a shame to ruin them.

Technics and Beauty

The position on the farm for which I worked and sought most assiduously was that of rider on one of the mules of the long-tine rake. This was a structure about twelve feet wide, its tines extending forward about the same distance. Drawn by two mules, one hitched to a singletree extending from each side of the rake, the device gathered hay in essentially the same fashion as one gathered wheat by foot.

The mules, each guided by a rider, would pull the rake forward, its tines running under the mown hay. Soon the hay covered the rake in a conical pile. Then the riders would reverse the mules to pull the rake from under the pile of hay and so repeat the process time and time again all day long.

Men would pitch the piles onto wagons which carried the hay to the big barn, so constructed that a man's fork could lift its load of hay to the floor level of the mow. Another man in the mow would pitch the hay further in and a boy had the job of tramping (we said "tromping") it down. This was one of the less attractive jobs. Prickly bits of the timothy got down my sweaty neck and back. But in the coming winter the horses, mules, and cattle in the stalls below could eat.

A tine detached from the rake and standing erect on its base, its edges rounded, its grass and earth polished entasis on one side and its gleaming parabolic curvatures on the other—standing in a museum, this tine could be a Brancusi sculpture. The lines of this deceptively simple piece are abstract—as a functional form like the tine of the rake must always be.

A form of any kind designed to fit the human hand and body at work or the fatigued body at rest tends to be beautiful, especially if it comes from an old culture long unchanged. I have brought back from Spanish villages hoe heads much more efficient —and beautiful—than any available in America. This is possible because much of Spanish agriculture is more primitive even today than that of Boone County, Missouri, at the turn of the Century. The tool of a man's hand he perfects until it gets for him the maximum result for his last expended erg. When he achieves that design he has found beauty.

So it is with man's rest. A peasant chair will usually be comfortable. There is an ancient Mexican peasant chair of criss-crossed staves for a base and bent switches for a back—seat and back pig skin covered—which is as postured as anything modern hygiene offers—and much more beautiful. Our Boone County chair was of hickory wood, legs, uprights, and the one rung back; the seat of braided hickory bark. We sat in these chairs at the end of the day and on Sunday — save for Grandfather, who had a rocking chair. I never knew him otherwise: in the morning in the rocking chair on the shaded east porch nestled in the L-shaped house; in the evening on the west porch looking into the sunset as we came home from the fields. For thirty years that was his life. He died at eighty-one. I wonder if he needed a psychiatrist at fifty-one, but I smile at the thought of a psychiatrist in Boone County. We just accepted Grandfather. He couldn't work.

Sex on the Farm

No one in our family ever told me that storks brought babies or, for that matter, anything about how babies were brought. But I knew at an early age that storks did not bring horse and mule colts or cows' calves.

A breeder in the Boone County neighborhood would bring his ugly, braying little jackass and his big, black, handsome stallion. The stallion's smelling of the vaginal area produced from some of the mares the kick and squeal of heated readiness, from others cool indifference. Then for the mares in heat the rearing, mounting approach of the stallion or of the jackass, half awkward, the critical entry sometimes manually assisted to assure insemination.

Even the little jackass was almost grand in the performance of the only function for which he lives out his life. This little fellow must be closer to the first cause than others of our animal kind. His life and function are so uncomplicated. Why he should have become the symbol of stupidity is a mystery — buried deep, no doubt, in some aboriginal sex taboo.

We had our own bull — a beautiful black one, dreamy eyed, majestically aloof in his own private pasture. One late evening we were sitting in our chairs on the east porch when I heard a crash from the direction of the barnyard some 500 feet from the house. My Uncle Cad (for Cadmus, our branch of the American Hazards having come to Missouri by way of Virginia and Kentucky) let out a shout. We dashed for the barnyard, but too late. Our bull had torn through the rail fence to a waiting cow—one Uncle Cad had not intended to breed. In about 280 inexorable days she would have a calf after the manner of all cow and human flesh. I would not be there to see this one. But the year before, I had gone along to answer the call of a bawling cow, saw the calf helped out, surprised only to see Uncle Cad take a stick and cast the slimy placenta aside. And so I knew long before Dr. Sigmund Freud became a household name that sex was something not to be thwarted—at least not by a rail fence.

Why sows, the females of swine, should always be called old, I never knew. True, they looked quite mature at age three. In any case they made a most efficient garbage disposal system. In the kitchen all remains of soft food were put into pails of surplus milk. My cousin Maitland was old enough to carry these to the sty, which we called the hog lot. The contents of the pails were called slops. The pails were emptied into wooden troughs to which the voraciously grunting hogs, old and young, male and female, rushed in an utterly mannerless fashion.

I never quite brought myself to witness at close range the castration of the young male hogs, though I listened to the anguished squeals from the hog lot fence and knew that the operation was an early step in the long preparation for those delectable Boone County hams.

The Long Shadow of Dr. McGuffey

Sometimes we walked the mile to Harrisburg. That was when the horses were all working, or were tired, or the mares were going to have colts. Father proudly related that he always walked that mile to the school — and with a stick across his back, held by the crooks of his elbows to create an erect posture. In Harrisburg there was a principal general store smelling of open sacks of navy and kidney beans, bolts of calico, harness leather, chicken feeds, and thyme—an aromatic medley. The white school building, standing back in a spacious grove of trees, occupied one corner of the Harrisburg crossroads.

When I first saw the school house on my first remembered summer visit I felt like a tourist sleeping in an inn where Washington had slept or seeing for the first time the Roman Forum. Mary and her little lamb became alive on the shaded school house steps — so closely had a school house become associated in my mind with McGuffey's First Reader.

I think father remembered from his days at the Harrisburg school only the first two lines:

> The lark is up to meet the sun,
> The bee is on the wing.

But they served not only to rout me out of my earliest bed but also to define the nature of the universe — inexorably busy, demanding, as the close of the second stanza enjoined:

> O let me with the morning rise,
> And do my duty haste.

Such was the McGuffey ethic, epitomized in his quatrain,

> He who would thrive
> Must rise at five.
> He who *has* thriven
> May *lie* till seven.

Father and I were among the nine out of ten Americans who in the decades from the mid-nineteenth to early twentieth centuries got our first taste of literature from McGuffey. We possessed our copies of an estimated one hundred twenty millions sold between 1836 and 1920. In J. K. Galbraith's happy phrase, the Readers gave us our "conventional wisdom."

The face of America was changing more rapidly than McGuffey realized. Nothing in the Readers showed any awareness of the swiftcoming industrialism and urbanism. There is no awareness of the labor movement. Nothing in McGuffey reflects the issues soon to burn: labor's right to organize, strike, and picket. In 1896, O. W. Holmes spoke out for picketing in the famous dissent in the Massachusetts case of Vegelahn v. Guntner. But for two more decades the Readers were to expound virtues for a society essentially provincial and bucolic.

Of America's seventy-six million people in 1900 only 39.7 per cent lived in urban areas. Of today's two hundred million, 73.5 per cent are urbanized. In 1900 one American farmer supplied farm products for only five persons; today he supplies twenty-five persons. Did any education prepare America for such a vast shift —in only six decades—from a predominantly rural to a predominantly industrial and urban civilization? I think not—certainly not the Readers.

The conventional wisdom about teetotalism and prohibition captured Father and also the *Kansas City Star*. That paragon of financial journalistic success never took liquor advertising. Much of its revenue came from a large circulation in Kansas — a dry state to which Kansas City, Missouri, is still sometimes erroneously attributed. But neither the founder, William Rockhill Nelson, nor the majority of his associates were teetotalers. In the 1920's at a dinner party our charming hostess, Gertrude Prince, said to Henry C. Haskell, the Editor, himself a moderate drinker, "Henry, why is it that the *Kansas City Star* is so dry and so many of its editors are so wet?" Completely abashed, Haskell could say only, "Why Gertrude, that's a long story." Indeed so, and it is an American story — divergence between preachment and practice. No one could be against McGuffey's ideals but few could practice them in toto.

McGuffey and Pragmatism

We knew that McGuffey made drunkenness (now the ailment is called alcoholism), theater going, card playing, and dancing all of one piece. We never took the proscription of the theater seriously. Early, how early I am not sure, Father took us to the Grand Theatre in Kansas City to see "My Old Kentucky Home." Except for the first time I tasted real wild cherry phosphate, I remember no comparable early delight. That confined, luminous universe we call the stage, which lets us experience the unknown depths of ourselves from the black security of the orchestra, for us then the balcony, — that was my first love. Not to be an actor — just a spectator.

How could McGuffey have missed the stage? The Fifth and Sixth Readers include some Shakespeare, right enough: the pound of flesh scene, which McGuffey denominates, "Shylock, Or The Pound of Flesh"; the scene about the ghost of Hamlet's father; Antony over Caesar's dead body. But in an introductory biographical paragraph Shakespeare is "by many regarded as the greatest poet the world has ever produced." And the instructions which precede the Shylock say, "Let the pupil stand at a distance from the teacher and try to read so loud and distinctly, that the teacher may hear each syllable." And then more specifically, "Do not say pen'lt-y for pen-al-ty" and so on through qual-i-ty; per-ju-ry; law-ful-ly and more. Obviously the focus was on elocution, not on drama.

An education which affected so many Americans for so long must account for some of our present strength and for some of our present weakness. It seems certain that precept was not enough for unruly life. The Readers were still idolizing childhood and preaching frontier individualism at a time when a million children from ten to fifteen were gainfully employed in factories and sweat-shops. And at the very peak of the Readers during the last two decades before the turn of the century the new science of psychology was forming under William James at Harvard. Even more deadly to the concept of education by precept was James's new and all-American philosophy, *Pragmatism* (1907).

New indeed. "The truth of an idea is not a stagnant property in it. Truth happens to an idea. It becomes true, is made true by events: . . . The truth is the name of whatever proves itself to be good in the way of belief, and good, too, for definite assignable reasons." Critics said that pragmatism was not a philosophy but a way of doing without a philosophy. McGuffey would have agreed. He predeceased (1873) his Readers by almost half a century, after notable service as President of Miami (Ohio) University, of Ohio University, and, for the last quarter-century of his life, as Professor of Moral Philosophy at the University of Virginia. Inexorably as death took McGuffey, pragmatism and scientism closed the pages of his Readers.

Good and Evil

But teaching does not end with the teacher or his books. The pupils of one generation are the statesmen, the politicians, the business leaders of the next two generations. Of equal importance in a democracy, they are the voters for upwards of fifty years after the classroom. Specifically, the pupils of the McGuffey Readers of the last three decades of the 19th Century were the leaders and the voters of the critical first three decades of the 20th — the era of World War I, of the Russian revolution, and of the beginnings of the division of the world into armed camps of communistic dictatorship and capitalistic democracy. How well were Americans prepared for the swift, global march of history in the post-Victorian decades?

The ideals of personal excellence and goodness, so insistently taught first by Franklin and then by McGuffey, were unsupported by any history other than our own, if indeed by that. Gibbon's dictum that history is "little more than the register of the crimes, follies, and misfortunes of mankind" went unheeded — not applicable to a land thought to be so new under the sun as America.

The ideal sufficiently reiterated becomes mistaken for the reality. The six thousand year record lay back of us and wide open. Except for brief interludes, tyranny, ambition, war, and common misery had been the rule. But, dazzled by our ideal of personal goodness, we wrote off all the teachings of history as applicable well enough to the Old World and to the ancient past but not to us. And we made the mistake — one which has jeopardized us for an unforeseeable time — of thinking that since we were right we would by some magic prevail.

We were not prepared for a Marx, Lenin, Hitler, or even for a Khrushchev. We thought that power would not attend their pronouncements of malevolent intent. We thought that a good man, like McGuffey, who practiced his precepts, in some way represented the normal and that men who denied those precepts were all wrong or would fail. We have already paid dearly for our mistake. McGuffey tried to make us good. He did make us compassionate. But he left us unaware of a pluralistic world in which good and evil have no choice but to deal with each other.

World's Fair and War

In 1904 we went to the World's Fair in St. Louis. It was called the Louisiana Purchase Exposition in commemoration of the 100th anniversary of the purchase of Louisiana from France. One of the important attractions at the Fair was the "Boer War." When the great day came for us to take our seats in the huge amphitheater I had no idea what would ensue. Nothing much did ensue. There were some fancy maneuvers by horse-drawn artillery; some loud noises with belches of smoke from harmless cartridges; and some vague rushing about which left me in doubt as to who won. Of course I had no idea about the merits of the issues. My impression now, after almost six decades, is that we thought the English were right.

One piece of trivia about the Boer War at St. Louis bespeaks the biological delicacy of the era. A lady (we never said woman), referring to the event, called it the "Hog War." I, knowing more contemporary history and hog lot anatomy than the lady, felt superior when a young family friend of ours, Milburn Hogue, told us the story. But I think Father and Mother, despite the laughter, did not approve his telling it. One just did not mention the uncastrated male of swine in the first decade.

It is remarkable that war should have been selected as a subject for entertainment at a World's Fair. Imagine World War I having been depicted at Chicago's Century of Progress Exposition in 1933. In fact, it would have been impossible after World War I to simulate either the global movements or the sickening horrors of total war. The Romans could flood the Coliseum and literally reproduce the oar driven galleys ramming each other, the gladiators boarding literally to slay the vanquished. Even in modern times our motion pictures could do a convincing reproduction of a Civil War cavalry charge in *Birth of a Nation*. But after World War I, war on the stage must be reduced to the microcosm as in *All Quiet on the Western Front*.

I suspect that there is another reason why play-war was put into the arena at the St. Louis Fair in 1904. We thought in those days that war had become a museum piece. It was true that the bloody, disease plagued Crimean War (1853-56) had occurred, despite the best efforts of Queen Victoria and her beloved Prince Albert. But Tennyson had rendered that war unreal with his heroic *The Charge of the Light Brigade*. Our own Civil War we could not deny, but it had been too internecine to seem generic. And the Spanish-American War with its quick victory had been too short to count. We Americans in the first decade had the delusion that wars were over — for us at least.

So we could look at a play-war as unperturbed as we might view the world's most famous dinosaur at the Carnegie Museum of Natural History. War, like the dinosaur, was an anachronism — we thought.

Buffalo Bill

At St. Louis in 1904 war was for showmanship. Buffalo Bill's (William F. Cody, 1846-1917) Wild West Show was there. Shooting, roping, costumed Indians biting the dust, burning forts — all another museum piece out of an ended past. Last of the great scouts — Boone, Crockett, Carson, Bridger, Wild Bill Hickok — the old Indian fighter, Buffalo Bill, was a hero to us. We never doubted then that the Indians were wrong or supposed that they could have been treated differently.

The famous scouts of the wild west were the heroes of our first decade "Westerns" — the dime novels. Once a week I traveled the three blocks to Mr. Brinkley's drugstore at 38th and Woodland in Kansas City, Missouri, where ice cream sodas were served in glasses which fitted into German silver holders. I never became reconciled to the sad surprise when the straw signalled air at the bottom of the exhausted glass. The consolation was the week's new dime novel. I had to choose among Buffalo Bill, Kit Carson, Liberty Boys and others. The soda had been a nickel; the remaining dime permitted one novel. Kit Carson was a favorite. He had grown up in Howard County, Missouri, which adjoins our own Boone County, and so was a kind of neighbor, separated, of course, by two generations.

In due course, I would learn of the important Indian civilizations in the Americas; their songs and poems, painstakingly collected by scholars of the Peabody Museum of Harvard University; their sand paintings preserved in authentic color and design by the Bollingen Press, abstract as a Paul Klee; their stories of creation, more complicated than that of the Book of Genesis, more akin to the Asian cosmogonies; their antiquity in America; their migrations across the scant sixty miles of the Bering Strait, opened for passage as the glaciers receded some eleven thousand years past. But at the St. Louis World's Fair in 1904 and in the dime novels, Indians were for biting the dust except the good ones who elected to aid the white man's conquest.

The Mississippi, Craps, and a First Love

If the attractions at the St. Louis Fair presented some crude and confused notions about war and Indians, there was nothing unreal about the great wharves on the Mississippi at St. Louis.

Where the long sloping levee met the water a gangplank bridged the way to a new, and for me an uncertain, world.

I was eleven. As we passed up the gleaming wood and brass of the main hatch to our staterooms, I felt all the joy of expectation and all the pain of new experience. At some time, not remembered as an event, one loses the capacity for ecstatic or poignant reaction to new experience. I never cease to envy a child whose surprised face in a swift elevator shows the turmoil in the solar plexus, half pleasure, half pain — the body itself reacting to new experience. My own blasé solar plexus says nothing. Henri Bergson in that penetrating essay on the meaning of the comic, *Laughter,* put it that, "after a certain age, we become impervious to all fresh or novel forms of joy, and the sweetest pleasures of the middle-aged man are perhaps nothing more than a revival of sensations of childhood, a balmy zephyr wafted in fainter and fainter breaths by a past which is ever receding."

My *ecstasy* on boarding the river steamer at St. Louis, bound for St. Paul, was that of primitive man in his dugout — the escape from land to move on water. My pain was social. There were unaccustomed uniformed servants directing us here and there. The dining room was called "the saloon". But we were prohibitionists, and, except for Carry A. Nation, did not go into saloons. Every sophisticated eye was upon me, watching to see what I would do wrong.

The St. Paul was a stern wheeler. To borrow some snatches from Mark Twain's *Life on the Mississippi,* she was a handsome sight, long and sharp, and trim and pretty; two tall fancy topped chimneys, with a gilded device swung between; a fanciful pilot-house, all glass and gingerbread; the boiler-deck, the hurricane-deck, and the Texas deck fenced and ornamented with clean white railings; a flag flying gallantly from the jackstaff; the upper decks black with passengers. It was all very strange. Father was right to take me aft where we could see the great paddle wheel begin its turnings. The steam whistle sounded, seeming to come from both near and far — almost ominous. The paddle wheel moved, the deck began to throb the slow, swelling beat of a great body coerced by great power. We moved. My first airplane flight in World War I less than a decade later did not yield half so much uncertain joy.

I have lived my life in two cities made by two great rivers of the Mississippi system: first in Kansas City on the great bend in the Missouri and then in Pittsburgh where the Allegheny and the Monongahela join to form the Ohio. These are the principal tributaries to the Mississippi. There is something romantic about inland waterways — almost more romantic than even the open seas. That one can go afloat from Olean, New York, on the Allegheny to Great Falls, Montana, on the Missouri — four thousand miles — it seems remarkable — land having waterways to carry one so far.

Even at the turn of the century, river traffic had passed its zenith by some forty years. Time had been when three thousand steamers crowded the Mississippi system and a thousand called at St. Paul. The railroads had ended all that. Their tracks were in sight from our deck almost the entire passage from St. Louis to St. Paul.

Mark Twain was still living when we took our voyage. He had seen the river traffic at its height and deplored its decline even in 1883 when he published *Life on the Mississippi*. Some of his phrases came alive: majestic bluffs that overlook the river; the grace and variety of their forms; the steep verdant slope, whose base is at the water's edge, topped by a lofty rampart of broken, turreted rocks; the shining river; glimpses of distant villages, asleep upon capes; stealthy rafts slipping along in the shade of forest walls; white steamers vanishing around remote points. Such was our trip.

We had almost continuous vaudeville on the forward portion of the deck where the freight was carried. The best show was a landing to discharge passengers or freight. On the approach to the shore a great Negro would put down a pole perhaps eighteen or twenty feet long, and as the boat ran it to a vertical position he would call up the depth-reading to the pilot house above. "Mark Twain" was all I ever heard. That meant two fathoms, which meant twelve feet, which meant safe water.

Sometimes bells would ring frantically, the boat would pull back from the nearing shore, and we would try again for water deep enough for our landing.

An order from above, and the crane would swing the gangplank out and high above the deck toward the shore, a heroic figure balanced on the outer tip of the plank, great coiled rope (in nautical parlance, a line) in his hands. Then the throw of the line ashore, the catch by a shore-hand to pass the loop over a stanchion; an order from above; the line running through a cleat on the gunwale turned once and a half around the deck winch; another order, and the growling winch turned, drawing the line to the boat and the boat to the shore.

Soon a slight jar told even a landlubber that the great boat had touched shore. Another order from above; the screeching crane let the gangplank down to the sloping wharf; two or three passengers scurried off, stewards following with their baggage.

Then came the parade of the roustabouts — on our boat all Negroes — Old Man River Negroes, although I did not know it then. Sometimes if the freight were considerable, a second plank would be put out from boat to shore. Then the shouting, singing black giants shouldering incredible boxes, bales, rolls, and burdens would form a file of freight going off by one plank and coming on by another.

The whole procedure was over in minutes. Bells rang, orders sounded, the lines were cast off, we moved sternward into the river, and again our majestic swan resumed her northward passage.

Now was the time for play on the forward deck where the roustabouts awaited their next labors. One was named — self-named, no doubt —"Fewclothes". He was a great fellow, an extrovert or a magnificent pretender. "Throw down a penny to Fewclothes," he would call up to the passengers on the deck above, gesturing with appealing good will to the rags which left exposed big portions of his magnificently muscled body.

When the penny, nickel, dime, quarter (I was impressed when it was a half dollar) rang on the deck, no football scrimmage was ever more intense. There must have been rules, although I could not discern them. Finally, the bodies of the roustabouts would disentangle, leaving one great hand glued to the deck, the coin beneath. Then a pause while the victor made sure that all other contenders had withdrawn. Only then would Fewclothes start it all over again. The NAACP, which was not to come on the scene until 1909, would certainly have disapproved Fewclothes' exploitation of subservient Negro charm.

There was a sequel to the open deck show, one not visible to the passengers from above. The scene was midship in a nook from which one could have a close view of the steam engines and of the great shafts making their eccentric, reciprocating thrusts to turn the paddle wheel which moved us up the river on our four-day trip. The game in this partially secluded spot was craps — a simplified version of an earlier two-dice game known as "hazard."

I discovered the scene on a lone expedition to seek a closer view of the engines — and a great misfortune it was for me. The roustabouts, each in his own inimitable style, were rubbing or shaking the dice in their huge hands, rolling them out on the deck, following them verbally — sometimes hovering over them physically — with precatory appeals for the right number. The craps-game scene is always an exciting one — the circle of human beings avidly preoccupied, regressed in incantation.

A soft voice at my side said "The pot's 'most three dollahs, Boss, wud yuh stake me to a quartah?" I *had* two quarters — my capital for the trip. If my man had won (perhaps he did) I would not have known it, and if he had shared the winnings with me, his financial backer — a commitment not clearly made — I would have had a dilemma because neither McGuffey nor Father nor I believed in gambling. In any case, and whatever my motives, I lent him one of my two quarters — because I lacked the courage to refuse — naively expecting to have it back presently and then to run back to the security of the upper deck.

The acute sorrow of my loss persisted a full day and then diminished only gradually as grief does with time. I toyed with several wild schemes for recoupment and then resigned myself to silent suffering. It was unthinkable that I should tell anyone.

Supper, a term we then used for the evening meal, was some consolation. The dining saloon of our river boat was fitted with long tables, rather narrow, accommodating twenty persons or more to the table. The Mississippi Valley still reflected in the first decade of our century the American equality so much noted by European observers almost a century earlier. The nonexclusive dining table was one of the symbols of egalitarianism.

The meat — roast beef, fried chicken, fried ham — was passed by white-jacketed Negro waiters. The vegetables — mashed potatoes, yellow string beans, peas, squash, cole slaw — and bowls of gravy and trays of pickled things were on the tables to be passed around by the passengers. Hot biscuits and corn bread were served by the waiters. The dessert, of course, was a pie of some fruit but, for us an innovation, à la mode.

After the first night I was eager to finish supper because on the deck I might encounter a little girl. Mary tells me that the dress I describe was, and is, called a jumper. A skirt of accordion pleats, white ruffled blouse, and velvet yoke—the earliest feminine attire to work magic on me—a first. Now that I think of that childish infatuation, I have great respect for those prepubescent stirrings and their amorphous pain.

By day the river seemed to flow under us and the boat just to stand. This was especially so where the river was wide and the distant banks were scarcely perceptible because the river bottom lands were flat and formless. At night the river beacons shone out on every point and at every hazard. As we came abreast of them we knew that we moved. Then occasionally came the thrill of the searchlight groping ahead or aside for some landmark the pilot needed or finding a wharf where the now tired roustabouts would discharge a late cargo.

The banks of the river were not always just part of a level horizon. At Rock Island, Moline, and Davenport the river bluffs were spectacular. We had passed Quincy, Keokuk, Burlington, and Muscatine. Then Dubuque, LaCrosse, Winona. The river was narrowing. More log rafts, incredibly vast, pushed and guided by steamers like ours, passed, sometimes close by on the river, now tightly contained between implacable bluffs. All life aboard was now routine. Landings, loadings, day scenes, night scenes, the whistle blast, the boat's throbbings — nothing was new. The last morning came — and St. Paul.

Amid the confusions of landing I had missed seeing how it was done. I must stay with Mother, my sister, and Father. The official at the gangplank was saying good-bye. It was over and I was unhappy but not for that. It had never occurred to me that I would not see the little jumper dress again. I cannot be sure now, but I think I had never spoken to her. But the relationship was such, in my opinion, that I might have waved good-bye. That would have been sweet intimacy.

Long after, and long since now, I learned the psychological meaning of projection, that unpleasant process by which a frustrated person seeks to cause others to share his ill humor. All the first day's joys of a new city, of new ventures in what was to us the North, were of no avail. I was in deep depression. Father tried his magic wiles, Mother looked her loving distress, my other-directed sister was oblivious, but it is doubtful that a psychiatrist would have got from me the cause.

Going to Town

We had had a special interest in two river towns, Hannibal, Mark Twain's "white town drowsing in the sunshine of a summer's morning" and just above on the river, Quincy, Illinois, standing high on the slope of a hill — a brisk, handsome, well-ordered city . . . interested in art, letters, "and other high things," according to the account in *Life on the Mississippi*. Father had gotten his own "business college" education at Quincy in Gem City Business College.

The proprietary schools held the field in what was called business education during the second half of the 19th and early 20th century. The curriculum included shorthand, typewriting (first practical model of the typewriter, 1873), bookkeeping, penmanship, commercial law. These schools recruited heavily, particularly in the rural districts where their representatives urged that "business education" would open up — by way of stenography — commercial opportunities for young men. Male secretaries were usual at the turn of the century. Many firms refused to employ female secretaries for a complex of reasons, prominent among them being the assumption that women could not keep secrets.

Nevertheless, opportunities were opening for trained women— we said "young ladies." And for the girls the business schools offered an escape from the farm, which both parents and daughters desired. High schools were not yet usual in rural areas; business and the city had romantic appeal. Farmers and their wives wished a life of less hard work, or more grace and refinement for their daughters. An education which offered the opportunity for an honest living amidst the advantages of *city* living appealed to rural practicality.

I suppose there were some risks in bringing farm girls to the big cities. Apparently Father took precautions. Many times I heard him dictate letters to students whom the school's field representatives had recruited. He would say, "Carry the enclosed school catalogues in plain sight. Our representative will do likewise. Thus, you will meet our representative in the union station and he will conduct you to a good family home where we have arranged room and board."

In the decades which bracketed the turn of the century, business enjoyed great respect. John Pierpont Morgan the Elder and Andrew Carnegie were national figures of heroic proportions. Although some railroad and industrial practices were impliedly condemned in the Interstate Commerce Act (1887) and in the Sherman Antitrust Act (1890), the idea of unlimited American business potential was still prevalent. Edwin Markham's *The Man With the Hoe* had raised doubts in 1899. Theodore Roosevelt's Northern Securities case (1904) had branded the great corporate amalgamations as enemies of the people and Upton Sinclair's *The Jungle* had shown the heartlessness of the big packers. But Americans still had faith in business and business opportunity.

Horatio Alger had died in 1899, but his one hundred-twenty juvenile books, all depicting a poor boy, through virtue and work, achieving wealth and fame, had left a folk-thought about business which a poem, a novel, and a Supreme Court decision did not immediately dislodge. In fact, the American admiration for business, including big business, did not suffer serious doubts until the Great Depression of the 1930's.

I encountered rural eastern Kansas myself as a recruiter for the "College" in an interlude after return from World War I and re-entry into Law School. My prospective recruits were given me by the school—names which came in response to advertisements in the weekly rural edition of the *Kansas City Star* and in the country newspapers of the territory.

The Model-T Ford was then the American car. I bought a single-seated runabout with a collapsible top—my first car (1919) although we had had a family car since 1908.

Eastern Kansas, unlike the great wheat plains of central Kansas, is hilly in places and frequently has quite charming landscapes. In 1919 the roads were almost wholly of dirt. Seneca, Netawaka, Oskaloosa, Ozawkie, Centralia, Goff, Soldier, Circleville — whether the names were Indian or other — the road was dirt. But the summer was dry and hot in 1919, as it should be for the corn and wheat to ripen for the harvest. The dirt roads were hard but with a certain resilience never characteristic of concrete. In fact, it was not until the balloon tire (1922) that automobiling on concrete became as exhilarating as on a good, dry, dirt road.

After an initial success or two I approached my prospects with absolute confidence. Runabout top laid neatly back, its cover in place, I made my way singing badly, or whistling better, in the cool of the evening. That was when I must work — the farmer's day of toil over, his wife and children, including my prospect, gathered around him on an aging porch, chickens often at my feet, bawling cows interrupting my address. But I needed only be modestly urbane and not abashed by that tight-lipped face of flint—American Gothic—because back of the face was the American yearning to change status; back of the tight lips a twinkle in the eye was ready. I stood for education, business, and the city. They were usually enough to make the sale.

We did not fully understand in the early 1900's the speed with which urbanism was approaching. In 1900, 1910, 1920, we were on our way to the city. It was not only that boys and girls wanted to leave the farms. They *had* to leave because they were no longer needed. They had been displaced by machines and better methods. If I had seen all that clearly in 1919 I would not have felt, secretly of course, so immodest about my good record in business college recruiting.

Humor by Lamplight

It was after President McKinley's assassination (1901) that we moved into our new house. We were Democrats, but we knew that the dead President had been a good man because his favorite hymn was "Lead Kindly Light." Father thought that Theodore Roosevelt was a risk for the country —"a little wild." Father did not go as far as Mark Hanna, who said bitterly in a Pullman Parlor Car, returning from McKinley's funeral, "And now that damned cowboy is President of the United States." In any case, Father would not have employed the word, "damn"— adjective, adverb, verb, or any tense thereof. Mother would sometimes say "dog-gone" when Father was not around.

The new house was just next to the old one. By now we had running water on our street so we had a bathtub on the second floor. But an outhouse with two holes graced the rear of the lot. Once quite a gathering of neighborhood children were assembled in a game in our yard. One little girl, who came from a more sophisticated community, several blocks away, said to me, as I returned from use of our sanitary facility, "Do you feel better?" I was speechless. One just did not speak of such matters in any society, so far as I knew. Of course, I never told anybody about the shocking incident.

In the living room of our new house stood a round oak table on a massive pedestal. It was covered with a somber reddish fabric with threads of black running throughout—handwoven by Mother in her pioneer Iowa home. She met Father when she was singing Buttercup in an amateur production of *Pinafore* at Dexter, Iowa, where Father was teaching in the local normal school. Mother's voice was a nice full-bodied soprano. I never heard Father carry a tune, but, of course, I did not know him when he was a seaman in *Pinafore*. On the table stood an oil lamp with ample green glass shade. The whole effect of the cloth of dark red and the green shade projecting most of the light downward was quite pleasant. Such a lamp was called a "student lamp."

Mother took my sister and me to a furniture store to buy a big chair to go with the table and the lamp. It was to be Father's birthday present. I felt complimented to be included in making such an important judgment and Mother was uncertain about making a substantial purchase alone. The store was on Main Street, south of 12th Street (later Kansas City's wide open night-life street), and just off the more elite shopping district. William Morris (d. 1896) had made his furniture designs and had produced the chair which became a household word and ubiquitous possession, but we, and probably the store, had never heard of him. We bought a huge rocker with enough oak wood in it to make six chairs of contemporary design, with springs and padding for seat and back, covered with taut black leather. It cost $36.00

I had no idea whether the chair was comfortable or not. Father sat in it a great deal. He had by now graduated from the Kansas City School of Law, a night school of the proprietary type, today a part of the Kansas City branch of the University of Missouri.

So he had more evenings with us at home to sit in the great rocker under the green lamp to read and often to laugh at the humor of that era—especially at Artemus Ward (Charles Farrar Browne), Josh Billings (Henry Wheeler Shaw), Bill Nye (Edgar Wilson Nye), Petroleum Vesuvius Nashby (David Ross Locke), Uncle Remus (Joel Chandler Harris), and Mark Twain (Samuel L. Clemens). These men were contemporaries—10 to 20 years older than Father; 60 years or so older than I. Their humor could be raw and poignant in turns—the humor of a pioneer society beginning to laugh at itself. Only Mark Twain's writings survive to remind us of the humor in exaggeration when, in *Connecticut Yankee,* he says of Alisande,
"She was a comely enough creature, and soft and modest, but if signs went for anything, she didn't know as much as a lady's watch."

Jokes with a Purpose

There is something at once appealing and repulsive about American humor. Father certainly introduced me to the main stream of it — from James Russell Lowell (*Biglow Papers,* 1848) through Mark Twain. I acquired on my own the moderns, to name only Mr. Dooley (Finley Peter Dunne, 1867-1936) and James Thurber (1894-1962). What I learned in the green shaded student lamp era around the turn of the century was that profundity need not be dull. To say this less pretentiously, humor helps in exposition. Humor is not adequate for every situation. Death, disgrace, despair do not yield to humor. But these are personal pains. Even despair, when a whole people is involved, yields to the humorous recital.

I know a great many jokes (episodic accounts which end in surprise—one of the fundamentals of humor). But if I were asked to tell a joke, I would probably fail the request. This is because I remember humor only in the context of a serious point. For example, just now I am working hard on urban renewal and rapid transit in Pittsburgh, Pennsylvania. Pride is a first requisite for community improvement. So I remember a Boone County, Missouri, joke about a farmer who sold a mule to his neighbor. The next day the purchaser brought back the mule cut and bleeding on its foreparts and flanks, saying that the mule must be blind otherwise it would not run into the barbed-wire fence to cause such injuries. "That mule ain't blind," said the seller; "it just don't give a damn."

I have been at one time in my life deeply engaged in labor negotiations, in which frequently the situation is tense and confused; perhaps tense *because* confused, since, in such negotiations, tempers rise and the issues, often simple enough, get lost. Then comes to mind the tale of a little village, one of whose 100 or so citizens owned a jackass. The little animal was a community favorite because the surrounding farmers brought their mares to town for breeding to get mules, and this produced other business. So when the community asset strayed, the whole town turned out to find him—and failed. The next day the village half-wit appeared leading the animal down the town's single street. The delighted citizens gathered around, saying, "How did you find him?" "Well," said the boy, "I said to myself, if I was a jackass whar would I be, and I went thar, and thar he was." Humor like this has a bite. One must be careful, because after the tension is broken, as it will usually be broken by such a story, there will be questions the next day about who was the jackass and who was the half-wit in our negotiating group. But what the story does is to say to all and sundry, on whatever side of the intellectual melee, that relaxation, insight, and empathy will do the work of the conference better than tempers and shouting. But imagine using *those* words with an effect equal to that of the story.

A Little Learning

We had a little library in addition to books on American humor. One set of nine volumes — published by P. F. Collier, and still a monument to the bookbinders art of the last century—contained works of Bulwer-Lytton, including, *The Last Days of Pompeii.* There was, I think, only one volume of Charles Dickens, *Martin Chuzzlewit*—a strange title for a book, it seemed to me. Then there were ten volumes called *A Compilation of the Messages and Papers of the Presidents — 1789 to 1904* edited by J. D. Richardson.

Of course *Uncle Tom's Cabin* and *Black Beauty,* the story of how to treat a horse by Anna Sewell (1877), were there. Mother read them both to us, pausing to cry over the plight and escape over the ice of the Ohio by Eliza and the sad fate of Tom at the hands of the brutal Simon Legree. So we were among the millions of Americans for whom the moral issue of the Civil War was dramatized by Harriet Beecher Stowe. I have myself seen—over a hundred years after the book was published (1852)—one of the many dramatizations, this one performed at a summer theatre in Jennerstown, Pennsylvania. It was offered as melodrama, but the audience did not succeed in remaining wholly dry-eyed.

We were post-Puritans, if one can know when, if ever, Puritanism ended in America. *The Scarlet Letter* had been published (1850) a bare 50 years before Father was reading the humor of Artemus Ward and Bill Nye. It had been published almost contemporaneously with *Uncle Tom's Cabin*. The Puritan soul of Hawthorne, pregnant of preoccupation with sin, was living testimony to surviving Puritanism no less than Mrs. Stowe's poignant emotionalism was predictive of reforms in America not yet completed—even to this day.

The Scarlet Letter won instant acclaim in America. It grew in esteem and continues as one of America's most respected classics. Yet we did not read it under our green shaded oil lamp. Why? For the most part my memory is clean and sharp. Even here I am not just speculating. I have a strong and persistent impression that I knew of *The Scarlet Letter* and that it was a book about a forbidden subject. If Hawthorne had picked some sin other than that of adultery to work out a scheme of irredeemable guilt — beyond the expiation of confession or the acquittance of God's mercy — then we might have read the book. But we were too Puritan for Puritanism's greatest novel.

And yet that aspect of Puritanism which espoused good education and new science was at work. Behind the three glass doors of our bookcase were ten volumes of Herbert Spencer, which, beginning with *First Principles* in 1860-1862, contained the writings of the ensuing 36 years. Why would Father not have spoken to me of this man, who, after age forty, with inadequate learning, health so poor that he could sustain mental activity for not more than one hour at a time, set himself the task of synthesizing all knowledge, all phenomena, all that can be known? Why did we buy the set—certainly a significant investment for us— and then never discuss Spencer? Father would have approved his doctrine of the Unknowable, because in his sermons, Brother Brown stressed the omniscience of God and the limitations of man. But as for evolution—men from apes—and such phrases as "survival of the fittest" and the "struggle for existence," coined by Spencer and soon to become that misinterpretation of Darwin in America known as Social Darwinism, Father would have had no sympathy. We had a conviction (at the turn of the century) that all things worked for good for those who loved the Lord, but we certainly did not know that on our shelves were ten volumes which took man up to an evolutionary mountain peak only to say that "an entire history of anything must include its appearance out of the imperceptible and its disappearance into the imperceptible." We believed in work and progress on earth; then we would go to heaven.

I am sure that Father would not have cared for Spengler or Sartre. I am sure also that the reason we did not see Spencer as their precursor was that we did not read the ten volumes behind the glass doors of our bookcase.

Brecht and I

We believed not only in work and progress but also that the world was just (by our standards, of course) and even friendly. This faith was shaken for me one day, at an early age, when, while I was chasing a brown butterfly in our garden, a black wasp made straight for my forehead. The poisonous sting was like a blow—and for no cause. The trauma forced me out of my chrysalis. I had encountered something beyond observable cause and effect. There was evil—unmotivated evil—in the world.

But it was only one episode, soon forgotten. Yet there was another. We had a picket fence along the street side of our house. It had a hinged gate on which a small boy could swing with that abandon which excludes the world. My most dependable between-meal delicacy was bread, baked by Mother, covered thickly with butter from my churning, the top spread with sugar. Sometimes there were candy-beans from Mr. Rene's curved glass showcase in the corner grocery, a block away, but not always. One did not come by a penny every day. The bread, butter, and sugar were good, and I had the confection in my hand, on that day, ready to eat it, when a boy came by and just took it away.

The wasp sting I could not conceal—the lump on my forehead was too big and red. The theft of the bread I did not mention.

It seemed to me something so foreign to our world that I could not properly speak about it. But now I could begin to generalize: a pretty little boy with long yellow curls (I hated it later when I was called "pretty boy") could not depend upon an admiring universe. Not everyone loved him. Years later I read Thomas Mann's Joseph series and even later I heard, and then studied, and then taught my students, Bertolt Brecht's "Three Penny Opera". "The world is mean and man uncouth." Brecht and I were both wrong, he because he thought the world hateful and futile, I because I thought it friendly and purposeful—but neither of us was entirely wrong.

Natural Enemies

Our grade school, a half block way—an index to Father's skill in picking building sites—had at first only four rooms. But soon there was a fine big brick and stone building. One early year I was the teacher's pet—a status I vaguely realized was not right. But I liked it. The next year was quite another story. Apparently the case was one of those in which one individual acquires an almost reflexive antipathy for another. Probably I exhibited the nostalgia I felt about the sheltered previous year and this was not the way to ingratiate myself with the austere mistress of the third grade at Horace Mann School. In any case, probably thanks to the wisdom of our principal, Miss Kate Biggs, I was sent clear across town by devious streetcar routing to be with Miss Lucy Smoot at Norman School. I would be all right there because Miss Lucy was the secretary of our Sunday School and, as I have said, always made the announcements when all of the classes were gathered in assembly. That arrangement lasted quite happily for one year; then I could return to my home school.

There was a significant sequel. In high school I encountered that same antipathetic teacher—this time in first year algebra—and promptly began to fail. She, herself, suggested a transfer to another teacher, Mr. King, who saw me through to a top category grade without difficulty to either of us. One rebels against the idea that there can be visceral, unconditioned enmities—natural enemies among human beings, such as that alleged to exist between the mongoose and the cobra. But however that may be, there *was* a teacher, who maintained a long and creditable career

in the Kansas City school system, and who disliked *me* so much,
or I *her,* or both, that I could not learn from her what I could
learn from others.

The King Dies—Forever

Our grade school had a summer library. I wish I could remember
who first sent me to it. There, in an interlude between the close
of school and departure for the Boone County farm, I encountered some version of the "Morte d'Arthur" of Sir Thomas Malory
(1470). Arthur was a hero to my liking—a Christian king with
a magic sword with a name, *Excalibur.* Even then I knew that
Arthur was a little stupid—but he was good. And what he lacked
in brilliance his Round Table Knights made up in bravery and
righteous quests. The invincible Lancelot, the impeccable Galahad,
and the incredible Merlin—I hung on their every deed. And I
knew that the Holy Grail was worth looking for, and I knew that
Elaine was beautiful, and that Arthur's Guinevere was even more
beautiful.

Then came the awful ending — double tragedy. Guinevere's
sleeping with Lancelot; I was not entirely sure of what happened
but I blamed her. Why I exonerated Lancelot or even Arthur I
do not know. (Much later as a lawyer I learned that such situations are complicated.) Perhaps the notion that it was Eve who
was originally at fault in matters of sex influenced me. A Sunday
School version of Genesis 3 was well known to me.

I might have survived Guinevere's promiscuity, but not
Arthur's death also, the result of grievous wounds delivered by
his benighted nephew, Modred. The Round Table was ended—
a dream of goodness and greatness had left only the pain of a
waking mind and aching heart. I was in deep depression, and it
seemed to me that the agony was unmentionable. To this day
I am not able to yield, for poignancy and power, to any other
lines than Tennyson's "Morte d'Arthur,"

> The old order changeth,
> Yielding place to new;
> And God fulfills himself
> In many ways,
> Lest one good custom
> Should corrupt the world.

Long Pants, Mister, Corsets and Skirts

Then came the day when we formed for the last time under the flag on the open court in front of our Horace Mann School and marched in. The Seventh Grade would graduate. I was wearing my first long trousers. (We said "pants.") This decision had been reached with some difficulty in our household. But a powerful factor was at work.

A boy from a more elite neighborhood had transferred to our school from one named Woodland. He had become my champion, making it plain to all and sundry that any cause of mine was his. Why I needed a champion or why he volunteered I would tell if I knew. In any case he was not only a protector but also a mentor. He (Jay North was his name) got me on his older brother Tom's cow-pasture football team. I knew I was suspect and on trial, but a compliment which I still value came on a day when I made a certain tackle and Jay said to Tom, "See he's getting better." Actually I was not any good as a football player, and I knew it all the time. Jay was prejudiced. But he did something for me. As in the case of the wasp, he taught me, not by precept but by example, that one could not depend upon being liked. As a stranger on our school ground, he had to defend himself, and did. Perhaps he needed a friend as much as I did. I don't think my parents knew how much Jay had helped me but they must have sensed that I would be bitterly unhappy if I were not dressed as he was at our Horace Mann commencement.

It was over two miles across 39th Street from our side of town to Westport High School. Our part of Kansas City, Missouri, was not yet populous enough to have its own high school. There seemed to have been never a question but that I would go to high school and college, although Mother confided to me years later that Father had been so generous with Brother Brown's Michigan Avenue Baptist Church that my college financing was difficult. It was not a complaint, rather an apology (unneeded) to me.

I walked two miles and more. This pleased Father, who saw a chip off the old block. He had walked the mile from the farm house to Harrisburg but on a dirt road, whether dry or sodden with rain or snow. I had sidewalks. I walked alone. There seemed to be no one else from our neighborhood going to high school. So I walked alone.

To be called Mister Hazard, that was the first pleasure and the distinctive feature of high school. My father was called professor, but "Mister" was next best.

There was a new course called physiology. It was taught by a young woman of uncertain charm who, report among the boys had it, did not wear a corset. It was added that she did not need one. My own reaction was dubious. Should she not have worn a corset whether she needed it or not?

The effect of a corset can be seen in any painting of Lillian Russell (1861-1922) or in any American pictorial history, which will certainly show the Charles Dana Gibson (1867-1944) pictures of the ideal American girl of the 1890's. If the standard for a Miss America of today is 36-23-36, the corset of the American first decade would change those dimensions on the same person to about 38-22-35. This came about by reason of the shaping of the undergarment, which was fitted with resilient vertical stays of steel or bone and with lacings at back. When the lacings were drawn tight—an operation best performed by one other than the wearer—the resultant forces operated at all points from the hips upward. But since the stomach and the breasts are tractable, the effect was to reduce the waist measure and enhance the bust measure.

The science of the functional working of the human body *in health* — alimentary canal, arteries, brain, through the alphabet, to urinary system and veins—this was new in popular education in 1908. There was in our room a manikin which showed everything but reproductive organs of male and female. An aura of tension overhung the class—a dim perception of something new and untried in school. I really never learned whether Miss L. wore a corset or not. But I carry a strong impression that she dealt well with material which was delicate in those times.

At the very height of the suffragist movement a female style, called the hobble-skirt, appeared. It fell in straight lines from the hips to eight inches from the floor and was so tight below the knees that the girls could move only by mincing little steps. The circumferential dimension was about the same as that of the 1970 above-the-knee skirt—to the extent it prevailed in that year against the calf-length midi. The problem has been shifted from one of locomotion in 1910 to one of sitting down 60 years later.

The hobble-skirt went out soon. By the time our class graduated in 1911 the skirts reached the ankles well enough but with swirling flounces, and the hat had a diameter all but equal to the flounce of the skirt. In over half a century of spring, summer, fall, and winter styles the hobble-skirt has never dared to return.

No Foolishness

There was nothing foolish about the high school curriculum. It was assumed that I would take four years each of Latin and English; three years of what we then called Ancient, Medieval, and Modern History; also Algebra, Geometry, and Physical Education. I elected Physics, a course called Physiography, and Public Speaking, the last because there had been no time since the fully conscious beginning when I had not intended to be a lawyer.

The History and English took best. I was fortunate to encounter Henry Clyde Hubbart in his few years in Kansas City before he went on to Ohio Wesleyan, there to become the Head of the History Department. A questioning, non-didactic young man, he left me with a sense of the interplay between men saddled with power and events inexorably moving. Never since have I believed anything to be altogether new or altogether old in the political life of man. If I have this sense of history — perspective — why do I attribute it to Hubbart? I have had other great teachers, perhaps ten in all out of many, but today after sixty years, in a world frightened of nuclear incineration, in which I still try to think, write, and myself teach, it is his quizzical face and his inquiring voice, asking us, his students, for help with the enigmas of history I remember as clearly as I now see the inevitable relevance of every past to every present and future. Yet, why did I never write him or go to see him? What self-sufficiency tricked me into this grievous ingratitude? Why does the realization beset me now only as I write this book?

The four years of Latin (later a fifth in college) I cling to as important but for reasons much different from those which leave the history so sharp a memory. The Latin was unrelieved hard work. The history was filled with revelations and sudden insights. The Latin, from the grammar through Caesar's Commentaries to Virgil, was painful. Still, there was that opening day of the third-year class when my teacher for all four years, Frederick C.

Shaw, a gentle man (I never knew a Latin teacher to be other than gentle), used me as the example of a student who from poor beginnings had become "a pretty good Latin scholar."

I never used the Latin as Latin, but as early as my senior year in high school and later in college a few teachers began telling me that I could write well. It is my prejudice that the disentangling of those inverted sentences of Caesar, Ovid, Virgil, Terence gave me a sense of grammar and diction, still effective if no longer formal. My vocabulary seems adequate, although I am not a voracious reader. Often as I write it comes to me that there must be such and such a word, and when I look there it is. It is not that I love words, otherwise I could spell. Once I said to a secretary, Rose Pecora, "I wish I could spell all the words I know," and she, with a fine, natural Italian grace, replied, "I wish I knew all the words I can spell." No, I suspect that when I reach for a word, I find it submerged in the Latin pool.

Teachers and Teaching

But English was more fun than Latin, even the theme writing and the grubby business of composition. Miss Mamie Spencer was a good teacher of English composition, although I did not know it at the time. A joke in our student paper, *The Herald,* told us that Miss Spencer was teaching us that the simplest way of saying something is the best way.

Miss Spencer: "Give the plain English equivalent of the sentence, "The water pipes refused to yield their accustomed donation to the household activities."

Student: "The water pipes froze up and 'busted'."

The Editors of *The Herald* thought they were making humor. Actually they were expounding a profound truth, known to Miss Spencer and every great teacher of writing and every self-taught writer: simple, direct statement is more eloquent than eloquence.

We *did* read Emerson's Essays, some of them, and Thoreau's *Walden.* We studied the Concord Poets and got glimpses of the American literary scene under the guidance of Ruth Mary Weeks, daughter of that pioneer promoter of electric streetcars whom I have mentioned earlier. Later she was a President of National Council of Teachers of English. She was just out of Vassar—full of her subject but a shy girl. Her square stance at the foot of the rising tiers of students gave her a compensating belligerent pose—except for her smiling comely face. We learned because she knew. This was before the American educationists stressed methodology over content and set up schemes of educational methods—requirements which would preclude a Milton from teaching poetry or an Einstein from teaching mathematics.

I saw Ruth Weeks over the years because Mary, seven years after me, became her favorite pupil and life-long friend. When Ruth retired I wrote the *Kansas City Star* these and other things about her. In her remaining days she would say "that was the most widely read letter ever published in the *Star*." In any case I passed my final examination.

Louise Nardin, who later became Dean of Women at the University of Wisconsin, opened the gates of the British Isles from Chaucer to Shakespeare to Scott for me. She and I were mutual favorites. I think she was the first to tell me that I wrote well. She let me write a piece which I called "The Success of Failure" and try out for the graduating class oration. Elmo Robinson placed first with a brighter subject, I second. Of course, I was then unconsciously preparing myself for a lifelong fear of failure. To this day I keep old clothes around just in case of some adversity that would leave me glad enough to wear them.

I wished to debate and did represent Westport on its team of three in both the Junior and Senior years. I wished to act and did play the male lead in our Senior Play, as Stephen Fairfax in the "Raiders," a Civil War play in which it was necessary for me, wounded, to execute a fall. What a risk! But Mr. A. S. Humphrey, Elocution and Public Speaking, taught me how to drop to the left knee, then sit on the left thigh, and then let the torso fall forward—all so smoothly that I seemed to have fallen from a full standing position. *The Herald* said that "certain lines of his part which are usually ridiculous when rendered by amateurs, were portrayed excellently by Mr. Hazard and in all he made a dignified and commanding lieutenant." Despite this favorable notice the "Raiders" remains my first and last stage appearance.

College and Incipient Awareness

William Jewell College was, in my time, 1911-12, and is today, a good small college of Baptist origins and with some excellence

Dress rehearsal for "The Rivals" 1911; I have the sword!

Lulu Mae Hazard Woodruff.

in classical traditions. There are many such schools, products of the Puritan tradition in support of popular education. Many have fallen by the wayside. Those which remain have become increasingly nonsectarian.

William Jewell was at that time out of the main stream of new educational trends: economics, psychology, sociology. It was all right to have a year there with a try at Greek and some of good President Greene's Practical Ethics. The teaching was mostly didactic. I have no memory of lively classroom discussion such as we try to stimulate these days. The year at William Jewell was in deference to Father and Brother Brown, preacher in our Baptist church, from both of whom I was soon to have that intellectual separation which is both the happy and unhappy circumstance of growing up. I know it was good to move on to the University of Missouri, which was entering a golden age under a young president, A. Ross Hill.

I Encounter Davenport and Veblen

At the University of Missouri some good fortune assigned to me for an advisor Herbert Joseph Davenport, a Vermonter with a caustic tongue and a clear head. Young President Hill had brought him from the University of Chicago. He in turn had brought Thorstein Veblen, and the two for a few years made Columbia, Missouri, a shining star in what has been called, to offend my star figure of speech, "the gloomy science"— economics.

Just as physiology had taught me that there is more to the functioning of the human body than meets the eye and physiography had taught me that there are ageless forces constantly reshaping the earth's surface, so now I was to learn from Davenport that enterprise (such as Father's "business college" and house building) operates according to laws of economics and that juristic law, in one of its major aspects, conforms to other laws such as those of economics. Davenport's father had been a lawyer.

Once I asked my advisor, "Why should I study accounting?" He replied, "If you become a lawyer and have clients of consequence, you must be able to read their balance sheets." How right he was (I did study accounting under another brilliant member of that Missouri galaxy) and it was good to be under the tutelage of Davenport's leonine head and New England twang. No Puritan he. He would juxtapose the supply of *potatoes* and of *prostitutes* to expose the amoral nature of the economic law of supply and demand as the determiner of price. All my good and naive world was coming apart, as I watched quietly, telling no one.

We employed Davenport's own book, *Economics of Enterprise* (1913), whose rugged imagery taught me not only elementary economics but also more about writing. For example, these phrases from his description of that still classical figure, the economic man: He is "as solitary a hunter as a cat . . . as isolated a thing as a billiard ball, an atom, a nomad, a star . . . His plans may be far reaching but they do not intend the gain of any other; neither courtesy nor good will—nor, for that matter, ill will—can have any part in the case . . . there is no place for qualities like consideration or gratitude or courtesy or envy or revenge or ill will in the whole dull lexicon of gain." Though no superficial Puritan, he knew the Christian Ethic, without wholly approving it. He and his book taught it to me better than I would have learned it from all the issues of the *Wall Street Journal* or from the professionals who make a living from extolling free enterprise.

Herbert Joseph Davenport, I now know, did not add a great new dimension to the science of economics. He was a clarifier and a good one. Witness this learned jingle:

> The price of pig
> Is something big;
> Because its corn, you'll understand,
> Is high-priced, too;
> Because it grew
> Upon the high-priced farming land.
> If you'd know why
> That land is high,
> Consider this: its price is big
> Because it pays
> Thereon to raise
> The costly corn, the high-priced pig!

Davenport, while placing this compact exposition on price, cost, value, and profit in quotes in a footnote does not name an author. So we may assume it was his composition. But he was a teacher and expositor, not one of the great succession of Worldly Philosophers, as our contemporary Heilbroner calls them: Adam Smith, Parson Malthus, David Ricardo, J. S. Mill, Karl Marx,

Thorstein Veblen, John Maynard Keynes, Joseph Schumpeter.

Davenport championed Veblen at a time when the great man needed a male friend more than he needed the apparently endless succession of females whose proffered and accepted attentions had finally become too much both for the University of Chicago and for Stanford. He came to Missouri in 1911, heavy with honors for *The Theory of the Leisure Class,* in which he had dug for the first time deep into anthropological well-springs for economic causality and also in semi-disgrace for his philanderings. His long suffering wife had divorced him in that year. He lived in Davenport's household in Columbia, Missouri.

I was not Davenport's best student but he must have seen that none was more intrigued with him or with the new learning. In any case he urged me to take Corporation Finance from Veblen and then, by some dispensation, he gained for me, only a Junior, admission to Veblen's graduate course, Economic Factors in Civilization. In this course a dozen or so of us sat in a tight half circle before the desk on which he would place a great watch, silver case all but an inch thick, and often nothing else. He spoke in a barely audible tone—a poor teacher, but he never seemed at a loss for words. I have the certain memory that the little group did not diminish.

There was no text. The reading assignments ranged from Gregor Johann Mendel on heredity and genetics to William Zebina Riley on American railroads. The course was probably unstructured but *that* was intended. The neat formulations of economic theory he cast aside. Heilbroner says that Veblen asked economists to know that man is not to be comprehended in terms of economic laws but rather by how he actually behaves and why.

I called on Veblen more than once in his tiny office. He always offered me a very strong Russian cigarette, said to have been his only luxury. My testimony can be only impressionistic but it varies somewhat from the usual complaint about his constant uncommunicative mood. His colleagues at Stanford said bitterly that he was "the last man who knew anything." My memory is that he always seemed ready to answer my questions and that there was some coming and going of light in his pale eyes and some muscle play in his cadaverous, enigmatic face with its wisp of a goatee on the chin.

In the undergraduate course, Corporate Finance, at the last class session, he asked me to stop at his desk. "Will you be coming to class next Tuesday?" he asked with a quizzical smile. I replied, "Yes, it is the day for the final examination." He said, "True, and if you will put these questions on the blackboard, I shall not need to come," handing me an unsealed envelope. It was well known that he gave everyone a medium grade, M, doubtless because he never read the examination papers. He gave me the next grade up, an S. He knew it would not matter whether I opened the envelope. He was going to give me an S because he was excused from class.

Of course, I know more about Veblen now than when I was his student—this learned man, undoubtedly neurotic, who blew a chilly breath of realism into the Victorian penchant for having God in his heaven approving whatever was on earth, seeing our robber barons not as the instruments of economic law but as the agents of jungle law still at work. I can see him at the blackboard ruthlessly proving that men like James J. Hill and E. H. Harriman gave nothing to the society from which they took millions by their financial maneuvers. He taught me to suspect men and conventions.

Precisely what did I learn from Veblen? I do not know. Decades later when I was thrown with liberal economists I would say just that, and they would laugh, saying, "Veblen sticks out all over you." He destroyed my automatic respect for *status quo.* Something else—I was compelled to accept that a learned man, who, I intuitively knew, was a conceptual innovator was also a philanderer. My simplistic, moralistic world got another shaking.

As usual I did well in English. In one of the courses we used the *Atlantic Monthly* as a model of good writing. Agnes Repplier was a favorite of mine. Her learning, wit, and lucid writing filled me with form and substance. And something more—whether it was her skill or my maturing, or both, I do not know, but she made me feel an equal as I read. Again, a teacher, James Walter Rankin, told me I could write. We even discussed the possibility of some professional efforts, but other activities intervened. Rankin had been a colleague of Willa Cather in the Pittsburgh public schools. She submitted some of her writings to him even after he left Pittsburgh.

Book Salesman—Charlatan or Missionary

Until 1914, summers had been for the Boone County farm or casual moneymaking or just for vacations. In that year I went to St. Paul to sell "The Volume Library, a concise graded repository of practical and cultural knowledge, designed for both instruction and reference. Editor-in-chief: Henry W. Ruoff, Chicago The W. E. Richardson Co. 1911." I was one of a group supervised by an older man. We stayed at the Y.M.C.A.

I suppose the book was all right. It went through several editions, all of which can be found in the Library of Congress. It was in fact a one-volume encyclopedia which sold for $9.95 in buckram and $11.45 in leather. It was full of tables of comparative data about persons and events and conditions, past and present. There was an index, but there were few illustrations. I got 40 percent of each sale.

The Richardson Company provided us with a good and necessary sales gimmick. It would have been fatal to appear at front doors with the huge tome, nine by twelve—by three inches thick —in hand. So we had a chaste sample of key pages on thin paper, bound in limp leather, which fitted into a conforming bag slung over the left shoulder and concealed under the coat. Thus one could appear without impedimenta. I, however, carried a rolled umbrella, rain or shine, some instinct telling me that it would add an air of credibility to my otherwise unimpressive youthfulness.

Even so, there was a serious problem of gaining access to give the explanation. I remembered that years before a man had appeared at our front door saying, "Madam, I know you have washed your face today, but I will demonstrate to you that it is still dirty." Well, he did — with some kind of roll-in, roll-out cream, which did look different from its original color after it came out. But selling cleanliness in America — whether of face, hands, walls, floors, carpets, or ovens — has always been easier than selling knowledge. We are *for* education, but we *pay* for cosmetics and sanitation. How to sell knowledge — that was my problem.

After a few probings with mediocre success, I came upon a piece of good fortune—perhaps, sudden insight. In a middle class neighborhood, which, in Minneapolis, across the Mississippi from St. Paul, meant second and third generation all-American Swedes,

I entered a corner drug store one day for an ice cream soda. The fountain boy turned out to be an outgoing fellow. I told him about my book, demonstrated it to him, and, to shorten the story, he struck a blow for education by giving me the names of several neighborhood families who, he allowed, should have the book. Then came the sudden insight. I got from him the names of the children, their ages, and grades in school and the name of the school.

Now I had a technique. Approaching the door with nothing in sight but my umbrella, I would inquire, not for "the lady of the house," but for Mrs. Anderson. When she admitted identity, I would ask if Kathryn and Hans were at home because I wished to speak about their school work. The reader will now see why I am relieved to know that the Volume Library did stand up through several editions and was superseded only by more elaborate, highly illustrated, more expensive encyclopedias. The formula was successful, not invariably, but profitably. Almost always the door was opened and I was seated in the parlor.

I would mention the children's grades, speak about the home work, the need for parental aid, and the need of the parent for aid from my book. Then without flourish the sample would come from under the coat, the well-known pages would be demonstrated — ease of use, almost automation for discovery of truth. And then—this part still bothers me—a sixth sense told me when to state the price, take out the order blank, ask for the deposit, and hand the prospect my pen for signature—really making the decision for the concerned mother.

On one occasion my prospect excused herself "while I get rid of a salesman at my back door." On another, when my information was apparently incorrect because the only child was less than a year old, nevertheless the sale was made because, "the baby *will* grow up." That case still bothers me.

Occasionally, too often for my comfort, a sturdy *or* timid housewife would ask me to come in the evening to see the husband. This made quite a different problem. The husband would be a white-collar, middle-management executive as we call them now, a bit sophisticated, prepared to use on me supercilious banter or gruff formidability. But I was in college and most of my male prospects in those days had gone to work out of high school or even grade school. So now my tune shifted to how much I would need such a reference aid. (As a matter of fact I did keep my copy for some years.) I never sold books again. But it was a good summer—not a bonanza, but profitable in money, and more profitable in the learning that one never talks after the sale is made. To know when to quit talking—that is an art which applies to much greater affairs than selling books.

The Impossible War Comes

One of our Volume Library selling group, an older man already teaching history, and I were standing on the bridge between St. Paul and Minneapolis—a favorite relaxation, watching the Mississippi roll away on its long, romantic journey to New Orleans. A passing newsboy had the paper announcing the declaration of war by England on Germany, August 4, 1914. This was the last step in the series of events, after the assassination of the heir to the throne of Austria—Hungary on June 28, from which World War I ensued.

War had been repealed, we thought. The royal families of Europe were so intermarried that anything could be settled at the highest level; all European countries had such substantial holdings in each other and such substantial deposits in the Bank of England that no country would risk the freezing of its assets by war; Norman Angell in the *Futility of War* (1910) had so spelled out the nonsense of war that we thought war impossible.

Now in a flash, on the front page of a newspaper, we learned the hard lesson. Our history was to be the same as all history: war is the norm; peace is the normal *ideal* but the exception *in fact*. My historian friend was so upset that he could not work the next day. He had not been very successful in his selling, so it was easy for him to rationalize that his role as "sidewalk historian" required withdrawal from the book selling war in St. Paul and Minneapolis. Such delusive rationalizations I have had to fight off all my life. The dream world is so much more attractive than the real world.

I Encounter Manley O. Hudson

There was war in Europe. That could not be denied. But to millions of Americans, pupils of the good Dr. McGuffey's pacifism, the beginnings of World War I were just another ancient European quarrel of no concern to us. Manley O. Hudson, a Missourian, graduate of William Jewell College, first stirred my interest in peace by law buttressed by force. I had encountered him as a visiting speaker at William Jewell in the spring of 1912, extolling the democratic triumph of Sun Yat Sen's just formed Chinese Republic. If the ancient Manchu dynasty could fall to democracy, why should not the whole world soon embrace democratic peace? We equated peace with democracy. Only royal houses, kings, monarchs, and emperors made war. So it was as we saw it then.

When I entered first year law school at Missouri University, after my three years of arts and sciences, according to the plan at that time, *there* was Manley O. Hudson, fresh from Harvard Law School, teaching the law of property, but talking about world organization for peace. Later he served under Woodrow Wilson on the American staff at the World War I peace conference and a decade later became a member of the Permanent Court of Arbitration and soon a judge of the World Court. He was Bemis Professor of International Law at Harvard until his death in 1960.

Manley O. as we called him, took me to my first conference at which expenses were paid just to have me there. This was in the early summer of 1915 at Cleveland, Ohio—the European War in full scale. The meetings, sponsored by some organization for international peace, were of one mind. War could be prevented. The nations had agreed upon international postal regulations, why not upon everything else? Veblen's grim insights must have guided me. Toward the close of the three-day conference, I arose to say that there were strategic places about the earth, like Singapore, and narrow waters as at Gibraltar, and natural resources like the coal in Ruhr (this time was before oil and air power in a big way), and I allowed that such facts of geography and of life had produced war for some thousands of years, doubting in my hesitant, extemporaneous remarks whether our conference would be able to repeal history. I expected to be shouted down. But no, the older men, including Manley O., thanked me for raising some doubts. It was an early and rewarding experience of speaking a minority point of view.

I saw Manley O. in Paris after the World War I Armistice. We discussed the meaning of the 1917 Russian revolution. He said that our victory in World War I had made the world safe for political democracy, but industrial democracy was yet to be gained. It was a loose idea. I doubt that he then knew enough history or psychology of the Freudian type to appraise the Russian Revolution. But he was a brilliant international lawyer, teacher, and judge. When at some long last the role of law in global organization is chronicled, his name will stand high.

My roommates at the University of Missouri usually had something to do outside the room in the evenings. It was a bit of a sorrow to me not to be invited but I *was* left with a quiet room and I did read; among the extracurricular explorations was Bernhardi's *Germany and the Next War,* which appeared in America in translation in 1912. War in general he called a biological necessity—an aspect of the universal struggle for existence, power and sovereignty. He was probably misunderstanding Darwin. But, in any case, I was exposed to a man who would say in print in a published book that war was necessary and a necessary good for a worthwhile nation. Of course, he led me to Nietzsche and to von Clausewitz. Thus it was that I discovered alone – no teacher or parent telling me – that there were powerful men in the world having, as I saw it then, evil intent toward other men. I was not intellectually unprepared for World War I.

Insofar as slogans elect presidents of the United States, Woodrow Wilson was elected by the slogan, "He kept us out of war." The words themselves revealed the American naive view of history: leaders make war, never the people. The slogan implied that by some magic Wilson, the good leader, had kept us disentangled from the war of the European bad leaders. But as German espionage more and more became apparent within our shores and German submarines surfaced arrogantly in our coastal waters, we began to see the light. Europe was not something separate from America. It was, as Wendell Wilkie so eloquently articulated in World War II, "One World"– not one in the sense of unity and peace, as Wilkie and Manley O. Hudson hoped, but *one* in the sense that almost nothing can happen in today's world – anywhere – which does not involve the world – everywhere.

After a German submarine sank the Lusitania on May 7, 1915, and American lives were lost, we knew that the die was cast.

There were isolationists, including our Secretary of State, William Jennings Bryan, who held out, arguing that Americans should not leave our shores, or should leave at their own risk. But the American people sensed a German-intended world domination, which the German philosophers and statesmen had often enough themselves asserted. As early as 1905 the German Emperor had said at Bremen, "God has called us to civilize the world: we are the missionaries of human progress . . . We are the salt of the earth." How much it sounds like Hitler thirty years later! But America does not react to words—only to deeds, such as the sinking of the Lusitania or the attack at Pearl Harbor.

Thus it was that the President who had kept us out of war declared war on Germany on April 8, 1917, and exactly one month later I entered the first Officers' Training Camp at Fort Riley, Kansas. I had wished to enter aviation but Father interposed an unusually firm negative to that.

The first officers' training camps, dispersed throughout the existing military establishments of the nation, were America's answer to the standing armies of Europe. It was easy enough to draft troops, but how would they be led? Napoleon is reported to have said, "I have no such things as good and bad regiments; I have only good and bad colonels." I think we knew the magnitude of the responsibility, although later we were called, derisively, "ninety day wonders."

We were up with the bugle (reveille) at five; formed ranks; did setting-up exercises; drilled before breakfast. How I wish I could eat now with the gusto of those days! The appetite and digestion are still adequate but the waistline forbids. Then came marching, drilling, deploying, and maneuvering in the hills of the military reservation. (For the first 120 miles west of the Missouri border Kansas is not flat.) And after the sweltering day we studied the manuals, field service regulations, minor tactics, topography, map-making, and army regulations.

Again with the bugle we went to bed—all of a time, no irregularity. Regimentation was then of the essence of military training and practice. But in these long rows of silent cots it was possible to have a low-voiced conversation, after the lights were out, with the person on either side. On my left was a man some fifteen years older than I. He told me he was a professor of philosophy. He knew the German philosophers better than I. But we talked of them in the soft dark. For the most part, however, he talked to me of himself, his alcoholism, lechery, and sensuous episodes. One night he said, "I have come here in the hope of one glorious going over the top—to die." He was not concerned to save the world for democracy, but to save some last modicum of honor for himself. War to him was a way for honorable suicide. I wished to help him but I could only listen; this I did sleepily, and with the fatigue which a less complicated life permitted. In the interim between the training camp and active duty we lost him. I heard that some episode cost him his officer's commission. This was my first demonstration that not all men can act as they would. I had not heard of Doctor Freud at that time.

It was the bayonet practice which made me willing to kill and willing to die. That long, lethally pointed knife, attached to the muzzle of the rifle, bespeaks both offense and defense. My best remembered tactic is the dropping of the gun butt to the ground when the opponent is charging and then, at close range, with full body leverage, thrusting the bayonet knife upward into the soft underpart of his jaw. What makes a peaceful citizen willing to kill and willing to die must be a problem which has long intrigued military scientists. But for me it was the bayonet practice. I can recall as of yesterday the time when I knew that I hated the enemy and would kill him if I could and, by the same token, the time when I knew that my own precious life was not really precious.

But I was not destined to kill or to die. I could have died at the front later in France but by a shell—not in hand-to-hand combat. At the end of the 90 days of the First Officers' Training Camp, most of us were commissioned as second lieutenants; a few failed, and a few older men were made first lieutenants or captains. Then in early fall we returned to Fort Riley's war-time addition called Camp Funston, in honor of General Frederick Funston, celebrated for intrepid service in Cuba and in the Philippines.

Camp Funston was a ninety day wonder just as were the officers from the first training camp. Row upon row of wooden barracks greeted us—enough to house more than 50,000 men. We from the Fort Riley training camp were assigned to the 89th Division commanded by America's most celebrated soldier, General Leonard Wood. He was the hero of San Juan Hill. Teddy Roosevelt was his second in command. A graduate of Harvard Medical School before becoming a soldier, he was a great administrator of health and sanitation. It was under his administration that Walter Reed carried out the experiments in Cuba which found the mosquito the villain which transmitted the dread yellow fever, and so he found the way to eradicate the disease.

We felt well led under General Wood. He ordered us to carry riding crops because an officer would conduct himself more smartly with the crop in his hand. But General Wood was not a favorite of Woodrow Wilson's administration and something which amounted to official sadism occurred. When our 89th Division was ordered overseas in May of 1918, General Wood accompanied us to Camp Mills, the embarkation point near Hoboken. On the very eve of sailing the officers of the division were called to his headquarters where he read a telegram from the War Department relieving him of command of our division and sending him back to Camp Funston to train the 10th regular division. He spoke briefly, as a few reluctant tears, wrung by cruel sorrow, came from his soldier's eyes. I learned that a great man can be hurt.

Folk-Thought, War, and Insurance

In World War I an American Army division consisted of about 28,000 men and officers. It was the smallest complete battle unit, with balanced forces of infantry, artillery, engineers, signal and sanitary troops, motor and horse drawn transportation, staffs and auxiliary services necessary for a mobile force to do battle. My division, the 89th, was such a military unit, and I was assigned to the headquarters as assistant to the Division Adjutant. Why, I never knew. It turned out years later that administration was a field to which, first as a corporate officer and later as a teacher, I devoted much of my life.

When America undertook, as it did in World War I, to supplement a standing army of less than a quarter-million with a citizen army of over four million—half overseas in combat—thousands of officers, from the most seasoned regulars to the newest ninety-day wonders, found themselves performing assignments bigger than any prior experience justified. I learned that one does not question his ability in a case of obvious need. If higher authority directs—

or community or society asks—a service, one assumes competence and begins to perform.

Camp Funston—in Kansas, near the geographical center of the United States—housed at one time while I was there upwards of sixty thousand men—a sizable city, with all of the administrative problems of a community of that size. The men came from Missouri, Kansas, Nebraska, Colorado, and other western states. There was pathos, also alarm, in what one saw as these draftees —some from rural and mountain areas—were detrained between midnight and morning at the bleak siding at Camp Funston, thinking they had arrived in France.

Immediately they were marched through the showers, fitted with underclothes and uniforms, some inadequate for winter, which came early that year, socks and army shoes. There were endless incidents which we officers thought amusing, such as a draftee's, upon being asked at the outfitting station what size socks he wore, replying, "Don't wear no socks"—not amusing now in the 1970's when sandals or bare feet are the youth-mode.

At one time at Camp Funston my job was to convince the draftees to take advantage of our government's War Risk Insurance Plan. A soldier could obtain, if he so elected, up to $10,000 of insurance on his life. It was the intention of the American government that this low cost insurance program (about $7.50 per month for $10,000 of life insurance) would forestall after-the-war bonus claims. The bonus claims were not forestalled but that is another story involving the great American depression of the 1930's and the gradual movement of America toward various forms of "welfareism."

I was detailed to appear before any company of my division which was lagging in voluntary purchase of insurance—the goal was a one hundred per cent insured division. The company commander would assemble his men on some natural slope, as much in the nature of an amphitheater as possible, and I would speak to the some 200-odd men about insurance.

Throughout the rural areas of the middlewest there was deep-rooted folk-thought that insurance was gambling with death. Gambling was evil per se; and death was something in God's hands. One should not bet against God. I knew about this folk-thought because on the Boone County farm I had heard my grandmother solemnly relate how she had saved grandfather from the clutches of an insurance agent and was now planning to save her modern-minded son, my Uncle Cad—at that moment talking to a rural insurance agent at the stile. (The stile was a set of steps rising from the inside of the fence to a platform on the public road side. The platform was for ladies to mount horses—side-saddle. Alongside the stile was a turnstile through which men could go to mount horses from the ground. A small boy had to use the ladies' platform.)

War is an agency of change. It was soon apparent that the draftees were going through the process of becoming willing to kill and to die which I had experienced in the Officers' Training Camp. God had to some extent been replaced by the enemy as the cause of death. So my problem was to create a feeling that it was good and proper and American to be insured at the very favorable rates our government offered. As in the case of selling books, the trick was not to say too much.

Then I must answer questions. The most difficult one went as follows: "If I buy this insurance and then don't get killed, do I get my money back?" The challenge was to avoid treating this as a stupid question. It was not such to most of the 200-odd, silent, serious, aware-of-death men before me. Only a flicker of a smile here and there in the audiences would show the tiny minority who knew about insurance. What was I to do? Deliver a lecture on the tontine, a discourse on the theory of probabilities—to men who but weeks ago had been following Missouri mules in the corn rows or punching steers in the west?

I used an analogy. Junction City, Kansas, was a rural metropolis, the nearest to Camp Funston, and the soldiers could get occasional passes to visit the town. So I would say: "Suppose you have an enemy who has vowed to harm you. This threat is not of much risk in camp because your buddies are all around. But then you get a pass to visit Junction City at night. So you offer $2.00 to a big fellow to go along. You go to Junction City and do whatever you do there. Your $2.00 guard goes along. You return. Your enemy never shows up. Would you ask for the $2.00 back?"

There was one other inevitable question. I always left the void for this question because I knew the answer would bring a tension-relieving laugh. Toward the end someone would ask: "Can I

leave the insurance to anyone but a wife, or parent or relative?"
Answer: "Yes, you may leave it to your sweetheart." We said
sweetheart, not girl friend, in those days. That was usually the last
question and the answer adjourned the meeting in good humor.
I have a poignant memory of some thousands of those faces—
many of them soon to die—making their plans to die, quietly,
bravely accepting war and the probability of death.

For the final mopping up on our War Risk Insurance program
I wrote a play, laying the scene in 1950. That seemed a long way
off in 1917. It seems a long time past now. The dialogue, as I remember it (the manuscript seems to be lost), compared the well-
being of a veteran who had insured himself with the unhappy
estate of one who had not. The policy provided for disability as
well as for death. John C. H. Lee, later our 89th Division Chief
of Staff and in World War II head of the gigantic Service of Supply,
returned my play marked "Excellent", and orders were issued
that a theatrical company, then part of the camp entertainment
program, should produce it. This was done to huge captive audiences, along with such attractions as the Boston Symphony, my
first enchanting exposure to such music, and ex-President William
Howard Taft, who was touring the camps as a morale builder—
and a good one he was with that infectious chuckle. That play
was my first and my last.

We went overseas insured to the hilt—99 per cent according to
George H. English, Jr., a scholarly lawyer who wrote in his History
of the 89th Division, "a record equalled by only one other division
and excelled by none." Our division did suffer over seven thousand
casualties, one fourth of its strength. Widows, parents, relatives,
"sweethearts" received the funds, which, of course, could not
assuage the grief. The disabled of our number had their lifetime
insurance benefits. Money is no substitute for life or health but
it helps.

Overseas to the Front

On June 4, 1918 we sailed—nine great transports, guarded by a
British cruiser and American torpedo boat destroyers. Two naval
airplanes circled above us and an observation balloon searched
the seas for submarines.

I had never heard of Picasso or Braque, nor did I know that

Genghis Khan's mounted Mongols moved with twigs and leaves in their caps to distort silhouettes against the skyline, nor was I then able to perceive identities as quickly as I do now, and so I did not liken our camouflaged convoy, moving in three columns, each ship holding a precise spacing to the others, to the moving of Birnam Wood on Macbeth at Dunsinane. But I was aware of our great abstraction at sea, looking as if some giant sized brush had played, at once whimsically and meaningfully, upon the sides of the great vessels, with all of the sea and sky for underpainting. I was to think more than once that war did not preclude beauty.

Off the Irish coast British torpedo boats joined us for protection against German submarines. They darted around our convoy, in and out, rolling precariously, it seemed, in the heavy seas, acting for all the world like hounds on the scent. They did not add to our sense of security. We knew that they were there because the German submarines were there, and German submarines occupied a high place in our category of war risks. But we docked at Liverpool intact.

Deep depression attended our arrival. The mighty German drive of March 21, 1918, had pushed the British under General Gough back through their second and third lines of defense and then to the west bank of the Somme. This was the great offensive which forced the entente Allies at last to unify their military commands under the French general, Ferdinand Foch, who was given unlimited authority. On the eve of our arrival in Liverpool on June 16, the German general, Ludendorf, had pushed his troops through to the Marne.

There was no effort on the part of the British we encountered in the Liverpool area to conceal the doubt that the Americans had come in time or in enough force. In fact, some veterans, casualties of earlier battles, resented the advent of the Americans, saying bluntly to us that we could only prolong a war, already lost.

But the dining room at —I hope I remember rightly—the Delphi Hotel in Liverpool had a little orchestra of aging males, one of whom periodically would march off the podium blowing his saxophone in an unconvincing show of gaiety. Equally unappealing were the pastries which in the brave shop windows looked appetizing, but that look belied their lack of savour—no butter or sugar.

By train through entrancing English countryside to South

Hampton, we were packed onto transports for the rough passage to LeHavre—by night, of course. Soon we were traveling across Normandy in June and just as on the train trip through England, so now I thought, where is the war, so beautiful was the land, so peaceful with its orchards, cattle, green fields, and white villages with black Norman steeples. Two days we traveled, men in the French little boxcars for Hommes 40 or Chevaux 8, officers in third class passenger cars. At each stop our meticulous Brigadier General Winn, Division Commander, set us an example by dismounting and pacing for exercise along the railway platforms.

Now we had arrived at the training area with our divisional headquarters at Reynel, a village some thirty-six miles from the front. No tourist without a special reason would go to Reynel, but if he were driving from Cannes to Paris on the old Napoleonic road and passed through the town of mustards and mustard jars, Dijon, as he should, he would have our tiny village on his right by a hundred miles or so.

Reynel was, as all French villages seem to be, a place of crumbling stone houses spaced along a road which comes from another such village and goes to another such village. There was a chateau in Reynel which we used for headquarters' offices and the officers' mess, where many, like me, first encountered the benefits of wine with our meals. Captain Tom A. Velie, who commanded our Headquarters' Troop, was a debonair equestrian, sophisticated and fine. He explained to us, those within his hearing at the mess, that one did not drink water, coffee, and wine indiscriminately and in close sequence. Our palates were uneducated. Captain Velie was a thoroughbred. By example he taught us the graces.

I was lodged in the cottage of Madame Chaudron. One entered the front past a sizeable manure pile, indicating, as always in the case of peasants in such villages, her relative opulence. A captain and I shared a bedroom on a second floor with separate beds into which one would sink all but out of sight in the feather mattress. It was cool in France and we opened our tiny window to the brisk night air. Never again until we came to our part of occupied Germany after the Armistice did we have such comfort.

Madame Chaudron showed us how she lived, cooked, slept in one sizeable room below, her bed niche by the fireplace, closed by curtains and all windows shut and barred against the distempers of the night air. She was lean, hard, and active, reminding me of my own grandmother on the Missouri farm. Every day a troop of twenty or more of her kind went from the village to the fields—old people, some bent forward from the waist 90 degrees, to pursue peasant agricultural routines older than any record.

One night, Madame, the captain, and I celebrated. He had brought in his part of a wild boar killed on a hunt in the not too distant woods. She asked for flour and sugar from the American commissary and produced delicious bread and pastry. The boar meat was floating in its simmering marinade. There was a lettuce salad. We had unlimited wine and limited conversation, although she complimented me on my pronunciation of what French I knew. Madame was fond thereafter of depicting the scene by the little fire on which she had cooked the boar. "Moi ici, Capitaine là, Lieutenant là—tous malades."

On July 15, 1918, the Germans launched their expected fourth offensive preparatory to the final drive on Paris. So our D-day came. We moved the short 36 miles from the Reynel Training area into a sector of the front line which had been quiescent for most of the time since 1914—a stalemated area between the supposedly impregnable German Metz and the supposedly impregnable French Toul. Our combat area was known as the St. Mihiel salient north of Toul.

When we entered the trenches of the St. Mihiel salient, offensive and defensive foot soldier tactics were of equal potency. Rifles, bayonets, hand grenades, trench mortars, guns were at a stand-off. Therefore foot-troops were dug in, and had been dug in for most of four years, viewing each other through periscopes, or as covertly as possible over parapets, across a no-man's land of a mere few hundred yards, sometimes feet, in extent. The stalemate was broken only when massed artillery firing would pinpoint a segment of trenches, rendering them uninhabitable, or a major nighttime raid for prisoners or information occurred.

In warfare, administration is essential as in all complex human activity. A written record of the fact and occasion for every movement, accomplishment, failure, change of condition, sickness or death must be made and reported. Except in the heat of battle, orders are not shouted; they are written. All such records and orders, in one way or another, originate in or pass through the office of the division adjutant, in our 89th Division held by Lt. Colonel Burton A. Smead. Colonel Smead wore a small goatee, which, when he sensed the need for action, and that was often, seemed to elevate itself, independently of the position of his head, commanding attention like a raised hand. My position was Assistant Adjutant.

We had some 40 soldier-clerks in our command. Typewriters, adding machines, duplicating machines, files, card records and more were in tightly organized, stout field cases, which we could close in five minutes for a move or, on arrival, open and start to work, whether in the ballroom of a captured chateau or in a tent on a sodden field.

Mustard gas is miserable stuff—lethal in the lungs and equally lethal if enough of the body skin is affected—bitterly maiming if body parts such as genitals are reached by the gas in liquid form. The gas comes over in exploding shells. Unless there is a wind, it remains in the target area, liquefying if the night is cool, as it was in the St. Mihiel on the 7-8 of August, 1918, lying there odorless, to burn the soldier who sits or lies where it lurks, and then in the heat of day to gasify again to fell its victims hours after the danger has apparently passed.

Units of the 89th were greeted, on their first entry into the front line, with a bath of mustard gas. We had succeeded the 82nd Division in the St. Mihiel and received the retaliation for a massive raid which some of its units had staged earlier. The German retaliatory gas attack, at the very moment of our entry into the front lines, found us unprepared to learn at Division Headquarters the exact extent of our casualties. There was a system for reporting, but it broke under the stress of such instant pressure. This initial emergency set the tone for my activities throughout the fighting.

Mostly Alone—Myself for a Model

Colonel Smead and our Division Personnel Officer, Joseph E. Brown—son of that Brother Brown I have mentioned—who was responsible for the reporting system, and I talked it over. Our Division Commander had sent over a note directing Lieutenant Brown's removal. A commander must know at once the number of his casualties because he must at once requisition replacements.

I had a personal interest—not to see Brother Brown's son disgraced; besides I was proud that Smead and Brown consulted me in the crisis.

If thereafter I could get to the advanced field hospitals fast enough, I could get the reports, personally count the dead and wounded, if necessary, and bring back the needed information. I wangled from our Division Quartermaster, kindly Colonel Warren W. Whiteside, a huge, beautiful Harley Davidson motorcycle. I had never ridden a motorcycle, but that was my secret.

A division of infantry in battle in World War I was disposed roughly in the form of a triangle standing on its apex, with division headquarters there; brigade headquarters forward and inwardly of each leg; regimental headquarters still forward and just back of the base (front line), along which the infantry companies and combat groups were in direct contact with the enemy. The dead and wounded were carried by stretcher bearers to the nearest field ambulances for transport to nearest command posts or field hospital. Such field hospitals and first aid stations were often under fire. At one of them I saw my first shell-shock victim. He was a medical officer of high rank standing in the open as a field hospital tent was being erected. I stood nearby as German shells fell, one long, one short, one left, one right. This was called bracketing. It meant that a German plane pilot was observing the location (perhaps too exposed) and signalling to German artillery. If all went well for the Germans, the fifth shell would land on the target.

The medical officer was a big man with a leonine face. I stood near him, awaiting the casualties, who would soon arrive, and admiring him as an officer of high rank who had come well forward to direct the work in his charge. The fifth shell would come momentarily. We were in the open—no place to take cover. One might as well stand; certainly he could not run. Then, suddenly great tears were running down the strong face and the big body was shaking. Some medical personnel, who must have known the symptoms, led him away for evacuation to the rear—a casualty with his body skin intact. I believe that we do not know yet whether bravery is a matter of body chemistry or a morality, if there is a difference. If I ever knew whether the fifth shell dropped, I have forgotten.

The distance from division headquarters to any one forward

post could be as much as five miles as the crow flies. Given the meandering roads, their often shelled out condition, and the number of posts to reach (our divisional front might stretch for almost 10 miles), I needed speed. We allowed ourselves only 24 hours for the numbering of casualties. Cars, trucks, ammunition carts, heavy field kitchens went far forward. They had to in order to get ammunition, food, and supplies to the fighting lines. But these heavy vehicles were often immobilized in wartime traffic jams as frustrating as those on peacetime city streets. With my motorcycle I could make speed on the intact roads, weave in, around, and through traffic jams; and if the road, lacerated with German shells and our traffic had become an utter quagmire so that balance on two wheels was impossible, I could plod alongside my motorcycle, keeping it moving under low power and holding it generally upright by hand. And so from Lucey to Menil la Tour to Lironville, Limey, Flirey, Beaumont, Rambucourt, Bouconville, to such villages, mostly destroyed, I went throughout St. Mihiel on my motorcycle to gather first-hand the grim data, ignoring the system of conventional reporting. We saved Lieutenant Brown's skin. He ended his military career honorably as a Major.

My daily rounds took me where the destruction of warfare had just occurred. A destroyed French village is gray—non-descript, indiscriminate, unmoving gray. If there is some brown on the stubs of walls still standing, it is from the mud sloshed up from stumbling, dying men, straining horses, slewing trucks. If there are bits of red, it is blood. If there are disintegrating designs on walls still standing above a man's head, they are irrelevant reminders of an age, seemingly gone forever, when there was Chocolat Menier or a traveling circus. If a house and roof stands, it is forbiddingly lonely. If a church belfry stands amid general ruin, its supports torn away so that one sees the innards of the stone and mortar anciently put there by pious hands, it is a miracle —to the faithful. A destroyed French village is gray—it is nothing.

As if war had no right to claim the entire attention of the soldier, he was followed in World War I right to the eve of personal combat by paperwork, chaplains, social workers, and, in general, a surprising amount of the business of ordinary life. Perhaps even the paperwork was good. The couriers who brought it to the trenches and took it away risked their lives, just as did the ambulance drivers and stretcher bearers. Certainly the chaplains died now and then—just to be there. And some of the social workers were a positive inspiration. I needed to pass in the St. Mihiel salient more than once a certain dead-man's corner where German artillery regularly effected fatal hits. Exactly there, a few yards away, in an improvised, barely camouflaged shack, Salvation Army women cooked doughnuts. Paperwork, couriers, chaplains, stretcher bearers, doughnuts—who knows which of these may have been just the diversion, seemingly irrelevant at the time, which conserved some modicum of spirit—just enough for the next bloody business?

Did I do my duty in America's first war to stop the Germans? Formally, I suppose so. I volunteered for the First Officers' Training Camp. I had a letter to the commanding officer from an influential citizen in Kansas City, but never presented it—not very courteous to my benefactor. I don't remember why—too timid probably. My assignment was to the artillery—not the safest but not the most dangerous service. I was assigned to the Adjutant General's Department, where I went through three grades to become a major at an age young for the National Army, but just because the chart of organization called for that rank. The only request I ever made — for the motorcycle — carried me to more rather than less danger, and in carrying out my projects I never stopped or went around or back until I had what I went for.

But I was alone. No one told me what to do, or guided me, or set me any direct example. From time to time I would say to Colonel Smead, "I must go there and there; please order me." "I order you," he would say, both of us grinning. I had an inordinate fear that if I were killed, someone would say, "What was that staffer doing there anyway?" Other men in the 89th were crawling across no-man's land in the black of night to take prisoners and returning sometimes carrying their own dead and wounded, but they were together. Little groups charged machine guns in the open—sometimes one survivor made the final rush to silence the lethal thing, but he had started with others.

Guy Chapman (later a dear friend), whose *A Passionate Prodigality* is called by Peter Viereck "one of the best war books in the entire history of the human race, from Homer on", clearly fought for front-line assignments and clearly knew the somber joy of human fellowship in war. In one beautiful passage, he writes, "Your death means no more than if you had died in your bed, full of years and respectability, having begotten a tribe of young. Yet by your courage in tribulation, by your cheerfulness before the dirty devices of this world, you have won the love of those who have watched you. All we remember is your living face, and that we loved you for being of our clay and spirit." There is my question—now so very long afterward—should I have demanded the right to be with others at the points of gravest danger and of more certain death? Of course, there is no answer. One lives with such questions.

We came out of Euvezin on October 7th, 1918, bound for Commercy and a rest after two months in the front line and three weeks of the fighting advance in the St. Mihiel. I was to go ahead in search of the personal mail of the men of the Division, held up, of course, during the fighting. But now the roads behind the lines, though intact, were as congested as the ruined roads at the front, the traffic jams too much even for a solo motorcycle. Colonel Smead managed an order for an airplane. I located the mail at Bar le Duc, got it on time to Commercy for distribution to the Division, and had the pleasure of seeing headquarters troops gather around a sergeant, standing on a table under a peaceful tree in Commercy, and calling out the names of the lucky ones. I had the pain too of faces empty as their hands—after the last name was called—and the greater pain of unanswered calls—not heard in some battlefield grave.

It turned out that on several occasions an airplane saved one of my missions. Getting such a plane was a matter of mere chance. The small American Air Force flew British or French planes. We knew that the Germans had general mastery of the air over our sectors. A favorite technique of German pilots was to find a long line of military vehicles, stalled in a traffic jam, and fly low along the line—strafing. It was an ugly sight—a Fokker plane, with its machine gun synchronized to fire through the arc of its propeller blades, rising low above an horizon of trees to attack our immobilized vehicles. We tumbled under the trucks, I borrowing space under the nearest one because my motorcycle was no good as a shield against machine gun fire.

World War I planes had speeds of around 100 miles per hour.

My flights were in a deHavilland, with open cockpits for a pilot and one other. In a little more than 50 years, aircraft technology makes that plane seem an oxcart of the air, yet it could and did land on almost any moderately smooth bit of terrain. It was my job to scan the skies aft of our plane for the dreaded Fokkers.

In War Men Die in Sight of Peace

After only two days our rest at Commercy ended, and we were moving again. We did not know that General Pershing was launching the American offensives, under the Supreme Command of General Foch, which would take Sedan and help break the German will to continue the War. In war soldiers and officers—up to a rather high level—are like individual players in an orchestra. Neither can ever appreciate the grand strategy of the entire performance.

In war, surprise is a major element. If every soldier knew the whole planned strategy, or even the immediate tactics, then the opportunities of advance discovery, and therefore nullifying countermoves, by the enemy would be immensely increased. We had dramatic proof of how much the enemy knew about our 89th Division, despite our strictest security precautions. Colonel Levi G. Brown, acting as head of a section of the Headquarters Staff in charge of operations, known as G3, went forward to explore the location of front lines held by the 32nd Division, which we were to relieve. This was in an area known as Meuse-Argonne, heavily wooded in part, and heavily fortified and tenaciously defended by our enemy. Colonel Brown and an orderly rode their horses literally into no-man's land in plain sight of the Germans. They had been repeatedly misinformed by American front line troops as to the exact location of its true front. This is not as absurd as it sounds. A battlefield at the very front is not neatly marked out by white lines like a football field.

Colonel Brown's horse was killed. His orderly was wounded, but escaped back to the American front. The Colonel was captured—the highest ranking American prisoner of war. When he returned to us in Germany later, he reported that German commanders told him precisely of all the 89th's moves at the front, thus demonstrating the excellence of the German Intelligence Service. What the German commanders asked of Colonel Brown was his opinion of whether American successes on the battlefield would tend to obscure Woodrow Wilson's Fourteen Points, announced the previous January. One of Wilson's early proposals had been peace without victory.

For some ten days before the last big push our Headquarters were at Epinonville. General Pershing visited us there. He was staking much on a division which had proved itself in the St. Mihiel but had had insufficient rest between engagements. Within broad limits, however, the human body, under stress, does what is necessary—not always the spirit.

I had personal contact with such a case. He had been with us from the early days of the 89th—an older man, probably in his forties, a smart and handsome soldier, model officer, brilliant on the parade ground and in all preparatory exercises. But in the St. Mihiel offense he had become ill and again in the Meuse-Argonne—physical incapacity just as the fighting became rough. His colonel, a brave and patient man, asked that the defaulting officer be removed. Instead our commanding general sent me to place him under arrest. As I brought him through the shell scarred woods he spoke to me softly, pointing out places—a concrete pill box, which had been spitting German fire the day before, rough howitzer craters across which bayoneted men must rush the enemy—places where his spirit had failed. But he did not say "failed"; rather, he plaintively asked me to agree that there were such places as would make a man ill. I could not agree or disagree. I had not myself been at those places.

The usual technique in cases of military cowardice is to shoot oneself *accidentally* through the foot. Perhaps my arrested officer could not bring himself to even that token of bravery. The armistice came some days later. Ultimately a court martial stripped him of his rank and fined him—a lighter sentence than would have been imposed if the fighting had continued longer. Such cases are more tolerantly treated when mental illness is better understood.

On the morning of November 11, 1918, the infantry units of the 89th were in battle formation along the Meuse River across from Stenay, which had been for two and a half years a German Headquarters, occupied at the time of the Battle of Verdun by the Crown Prince. Some of our units had fought their way across the river and had occupied a portion of Stenay before 11 o'clock.

Official word of the Armistice was received by our Division Headquarters at 8:30 A.M., and the cease-fire order was to be effective at 11 A.M. I was on hand at the Meuse river front to account for casualties, since even at divisional headquarters we did not relax. One unit, engaged in the capture of Inor, a town across the river, did not receive the order until 12:15 P.M. At noon a German detachment, with knowledge of the cease-fire, and assuming that the Americans also had knowledge, approached the town to make an inquiry about billeting. Our troops fired upon them, wounding the lieutenant in command of the little detail, who then drew his pistol and killed himself.

It was hard to believe that the shooting was over. At a company headquarters I heard the commanding officer issue verbal orders: "I want every man to dig a foxhole and stay in it." He was taking no chances. There was no dancing in the streets along the Meuse when the Armistice came—just silence, mud, ruin, lifeless faces of exhausted men, and dead German horses from which the retreating Germans had hastily cut rump steaks.

"We Loved our Kaiser"

The 89th had been a hard hitting, effective division and so was given the honor of a place in the American army of occupation. Other divisions with longer service in France, such as the 1st and 2nd, moved in ahead of us, following the retreating German army by one day's march. Our line of march was through Luxembourg. At Mersch a triumphal archway had been erected and huge letters read, "TO OUR DELIVERERS." The good citizens of Mersch offered to fraternize. One, dictionary in hand, approached me saying, as he turned the pages, word by word, "You to drink with me." It was one of the few times in my life when I turned down an offer to have a drink. We had orders against fraternizing. But that night the good housewife where I was billeted put a bed warmer at my feet. Sweet victory—my first civilian bed after the war.

As usual I had a special assignment which sent me ahead of our division this time to Coblenz on the Rhine.

Bunting was hanging from public buildings. I thought, "This goes too far—Germans greeting their conquerers with bunting." Soon I learned the facts. The German people had feted the retreating German army because it was intact. It is one thing for armies to be utterly crushed and a commander like Hitler driven to the ignominy of suicide, as in World War II; quite another for armies to remain intact and enemy commanders to retain the dignity of command, as in World War I. I had arrived in Coblenz before the bunting for the retreating—stubbornly intact—German army could be taken down. But equally incongruous, so it seemed to me then, early as I was, French merchants were also in Coblenz to promote sales of French goods and to tell German merchants what prices to charge the coming American doughboys. War and trade are two prime characteristics of civilization, as Bertolt Brecht has said in "Mother Courage".

Our headquarters in the Army of Occupation were at Kyllburg in a mountainous district of bold headlands and deep valleys, called Eifel. The principal river is the Moselle, which flows into the Rhine at Coblenz. The principal city of the area is Trier, where a portion of an ancient Roman gate still stands.

In contrast to the bleak and ruined French villages, we were now in the midst of smiling landscapes, dotted with intact and picturesque villages, from which the inhabitants went forth each day to tend the important grape and other cultivations. Our 89th area was some 50 by 30 miles in extent. We administered it through existing German civil authorities. There was a lot of work, but it was dull.

We were kept in touch with the outside world by the *Stars and Stripes,* official newspaper of the American Expeditionary Forces. We followed Woodrow Wilson's fateful decision to lead the American peace delegation to Versailles, watched in print his triumphal public acclaim in Paris, London, and Rome, and saw his idealism shattered on the sardonic realism of Lloyd George, Clemenceau, and the Italian Orlando.

Woodrow Wilson's Fourteen Points, enunciated to the American Congress almost a year earlier, had made him the undisputed moral leader of the world. No wonder that the German captors of our Colonel Brown wished to know about President Wilson's ability to hold the allies to his own high moral fervor. They suspected what we Americans learned all too soon: open covenants openly arrived at; freedom of the seas in peace and war; removal of economic barriers between nations; reduction of armaments to needs for domestic safety; adjustments of colonial claims with concern for the wishes and interests of the inhabitants—they suspected, and we learned, from our own allies, that no such world was yet for mankind.

In February, 1919, after we had been in our sector of occupied Germany for two months, we received orders to start schools, with special emphasis on the correction of illiteracy in our Division. An illiterate was defined as one who could not read a newspaper or write an intelligible letter. We found such men to number about 3 per cent of our total force. Our Division historian credits the schools under the direction of our chaplains with considerable success. One soldier said, "It's no use. My sister (a school teacher) tried to teach me to write. It can't be done." The record has it that he wrote his sister several letters before we left Germany.

Our schools had their usual special evening occasions and I was detailed to address several of the sessions on the meaning of the American position at the Versailles Peace Conference. Of course, I did not really know what a tragic defeat Woodrow Wilson was suffering. I left my audiences with a vision of the future as dim and uncertain as my own. The effort would have been better omitted. Wilson's case for a world safe for democracy was already lost, had I but known the truth.

In Kyllburg in late 1918 and in the early new year, we were well aware of the fact that William II had abdicated on November 10 and had fled to Holland for sanctuary. I was not then a student of revolution. I did not understand the significance of the November 7, 1917, Russian Communist Revolution and had regarded Russia's precipitous withdrawal from the war only as a fact of greatly adverse military significance for the allies. In Kyllburg I was not aware of how closely Germany escaped communism just after the Kaiser's flight, and I did naively suppose that the whole German people had suddenly seen the light of day and become Woodrow Wilson democrats overnight. In such a state of ignorance I entered the public library at Trier one day bent on some piece of information about the area we were administering. Gradually I became aware of the eyes of the woman attendant at the desk. They were leveled on me, filled with hate. Quite irrelevantly to our business she said, "You Americans think that we Germans like the new government you have brought us. We do not! We loved our Kaiser." In one respect she was as naive as I—in assuming that the American army had brought non-monarchial republicanism to Germany. The seeds for that had long been germinating. But I remember the hate in her eyes.

It was General Pershing's custom to review American divisions just before they returned to the States. Our date was April 23, 1919, and the place was to be a vast expanse of land outside Trier on which a Zepplin hangar stood. I was to be aide for the day to Major General J. T. Dickman, who commanded the Army of Occupation. There was much preparation, including, on my part, some extra equestrian exercises, since a portion of the program would involve mounted movements. In World War I, an army officer, even though his staff assignment might be necessary, must be ready to mount a horse or take a day's march.

The great day came. We members of the official party, including General Dickman, were assembled on a knoll overlooking the vast field on which every unit of our 28,000 man division stood in rigid attention as General Pershing and his immediate aides rode dramatically onto the field. General Dickman's party, which included me, had some uncertainty. The protocol required that we ride forth to meet General Pershing, but it so happened that Newton D. Baker, the Secretary of War, had arrived on only slight advance notice. There he stood, a plain little man smoking a curved stem pipe, but he was the highest ranking military person in the whole spectacle. Protocol did not allow the unmounted Secretary of the Army to go out to meet Pershing and, by the same token, Dickman could not leave the presence of the Secretary. Some courier apparently got the word to Pershing, because, as Secretary Baker relieved our tensions by relaxed small talk, General Pershing suddenly wheeled and, riding at a smart clip to our knoll, dismounted and approached the Secretary of War, saluting smartly. He invited Secretary Baker to join the reviewing party. The Secretary declined, saying, "No, thank you; please go forward with your review; I'm just a visitor"—all in such a gracious, unpretentious manner as to put us all at ease. We mounted the horses, held near at hand by our polished, shining orderlies, and rode off to begin the inspection with the Commander of the American Expeditionary Force.

We made the inspection on foot, led by General Pershing. The pedestrian mode was a bit hard on General Dickman, who was somewhat overweight, albeit a distinguished battle commander with a fine combat record. When I delivered him to his special train for Coblenz that night he sank heavily into his first-class compartment seat and returned my smart parting salute a bit wearily. General Pershing had walked through the ranks of our division, spread out over such a space that from the aerial photograph now at my hand a whole regiment makes only a dot. He stopped frequently to talk with a company commander, and more often than not I would hear him inquire about the venereal disease record of our company. His point was that unreported venereal disease impaired military efficiency and that company commanders should be zealous in the detection and medical treatment of the disease. Even then it came over me that a military man must be single-minded. Here we were in gorgeous parade array, poised for the joyous journey home, but trim, tall Missourian John J. (Blackjack) Pershing was concerned only with our military efficiency.

Home from the War

We were to leave Germany to sail into New York Harbor almost a year to the day of the beginning of our overseas venture—12 months, of which six were spent in the mire, misery and sometimes majesty of battle, and six in the softer ways of occupation in physically unscathed Germany. As usual there was an advance mission for me—to Paris to expedite the production of our Division insignia, olive drab arm patches with a black W (or M, depending upon position) contained within a circle of black cloth. The sign stood for Midwest Division or for the names of our three commanders, Wood, Winn, Wright, or for Wright (right) Wood (would) Winn (win), since there was that moral flavor to our enterprise which critics now blame for some of the American unpopularity in the bipolar world of today. As in all full scale wars, production of such marginal items as insignia had a low priority. But we had a promise from a factory outside of Paris and it was my job to put on pressure for delivery before our sailing date.

In Paris, Manley O. Hudson, my first year law teacher at Mis-

At the first officers' training camp at Fort Riley, Kansas, 1917.

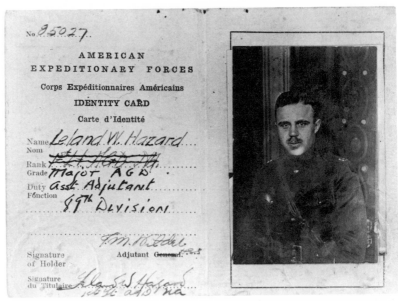

Identity Card — American Expeditionary Forces.

We are welcomed in Luxembourg on our march into Germany.
Captain Hazard at the right. December 3, 1918.

Gate at Kyllberg, Germany, in the Eiffel Mountains. The street leads
to the towered 89th Division Headquarters. This etching by
E. de la Fontaine (1911) was my first art purchase.

Major Hazard and Alvin M. Owsley, Commander
of the American Legion, at services in Westport
Baptist Church, Kansas City, Missouri, during
the Legion's Convention, 1921.

souri, was busily learning French while finishing his work on President Wilson's delegation at the Peace Conference. He took me to lunch and spoke hopefully of the Russian Revolution, as intellectuals were inclined to do in the early stages of the Russian Communist take-over.

I got the epaulets, sufficient for the troops who were to sail on our Division Headquarters ship, the Rotterdam. On the night train to Brest I had a space in one of those French pullmans (wagon lits) with four open thinly padded berths for sleeping in full dress. One lower was occupied by a Y.W.C.A. service woman, the other by me, and the two uppers by two French civilians, one of whom fell out of bed, apparently without damage, for he made only the uninspired remark, "Je suis tombé." The next morning we boarded ship and our troops promptly began sewing on their "patches". General Winn was pleased because we would be the first American unit to arrive in the States fully equipped with insignia.

The voyage home took fourteen days. We were all quite gay. Elsie Janis, a famous and gracious entertainer, was aboard with her mother. There were dances. The slow days passed, and then New York, and then Camp Funston, again—where we paraded naked before medical officers who recorded our physical conditions. There was then the now quaint notion that society's obligation to veterans should bear some relation to the damage done to them by the War. Now we know that society is rapidly becoming responsible for whatever malaise besets any of its members, war veterans or not.

In Kansas City I could see that Father had reached a plateau. The War had increased the need for women secretarial and clerical workers; there was prosperity; so the business college and Father's rental properties were doing well. But there was that inexplicable understanding that Father would just be working out his time from then on. Mother's asthmatic breathing was more pronounced. Her loving concern had never been didactic, and she seemed even more precatory, hoping, while she played the Martha role, that all would turn out well. My sister had lost in the War her fiancé, Sanford Brown—another son of that same Brother Brown and my never-forgotten childhood and teenage friend. It was a less than happy summer. My sister thought that the War had not improved any of the boys we knew, including me. She had, and still has, the blond, delicate beauty of Hazard women, also a stubborn practicality. After a period of mourning she married and to her role as mother of two successful children added important public activities in Kansas City's political reforms. She was at one time President of the Women's City Club. But the summer of 1919 was hard. I took her for her first trip to New York and Boston on my way to enter Harvard Law School.

The Glory that was Bologna

The phrase applies to Europe's oldest University, established in 1088—Bologna. It has been analogized to Harvard Law School because of the vigorous discussions in the classrooms. But I was not prepared for such excellence. By the end of the first semester I knew the depth of my problem. There were reaches of effort and requirements of application far beyond any standards I had met in any school. Fortunately I had encountered, after coming to Cambridge, a fellow member of the 89th Division, John Vogel, from St. Louis, Missouri. He and another student occupied the top floor of a house on Brattle Street, and there was an extra bedroom and study space across the desk from John for me. Now I set myself the task of keeping up in the second semester the pace of my mentor and of recouping what had been lost in the first semester. I think I built up in that period, brief as it was, whatever intellectual and bodily fortitude I possess for sustained attention to the work of the mind. I owe much to John Vogel, whose head for learning law was far better than mine and whose method of study I deliberately copied. Fortunately, I told him years ago of my admiration for his scholarship and of my regret that mine was not of equal quality. He replied graciously, and, I am sure, with honest intent, "But you were more imaginative," referring to the occasional discussions and arguments which infrequently punctuated our daily and nightly silences in the books. John Vogel became a quiet, solid lawyer in his native St. Louis. When I became active in the Missouri Bar Association, I never encountered him in the St. Louis lawyers' power structure. But why did I not search him out more often? My debt to him was great.

I now know, as I learned before my Harvard year had passed, that I was there in the second generation of the Law School's greatness. Although the school was established in 1817, it had pursued the easy ways of law teaching, following the didactic mode of the Justinian and Napoleonic scholars and of the English writers, Glanville, Littleton, Coke, and Blackstone. In 1870 Dean Christopher C. Langdell had come to the Law School. Reflecting the scientism of the late 19th century, he had repudiated the teaching of law by precept and turned the students' attention away from what the scholars *said* about law to what the judges *decided* in actual cases. He and teachers whose names are still great among lawyers, Thayer, Gray, and Ames, produced huge tomes of selected cases, which the student had to absorb and from which, by the help of class discussion, guided by the teacher, he deduced the concepts for legal reasoning. Thus law became, under Langdell's tutelage, not a body of knowledge, important as knowledge may be, but a way of thinking about the problems of social accommodation.

Of the second generation of the Law School's master teachers, I sat in the big classes (the total enrollment was upwards of 1000) of Dean Roscoe Pound, Samuel Williston, Zechariah Chafee, Jr., and Austin W. Scott. I do not know who influenced me the most, Williston, Chafee, or Scott. Pound was not the best teacher. He got into more contentions, it seems to me in retrospect, with the most brilliant students. It is well known that a poor teacher cannot survive at the Harvard Law School. The students will make his intellectual life intolerable. Of course, Pound did survive. He was one of the succession of great deans. His vast legal scholarship became known to me later, as I used his writings in the philosophy of law in my own teaching. But in 1919 and 1920, as he came slowly down the side aisle of the amphitheater classroom to teach us Equity, wearing his green eye shade (some churlish fellows said he affected that to prove how he had worn out his eyes in scholarship), he seemed less obviously a great one than Williston or Scott. I was not mature enough to know his greatness then.

Chafee was the most delightful, one of the few truly graceful teachers I have known. His subject, Bills and Notes, a dry commercial field, sparkled under his nimble mind. He gave me one of my most useful apothegms. Responding to a student who had pressed too long a distinction without a difference, he would say, not too often, "You are like the antiquarian given to arguing that the *Iliad* was not written by Homer but by another man of the same name." This gem must have been originated by some medieval schoolman in some monastery. But I heard it first from Chafee, and have never seen it in print, and so I gratefully give him the credit. I fear that I have used it with less restraint than did my teacher.

Scott was master of didactic teaching. Always on his feet, he would permit, *create* in fact, confusion, only to summarize at exactly the right time, comprehensively, the state of that portion of the law of Trusts then at hand. The summary was always so neat that one wondered why he had not done it himself. Scott, a pupil of the great Ames, produced the first edition of his case book on Trusts in 1919. Somewhat less voluminous than other case books, it seemed less formidable, and Scott uniquely covered it all, so that the student felt not surfeited but, rather, happily filled with the whole. The footnotes were replete with cases to disclose the vagaries of human nonsense. I reproduce one here.* I possess my student's copy of Scott's *Cases on Trust* and look at it occasionally for intellectual delight. There have been subsequent editions and

---

*In M'Caig v. University of Glasgow, (1907) S.C. 231, the court held invalid a trust for the purpose of erecting and maintaining forever artistic towers and monuments and statues of the testator and various members of his family on land devised by him. A similar bequest was held invalid in M'Caig's Trustee v. Kirk-Session, (1915) S.C. 426. In the former case, Lord Kyllachy said (p. 242): "I consider that if it is not unlawful, it ought to be unlawful, to dedicate by testamentary disposition, for all time, or for a length of time, the whole income of a large estate—real and personal—to objects of no utility, private or public, objects which benefit nobody, and which have no other purpose or use than that of perpetuating at great cost, and in an absurd manner, the idiosyncrasies of an eccentric testator. I doubt much whether a bequest of that character is a lawful exercise of the *testamenti factio*. Indeed, I suppose it would be hardly contended to be so if the purposes, say of the trust here, were to be slightly varied, and the trustees were, for instance, directed to lay the truster's estate waste, and to keep it so; or to turn the income of the estate into money, and throw the money yearly into the sea; or to expend the income in annual or monthly funeral services in the testator's memory; or to expend it in discharging from prominent points upon the estate, salvoes of artillery upon the birthdays of the testator, and his brothers and sisters. Such purposes would hardly, I think, be alleged to be consistent with public policy; and I am by no means satisfied that the purposes which we have here before us are in a better position." Scott, Austin Wakeman, *Select Cases and Other Authorities on The Law of Trusts,* The Plimpton Press, Norwood, Mass., 1919, pp. 290-291.

there is also a *magnum opus* on Trusts which, at this writing, Austin Scott continues to revise. He is the last of the second generation of superb teachers at the Harvard Law School. There are subsequent generations of teachers and of students who "knew not Joseph." I am a fortunate one who did.

Samuel Williston always sat. Master of the Socratic method, he was, as Learned Hand says in comment on Williston's autobiography, *Life and the Law*, "the picture of one who had neither vanity, nor its counterpart, self depreciation; neither pedantry, nor intellectual slackness." It was like a play to see and hear him spin a supposititious case, "I offer to sell you my black horse, Dobbin, for $100 provided that you . . .", and then a student would rashly propose the answer in some proposition of the Law of Contracts only to find from Williston's gentle questioning that he had missed controlling nuances which made the answer the reverse of the student's original pontification. I think that Williston's planned questions, each so apparently ingenuous, so pacific that some student would invariably bite, were as much like swordsmanship to the death as verbalism could possibly be.

What was my surprise then when, twenty years later, his biography disclosed lifelong nervous ailments with insomnia, intelligently controlled at times with the drugs then available. This serene man, whom I still picture sitting Buddha-like, only the deep chest and noble head visible above the podium desk, was seldom wholly well. Yet we felt a power of teaching such as the pupils in a corner of the agora must have felt in the presence of the originator of the Socratic method.

At the end of the long year, the examinations over, the result unknown, I met Father and Mother and my sister, Lulu Mae, at Spring Lake, Michigan, for a vacation. Father was overweight, a sign of stress which soon was to materialize in a temporary nervous collapse, which today would be called depression. Even at that late date we knew nothing of psychiatry. There was no obvious cause of Father's symptoms, considerable weeping and protests of his concern for his family. We all agreed that he would go to the Boone County farm with my sister to help with the extra work. After six months he himself decided to come back and functioned well for another 20 years.

One episode on that vacation taught me something. I was a

fairly good swimmer, having done a mile several times in the past. The 1890 resort hotel had a long turf sloping down to the lake where one day our family was seated with vacation-made acquaintances. I went to the dock for an evening swim, jumped off, and nonsensically decided to swim without an accompanying boat to a point of land about a quarter of a mile away. Half way across, I thought of the depth, 90 feet, looked forward and back—equal distances—and then a panic cry for some help came right up to my Adam's apple, where I, by an act of will, stopped it. A swimmer can always rest on his back with almost no effort. This I did, and saved myself the experience of drowning. Ever since I have known what may have happened when the news account says of some good swimmer that he inexplicably sank. I went on to the far shore and Father came in a boat to accompany me back. As had long been my custom, I said nothing of the crisis. But many times I have practiced relaxation in a crisis. Often I have said to my colleagues in the practice of law, confronted with a critical decision, "When you don't know what to do, do nothing," which is to say turn on your back and rest, while strength and inspiration for the next lap comes.

I had already decided not to return to Harvard. My own funds had been enough for one year only. In Cambridge I learned of students who had not taken the law degree and had gone into practice. In most states one may take the examinations given under state controls and, if he passes, gain a license to practice law. (A rule which requires a degree from an accredited law school would be socially important but there was no such rule in Missouri in 1920.) Perhaps I was clairvoyant. In any case, it soon became apparent that Father could not help me financially for another year in school. (I did not even raise the subject.) I was welcome in the household, where room and food were provided generously without question. I studied hard the summer of 1920, sometimes discussing and disagreeing with Father on points of law in my preparation for the State Bar examinations. My grades from Harvard came, passing, but without distinction. I passed the state examination in the fall.

PART II
In the Testing

Two Kinds of Lawyers

I had a license to practice law in Missouri, but one needs clients or employment from a lawyer who has clients. I had neither. This worried me; it worried my family, including my sister Lulu Mae, who mentioned a certain Arion Jordan, member of our church and secretary to a lawyer named Jacob L. Lorie.

So prompted by my sister, and secure in the church background, I gained an interview with Jake Lorie. There would be no salary but a nice office in his comfortable suite. My employer would give me some minor law work which he could not handle or preferred not to take. More important, since he was more a money lender (out of a substantial family fortune) than practicing lawyer, he would give me abstracts of titles to examine. Jake Lorie was a good lawyer. Graduated from the University of Michigan Law School, he "knew the law," as we lawyers say. Yet Jake Lorie was not aggressive. He was deeply devoted to his mother—over and above the attachment usual in a Jewish family. He would telephone her several times in the day, and leave the office early to take her a-riding in a 1921 Cadillac. He knew all the rich Jews in town, but did not have much of their business.

The abstracts of titles I examined were critical to my legal development. Lawyers may be classified among several categories, one of the simplest divisions being courtroom lawyers on the one hand and office lawyers on the other hand. Almost everyone is familiar with the dramatics of the courtroom lawyer, certainly since television. Not as many know what the office lawyer does or why. The examination of titles to real estate makes a good illustration.

Title to land in America rests upon an original grant from the sovereign, in the case of some of the colonies by act of king or

English Parliament; in the case of states beyond the 13 colonies by grant, sometimes called patent, from the federal government. From then on one must find a perfect chain of title made by deeds of conveyance from successive owners or by some other legally valid process by which ownership can pass from one to another.

Title searching can be dull work. One must make a diagram of complicated land descriptions and a check list of land title law points—and, above all, stay awake. One nod, and the client may pay for land which he will not own. The chain of title transfers from the original grant by government through centuries and the decades—that is what the lawyer must examine. If he misses a missing link or fails properly to evaluate a weak link, his client will lose money and the lawyer will lose reputation. Professional mistakes spread rapidly within the profession and beyond.

When Jake Lorie gave me a title to examine, it was because he intended to lend money on the security of the land. If I missed a point he might have no security. Likewise, when our family friend, Milburn Hogue, brought me an abstract, he intended to spend money from his meager fortune. I must be right. This sense of responsibility came to me early—in Jake Lorie's office. A courtroom lawyer may blame his mistakes on a stupid jury or a biased judge; a doctor may bury his mistakes, as the trite saying goes; but an office lawyer who has made a mistake in a title search can only stand naked and ashamed before his professional brethren and his client, for the mistake will be as apparent and inexorable—beyond any apology—as an error in multiplication or addition.

After I had gained a bit of reputation as a title examiner, a rather distinguished lawyer, but one not mentally adapted to title work, came to me for help with a bad title mistake. His white face, nervous hand, and plaintive efforts to explain made the interview an agony for him and for me. I myself once made a bad mistake— a disgustingly simple mistake. I just overlooked an entire 40 acres out of a 160 acre tract. It was not even a mistake of judgment. It was an oversight, as inexcusable as a mistake in addition. Providentially I consulted a colleague, prompted by some vague sense of difficulty, and he saved me before any damage was done. Not all lawyers can stand the silent pressure for exactitude. Occasionally one becomes alcoholic, or an insurance salesman, or goes to the state legislature. In any case, the office lawyer, called Solicitor in Britain, and the courtroom lawyer, called Barrister, are likely to be men of greatly differing aptitudes and temperaments. In Britain a lawyer must be one or the other. In the United States he may be both and occasionally one finds a lawyer who *can* be both. Most great law firms, however, have one or more partners who are known as the "trial lawyers" of the firm. The others are office lawyers and their work makes the six-sevenths of the legal iceberg which is never seen. Contracts, wills, titles, charitable trusts, banking and trade regulations, labor, taxes, mortgages, bond issues – the list is as long and varied as the affairs of men – these are the grist of the unsung work of office lawyers.

I encountered some first-hand testimony on the sharp temperamental differences between office lawyers and trial lawyers in my early practice. Massey Holmes was a Kansas City patrician, product of Harvard Law School, with a mind so facile and sure that one could almost see it work—like watching the flexing muscles of a gaited horse. James A. Reed at the time in question was a United States Senator from Missouri with an almost perfect record for success in the courtroom, whether as a prosecutor or defense counsel in criminal cases. In the late days of Reed's senatorship, which extended from 1911 to 1929, he formed a law partnership with Massey Holmes. We all thought it a perfect association: Reed, with mellifluent voice and noble countenance, in whose hands a jury, even a judge, were as putty; and Holmes in whose mind a legal idea was equally plastic. But the partnership was short lived; Massey Holmes told me why, after the partnership dissolved: "Now Reed's mind, if any, works this way. He will come into my office and I happen to be rolling a problem around. So I will say to him, 'Senator, what do you think about this case?' Then I will state the case hypothetically without saying which side we represent. Reed will use every artifice to drag out of me which is our side of the case, and once he knows, he explodes with ideas in our client's favor, but until he knows whom we represent, his mind will not work. I couldn't stand it," Holmes concluded.

Title examinations are dull work unless the examiner sees the romance in the dry record. Birth, death, illness, love, hate, penury, hostility, stupidity, brilliance; the need for earthly immortality; the need of the dead hand to rule; faith, love, in the sense of charity; hope for the next generation; contempt for the world; disillusionment with self—all are there, if one but reads between the dry lines of legal precision in deeds and wills and probates. If one permits a second, and somewhat poetical, self to function while the alert technical mind dominates, he will see what Robert Frost meant: "Good fences make good neighbors." He will understand what the Roman poet Catullus meant: "Justice comes from disputes over boundaries."

Church Consolidations and Mary

Michigan Avenue Baptist Church (that church of Brother Brown and the baptismal tank and the fishing boots) had consolidated with Tabernacle Baptist Church and then with Westport Baptist Church. These consolidations were a consequence of the growing automobile age. The neighborhood church has been abolished by the autombile. So in the early 1920's some of the deacons of the consolidated Westport Baptist Church, particularly Maurice H. Winger, a devout churchman and successful lawyer, involved me in the legal work of consolidating Westport with the oldest and most distinguished of Kansas City's Baptist churches, Calvary.

Some opportunities come just because one is new or young. Actually I was no longer young. To be approaching 30 seemed to me at that time to be approaching some end—not death but a plateau which would be death's equivalent. Quite a lift came to me when Maurice Winger involved me in the technical aspects of the consolidation of the two old churches. There were important properties of substantial value and the whole thing had to be done with technical competence. In any case it *was* done, and there were no subsequent disputes — the acid test of whether a lawyer's work has been well done.

Then I became a deacon in the consolidated church, the superintendent of the Sunday School, and a pillar of a sort. These assignments I accepted as challenges for study. I looked into Biblical lore with a lawyer's preoccupation in preparation of a case. I believe that I had long since lost any undiscriminating religiosity — perhaps in my sophomore year in high school, although I base that judgment upon the memory I have of arguments with my father of about that time. Certainly my interest was intellectual, not religious; yet to this day the intellectuality has never driven me to the scoffer's scoff. There is too much symbolism in all faith for dogmatic iconoclasm to prevail. Thus began a lifelong interest in the Hebraic-Christian tradition.

The brief period of churchman activity brought me Mary. Her mother, Jane Hasseltine Garnett, had been a pillar of the Calvary Church. Mary came with her to the consolidated church. A Phi Beta Kappa from the University of Missouri, first woman to be admitted to Mystical Seven, an ancient campus society, representative for the student body before the State Legislature, she was teaching in an early version of ghetto school in the heart of Kansas City's notorious gangland. I noticed her first in a rehearsal for a Christmas pageant. Soon the mind and the body proved equally alluring. Now, for almost five decades she has been wife, mentor, and mistress — in coordinate roles. It was a good wind which blew me Mary!

I Gain a Sponsor

Barely a year after Jake Lorie gave me an office, Maurice H. Winger gave me a salary as an associate in one of Kansas City's more aggressive law firms. The firm, then known as New, Miller, Camack, and Winger, was not the most prestigious of the City's law firms, but it occupied a whole floor of a building in the heart of the financial district. The huge lobby had wall-to-wall carpeting and important clients came to consult Arthur Miller in one big corner office and Maurice H. Winger in the other.

Maurice Winger, like Jake Lorie, had abstracts of title for me to examine, but many more. The firm represented several insurance companies, particularly the Northwestern Mutual Life Insurance Company and The Equitable Life Assurance Society of the United States. The times were prosperous—the early half of the second decade of our century. We thought that the American economy had discovered perpetual motion — ever upward. The insurance companies were lending on the farm lands and city properties of what we called the Middle West—Missouri, Kansas, Iowa, Nebraska, and Illinois, although the region is much larger, extending from the Alleghenies to the Rockies and bounded on the south by the Ohio River and the southern portions of Missouri and Kansas. Prices of farm lands were inflated, having mounted to as much as $250 per acre on lands which, as it turned out, could make a yield, by the then technology, on valuations of not more than $50-$100 per acre. In a few short years during the 1920's I found myself examining titles for loans made by the wisest insurance companies in America and then foreclosing the mortgages which secured such loans as the agricultural depression, which preceded the Great Depression in finance and industry, frowned upon our erstwhile smiling corn and wheat belt.

It was the predepression depression, besetting the Kansas City area, primarily agricultural, which brought me into association with Frank P. Barker. A few years older than I, he was an associate of our firm who had specialized in bankruptcy law. The partners and principal associates of a big law firm always need help—not because of incompetence but just because the load is too great. So I found myself, although I was considered Maurice Winger's man, getting assignments from others and especially from Frank Barker, to whom, as the incipient Great Depression deepened, more and more cases of insolvency, some of them great names in the business community, came "to go through the wash," as Frank Barker put it. Thus I learned bankruptcy and insolvency law in a period when such knowledge was to be quite profitable.

The phrase, "practice of the law"— or for that matter of engineering or of medicine — is a quite accurate term. The graduate lawyer with his license has much knowledge but the complexities of economic life are far beyond him. He learns by doing, meaning that he learns by practicing on real problems. This is why the client takes a risk when he selects a lawyer. Friendship, family associations, personality—these are dangerous guides. In the case of what I have called office work, the safest course is to go to an established institution—a large law firm, a large engineering firm, a doctor who belongs to the staff of a large hospital. Persons of small means often make the mistake of thinking that they cannot afford to go to lawyers of great reputation. Such lawyers will either take the case, and whatever fee the client can afford, or see that the client is sent to a competent practitioner. Good lawyers know good lawyers—and, by the same token, bad lawyers.

Despite all precautions there is always a risk in picking a professional. This is what J. P. Morgan the Elder meant when he said that the greatest risk in business is the legal risk. The high priests of any profession can be wrong. The client or patient must never forget that fact—and better still the high priests must never forget human fallibility.

Maurice Winger was the kind of lawyer we call practical. He was not a deep student, but he had a facile and sound mind. He expressed himself well. Businessmen liked him. His principal client was Walter S. Dickey, whose sewer pipe business—vitrified, salt-glazed sewer pipe—was making a million dollars a year, a substantial figure in the early 1920's. Maurice Winger was a good executive. I learned from him the importance of doing everything you can about a problem then and there. I was by nature a procrastinator, but as I spent more and more time by his side I learned how to divide the little things which often can be done or delegated at once from the bigger things which require reflection and deliberation.

Quite soon I became too much involved in other matters to examine abstracts of title. Maurice Winger, who wanted the intellectual help, took me into his confidence on matters of moment. Frank Barker engaged me for the opposite reason; he was a very hard worker and really needed the help. I had in abundance what every beginning professional needs—opportunities.

Maurice Winger and his clients taught me the responsibilities of counseling. Pete Reeder, our trial lawyer, gave me courtroom and jury experience, and equally important, since one of his clients was Fidelity and Deposit Company of Maryland, a bonding company, I became involved in the intricate questions of suretyship and subrogation. A bonding company which has paid the defrauded party's loss succeeds to whatever rights that party has against the defrauder or others involved in the defalcation. These are very nice questions. The amounts are substantial. The cases are tried in equity without a jury and one side or the other will usually appeal. Well before the end of my first decade of practice I was writing briefs and appearing in appellate courts, particularly in the Federal Eighth Circuit Court of Appeals, which sat at Minneapolis.

In brief-writing and in personal appearances before appellate courts I learned the inexorable necessity for brevity and precision. On this score Judge Kimbrough Stone told me a bit of court lore. He was the presiding judge of the Federal Eighth Circuit and I had appeared before him as I had appeared before his predeces-

86

sor, Judge Walter H. Sanborn—both fine gentlemen of the law. Judge Stone said to me in his chambers (the term for a judge's office), "We always know when a lawyer has finished his argument but nevertheless continues to talk just because his time has not expired. One of us will pass a note under the bench (the name for the high desk on the raised podium where the court sits) saying 'Now he is carrying empties.' " What more pointed analogy could he have used—containers full of nothing being laboriously transported. I could not be sure whether he was telling me that I had been guilty of carrying empties or whether he was paying me the compliment of talking about other lawyers.

A Federal Judge Gives Me a Lift

Whatever uncertainty about whether Judge Stone's "empties" applied to me, there could be no doubt about what Judge Otis said to me one day in his chambers, "I like your arguments." Only ten years my senior, graduate of the University of Missouri and its Law School, Phi Beta Kappa, he had risen rapidly to become an assistant solicitor general of the United States, and then, by appointment of Calvin Coolidge, United States District Judge, resident in Kansas City, Missouri. A big man, his facial features were regular, strong, and fine. When he spoke there was the nicest interaction between word and tone. He was capable of intense feeling but heart, head, hand, and voice each played its disciplined role so well that one felt only the majesty of the law and of the person. On one occasion the head of Kansas City's gangland, John Lazia, having been before Judge Otis on a federal criminal charge, remarked, "That sonofabitch almost makes me respect the law."

That same Johnny Lazia had the soft drink concession in the then Tom Pendergast machine-control of Kansas City. Others had other concessions: beer, slot machines, concrete, gasoline, music boxes, and so on through the list of night life and entertainment. Lazia had soft drinks. A circus which came to town for a few days, or a convention, any purveyor of soft drinks, temporary or permanent, if the business was of any consequence, must buy from Lazia's suppliers. It was the new form of gangsterism, called "muscling in" on legitimate business. The penalty for refusal was some form of violence. The reach of organized crime into high places is a continuing threat to our society, but, in utterly corrupted Kansas City in the 1920's and 1930's, city government itself would try to provide legal muscle to support the gangsters in the rare cases in which literal muscle failed. Judge Otis provided an unusual exception in our then benighted Kansas City, Missouri.

I appeared before Judge Otis frequently in the early 1930's. The decision in one of those complicated subrogation cases which I have mentioned, he delayed for months—unusual for him. One day he called me to his chambers to say, "Mr. Hazard, I have concluded that you should prevail in this case but I don't know exactly why. Will you be good enough to write for me the appropriate findings of fact and conclusions of law?"

The depression was deepening. Farm mortgages were in default. The temper of rural communities was ugly. Some trustees and state sheriffs were intimidated by mobs. I worked out a plan of foreclosure by suit in the federal court. It was necessary for the mortgage debtor to deny the debt *under oath*. This he could not do because the debt could be easily proved by the signed note; the oath would have been false—perjury, a crime. Hence, the debtor would file an answer, not under oath, hoping for some months or more of respite while the case was being reached. I would then file a motion for summary judgment, the debt in the court standing as not denied. On this motion the judgment of foreclosure could be obtained in about 30 days and would provide for the foreclosure sale by the United States Marshal—an officer often more highly respected than local sheriffs or private trustees.

There is a question which concerned me then and now: What is the lawyer's responsibility when times are changing more rapidly than the law? Certainly my procedure was altogether legal and helped insurance companies, whose payments were supporting widows and orphans and putting children through high school and college. On the other hand, I certainly put some farmers off their farms. Despite my awareness of the dilemma, it has always seemed to me that a lawyer must apply the law as it is in support of his client's interest and rights. That is what I did in the farm foreclosures. The New Deal soon made it possible for a farmer to take a form of bankruptcy under which he could stay on his farm by paying a reasonable rental. Judge Otis, who had sustained my motions for foreclosure judgment in ordinary legal course, held the farmer's bankruptcy law, called Frazier-Lemke Act, constitutional. The Supreme Court of the United States ultimately reached the same conclusion. Since the time of Solon, legislation has intervened in periods of depression to relieve debtors from the rigors of existing law. Father thought there should be legislation to relieve debtors who held investments in city properties on borrowed money. Such was his case. But no relief came and he suffered financial reverses in the 1930's. Fortunately he knew that I was prospering modestly and could help him if need be.

I had taken no part in the stock market boom of the 1920's. This meant that I had made no money by that method and so when the crash came in 1929 I lost nothing. In fact, on the day of the crash excavators were breaking ground for a house in which, I am sure, Mary and I would be living until this day, if circumstances had not taken us to Pittsburgh. French provincial, on a wooded slope, its steep roofs slate-covered, the house had two chimneys, one free standing, five fireplaces, one in an open patio. Mary and I gave parties for people we liked and the house co-operated well. The architect, Irving Parsons, a graduate from the University of Pennsylvania, husband of Mary's University roommate, Pemala Shackelford, came back from Sante Fe (he was tubercular) for the job. He was a whimsical, sensitive, vain man. Once in Santa Fe he took me to see a house he had designed, and to see particularly the main room, which, he told me on the way, was so exquisitely proportioned that people upon entering had been known to weep for the joy of its beauty. I did not weep; yet I understood. Architectural proportion can be as moving as music—for just two examples, Jefferson's Monticello or the 9th Century Church outside Athens at Daphni.

I am of the diminishing generation which knew the Great Depression: failing banks, Franklin Roosevelt's great early days, public works, relief, bread lines, the rush of legislation to save an economy in ruin. One day I encountered Father in a line waiting to deposit money in our Postal Savings Bank. We looked at each other sheepishly but understandingly. The banks were not safe. Father's tenants were in arrears in their rents and houses he had sold on deferred payments were being abandoned. There was fear in the land.

Mary.

Our Kansas City house.

The living room.

It's an Ill Wind

The Great Depression brought me a major business experience. Judge Otis was involved. F. R. Nichols was a genial trader in what he thought were bargain lots of steel and wire products. His company was called Nichols Wire, Sheet and Hardware Co. He had built it up, according to his own testimony, by selling galvanized steel sheets, which were "seconds" for the price of the prime product. Unethical, of course. How did he get away with it? "I would ship these seconds way to-hell-and-gone out in the Oklahoma oil fields. Some carpenter at the rig site, nailing up these sheets, would stop and say 'Oh, hell! This is a second' and then go right on nailing. They couldn't bother to wait for primes." Nichols would raise his chunky arm and fist and go through the motions of nailing, smiling a boorish smile. The world owed him more than he could take honestly, so he thought. In any case he was a fair-weather merchant. His idea of dealing with the Depression was to buy more products for resale—oblivious to the fact that the whole country was going into liquidation. The time was 1930. Nichols had distribution points in Missouri, Oklahoma, Iowa, and a wire producing factory at Davenport. There was mortgage debt over $100,000 and general indebtedness or commitments of $1 million—all in default and arrears. Creditors were restive. Arthur Eisenhower, a vice president of Commerce Trust Company, brother of Dwight Eisenhower, headed a creditors' committee and was acting as watchdog over the operations. G. V. Dryden, a completely cured alcoholic, who at the height of prohibition knew all the best bootleggers and always kept liquor on hand just to prove his immunity—and incidentally for his friends—was an excellent accountant. Creditors trusted his figures and had confidence that they knew the worst.

The creditors were a blue ribbon list of the great steel companies of America headed by U. S. Steel itself. By now I was geting what I still call a feel for the situation. I knew there was no short run solution. I did not ask Arthur Eisenhower, or G. V. Dryden, or even my senior partner, Maurice Winger. We were all apprehensive — Nichols, the creditors, Eisenhower, Dryden. The depression was deepening. Too much talk could have been contagious. Forced liquidation of the business in bankruptcy might have paid the general creditors ten cents on the dollar, perhaps nothing, since the bond holders had a prior claim.

A bitter Depression story was circulating: a raiser of hogs in Oklahoma shipped a carload for sale on the Kansas City market. They did not bring enough to pay the freight and the commission house sent the shipper a bill for the deficit. He replied, "Out of money. Sending more hogs."

In late 1930 I quietly prepared the papers for a federal court receivership for the Nichols Company. This was at that time a court procedure by which an insolvent company could continue to operate under the protection of the court through a court-appointed receiver. The creditors' old debts were frozen but anyone supplying goods for the continuing operations in the hands of the receiver would have a prior claim on the assets. There were many legal pitfalls in such proceedings and usually they were a prelude to liquidation and major losses for creditors — resulting only in handsome fees for the receiver and the lawyers. Furthermore, in both state and federal courts such proceedings were often used to favor political and personal friends of the judge, lay and lawyer alike, regardless of competence.

I was prepared for the risk and I convinced our client, F. R. Nichols. He was spending his time in ineffectual fulminations about salesmen's expense accounts, while himself constantly traveling, expensively, to cajole his creditors and to purchase more "bargain lots" of steel. One treasury representative of a large steel company told me, "Our sales executives always see him coming and know that they can sell him anything he thinks is a bargain." Things went from bad to worse, and I was counseling almost daily with Dryden on the maneuvers necessary to keep the creditors shipping goods. Customers ranged all the way from little tin shops to great oil companies in Oklahoma. Despite the Great Depression, some kind of economic life was going on, however haltingly, and precious customers could be lost unless we had the stocks to supply particular needs.

One day in February 1931, Dryden called on the telephone to say that a certain Arthur B. Van Buskirk from Pittsburgh, a lawyer for U. S. Steel Corporation, was in town and would I see him. I knew the day had come. In my office he deftly raised the question of the need for a receivership and when I agreed at once, his face opened like a flower. Then I showed him the prepared papers. We went into fast action, involving court proceedings in several states. Both of us knew just what to do. Within a few days' time the Company was in receivership; Judge Otis appointed Dryden as receiver; he appointed me counsel to the receiver.

The original client, F. R. Nichols, soon learned that a receivership meant much more than just immunity for him from the harassment of his creditors. I had to put him entirely out of the management and brought on a stormy scene in my office in which he said, "I know when I am being cleaned." He went to a lawyer, Byron Spencer in Kansas City, who assured him that my conduct was ethical — so Spencer told me later. One big creditor, represented by a fine Kansas City lawyer, Sam Sebree, tried very hard to force immediate liquidation. There was a widespread philosophy in the Great Depression that it was better to find out the extent of the loss as soon as possible and take it. I believed the Nichols business could be saved. Judge Otis decided in my favor and the receivership continued.

There were some close calls. When the Steel Code, the first under Franklin Roosevelt's NRA, barred "consignments" we *were* in trouble. A consignment is a legal arrangement by which a supplier may place on the premises of a merchandizer a stock of merchandise, retaining title and the right of repossession, meanwhile allowing the merchandizer to sell his customers out of the stock, provided he accounts for the sales. It is a device employed by suppliers where the customer's credit does not warrant a sale. We had such stocks in the amount of a half-million dollars — crucial to the orderly conduct of the business. I devised a plan. We formed a new corporation and induced the big steel company owners of the consignment stocks to sell the stocks to the new corporation. This satisfied the Code since it was a sale — not a consignment. Then we pledged all of the stock to the steel company suppliers, who could at any moment, since the debt for the purchase price was perpetually in default, foreclose, own the corporation, and so its assets, the former consignment stocks. As Judge Otis took up his pen to sign the order approving the scheme he said, "You would not cause me to violate the Steel Code, would you?" "No, sir," I replied, assuming the most angelic expression of which I was capable. I have never had much patience with bureaucracy; neither did Judge Otis; neither did the U. S. Supreme

Court because the NRA was stricken down and, unlike much New Deal legislation, never revived.

The whole business turned out very well except that F. R. Nichols died before the happy day when we paid off the bond-holders with interest in full and all general creditors with six per cent interest in full. The business, after seven years in receivership, could now be turned back to Nichols' heirs worth a tidy sum—an unusual outcome in the Great Depression. My performance did not go unnoticed in Pittsburgh.

How to Lose 40 Million Dollars

In 1927 Mary and I spent the summer semester at the University of Chicago. I was glad for an opportunity to see whether I could produce a better academic record than at Harvard, now that Mary had provided a stabilizing influence in my life. So we bought a Dodge, then a four-cylinder vehicle of quite luxurious proportions compared to the Model-T Ford coupe which had served us quite well, and drove to Chicago, where we had a pleasant enough apartment just off the campus and near the Lake Front.

Mary worked on her Master's degree in psychology, ultimately awarded at the University of Kansas, and I took law courses. One in Administrative Law under Freund served me particularly well a few years later when my practice carried me into big business. Mary had deepened my enjoyment of symphony, opera, and the theatre. I willingly sought out good performances. We drove the long distances from South Shore to North Shore to Ravinia, where Metropolitan Opera stars, especially Elizabeth Rethberg, performed in classical repertory. The sides of the pavilion were open and the landscaping and lighting were pleasant for strolls between acts. Chicago provided theatre and music far beyond any offerings in Kansas City. The tall, dignified, spiritless Frederick Stock competently conducted the Chicago Symphony Orchestra, and Mary Garden, trim as a college girl at 50, was still singing. I grew up culturally to some extent that summer in Chicago.

A little episode in the University Library contributed to my enlightenment. The great Gothic reading room had its open ceiling reaching to dizzy gabled heights. Men were on high scaffolds cleaning the ceiling and I was thinking how well they were restoring the original texture and colors. A girl across the reading table looked up as I did; our eyes met; she said, in a German accent, her pleasant face frowning, "What a shame to remove all the venerable dirt!" It was to be ten years before our first trip to Europe, but that remark helped me out of over-respect for the new and bright and sanitary—an instant of teaching across a library table, teacher and pupil strangers and never to meet again.

Maurice Winger wrote me from Kansas City saying that Walter Dickey, our richest client, had sued the trustees of the William Rockhill Nelson estate because of their rejection of his bid of $8,001,000 for the *Kansas City Star, Times,* and *Weekly*. Nelson, owner and publisher of those newspapers, had died in 1915 leaving a will which provided that after his wife and daughter died the bulk of his estate, principally the newspapers, should be sold "at the best price and on the best terms obtainable," the proceeds to become a trust for the purchase of "productions and reproductions of works of the Fine Arts." Kansas City's distinguished William Rockhill Nelson Gallery of Art is the result of this and other bequests.

Walter Dickey, at the time of this episode, was worth $40 million, the fruits of a monopoly (west of the Mississippi) in "vitrified, salt-glazed" sewer pipe. In the early 1900's municipalities had been busily installing sewer systems. Concrete pipe had not yet come into its own. Walter Dickey, rich, smart, hard—except for rather gentle eyes behind rimless glasses — was a power in Republican politics. He was unpopular — a lonely widower in a million dollar mansion. He wanted to be a United States senator from Missouri.

No newspaper could compete with the *Kansas City Star*. The distinguished old *Kansas City Journal* came to the end of its financial rope, and Walter S. Dickey bought it. Then he bought the *Kansas City Post* from Bonfils and Tamman, successful newspaper publishers in Denver but utterly defeated by the *Kansas City Star* in Kansas City.

The *Star* was ruthless competition, and the *Star* understood the provincialism of Kansas City. If a cat got caught in some obscure eaves gutter, necessitating a rescue operation by the fire department, and on the same day some Rome was burning in diplomatic crisis overseas, the *Star* would fiddle about the cat on the front page and treat the overseas crisis on page 14, if at all.

But Walter Dickey made one of the oldest mistakes known in the sagas of important businessmen. Despite his $40 million the newspaper so drained him of cash that he must borrow $7.5 millions. He had gone into a business he did not personally understand and was doomed to failure.

Maurice Winger and I handled the legal aspects of the bond issue, negotiated with Chicago investment bankers. It was like a Greek tragedy—one could see the beginning of the end. He was mortgaging his $40 million estate for less than a quarter of its value but that was too much. My bankruptcy experience had taught me the importance of liquidity. When a person or corporation must mortgage fixed assets just for cash for instant needs, that is a danger signal.

Walter Dickey had no choice but to bid on the *Kansas City Star* properties when they came up for sale under the terms of the Nelson Will on July 9, 1926. He was too deep in the, for him, strange world of journalistic enterprise. The trustees were eminent citizens: William Volker, our greatest philanthropist, J. C. Nichols, the city planning innovator, and Herbert V. Jones, the dean of the real estate men. Walter Dickey felt that the trustees were too much under the influence of the *Star's* management: Irwin Kirkwood, Nelson's son-in-law, August F. Seested, a tough business manager, and others who had been Nelson's able hired men but for whom he made no provision of opportunity to succeed to the ownership. Nelson's death did not deprive the *Star* of its power. One sour story could irreparably injure a citizen. No one lightly incurred the disfavor of the *Kansas City Star*.

Walter Dickey's bid was for $8,001,000—*all cash*—and for less than all of the property. Kirkwood, Seested, and other employees bid $11,000,000 for all the properties, payable only $2,500,000 in cash and the balance over a period of 18 years secured by the physical properties of the *Star*, worth only $2,000,000. The principal security for the deferred payments was the *Star's* earning capacity—an asset which could be lost by one false move such as the *Literary Digest* made in its poll predicting the election of Alf Landon, the *Star's* candidate, by the way, in 1936.

If the trustees in selling to the *Star's* employees acted improvidently, then they were guilty of a breach of trust. But could Walter Dickey bring a suit? Every lawyer who knew anything about the law of trusts knew the Attorney General of the State as representative of the public *could* bring a suit to set aside the sale, but in Missouri, few public officials would sue the *Star*. Could any member of the public bring such a suit? *If so,* then Walter Dickey was a proper plaintiff.

I began the investigation in Chicago and continued it after the return to Kansas City. Then I went to Cambridge for a month where we engaged my former teacher at Harvard Law School, Austin Scott, for help in the legal research. We found many English cases of the 16th and 17th centuries in which private citizens had brought suits to correct abuses of charitable trusts. In Cambridge we produced a preliminary memorandum in which Professor Scott affixed his name to the proposition that any member of the public benefited by a charity (in this case, the opportunity to view works of art) could sue to collect a breach of the trust.

I spent a long, lonesome six weeks in the Supreme Court library in Jefferson City, Missouri, to augment the memorandum which Austin Scott had guided in Cambridge. The result was a very long brief, 274 pages. Arthur Miller, head of our law firm, who was not especially predisposed to me, I being Maurice Winger's protegé, passed on to me a good compliment. Despite the length of the brief, a non-lawyer friend of his had read it as a matter of cultural interest and said that it moved forward like a novel.

The question was—would I, still decidedly a junior, participate in the argument of the case? I had spent so much time on the problem that I naturally wished to participate in the argument before the Missouri Supreme Court. Maurice Winger finally decided that I should. Later on a lawyer friend of mine, Dupuy G. Warrick passed on to me a comment from Judge William T. Ragland of the Court. My argument, he said, was the most learned which had been made in his tenure on the Court.

We lost the case. There was a problem—extralegal but real— Walter S. Dickey was, as I have said, an unpopular man. Few were sympathetic with his senatorial ambitions. He had used his great financial power unfairly. For example, he would defer, for long periods of time, payment of his accounts, including our lawyers' fees. Thus, he was in effect doing business on the capital of his creditors. If, as was the case, he owed a million dollars past due—

and perpetually so—then he was borrowing that amount without interest. Canny but not admirable.

Cyrus Crane, a fine lawyer, argued the case for the trustees and for the *Kansas City Star*. He spoke about these defects in Walter Dickey's character more than about the law. There was in the Missouri Supreme Court in those days rather wide latitude to be irrelevant.

The day came when Walter Dickey's bankers—creditors for the 7.5 million—took over. "They have allowed me $25 thousand a year to keep the place swept out," he said bitterly to Maurice Winger and me. The day came when his sons were seeking jobs—the elder one acrimonious that his father had wrecked his fortune in newspaper ventures. Then the day came soon when Walter Dickey—never a United States Senator—was dead in that million dollar mansion. I thought of David's lament for Saul and Jonathan, "How the mighty have fallen." Not so with the successful bidders for the *Kansas City Star*. They prospered; their debts were paid off; and today the *Star,* one of the most profitable of American newspapers, is owned in substantial part by those who edit and publish it.

After eight years of my practicing law, Mary and I were living in the house we built and loved. She was teaching at Sunset Hill School for Girls and had become its head. Wearing the bobbed hair which was the fashion of the period, she was barely distinguishable from the students—all girls, many of them from Kansas City's most prestigious families.

I slowly became aware of Mary's influence. She was discriminatory about people and ideas in a way which gradually took hold of me. "He is not intellectually interesting but he will go to the most timid lady at our party and put her at ease," she would explain about someone I was about to write off. To her, every person has always been the subject of a balance sheet—assets and liabilities. If the assets are enough, her tolerance of liabilities is unbounded. If there are no assets — meaning he or she is bigoted, ignorant, and graceless — then let him be rich as Croesus or the head of whatsoever great corporation, or let her be of the most impeccable social standing, Mary consigns him or her to oblivion in her world. And so with ideas: she is a hard nosed scientist with slight respect for folk-thought. Trained in statistics, while she was absorbing the poetry with which she has intrigued me, she is as skeptical of the pretenses of scientism as she is respectful of the role of facts in opinion formation.

Mary has a nose so straight that God must have used a ruler and eyes so intent that one pauses to wonder about himself. Once Prentiss Coonley at a Georgetown dinner party made the company look at Mary to see what he had observed about her eyes. In the midst of his effort to explain he verbally collapsed, saying simply, "Look at her. You see what I mean." It is not just beauty. There is lots of that. It is more. When she is intellectually aroused her face is irradiant; even dread concern or bitter grief does not dislimn its elegance.

Sex on the Campus

In the spring of 1929 I undertook a no-fee case in which public feeling was running high. At the University of Missouri a student of psychology and sociology, O. H. Mowrer—later to hold distinguished posts in psychology and education at Yale, Harvard, and the University of Illinois—released to some 300 each of male and female students a printed questionnaire relating to the changing economic status of women, the sexual code, and the moral ideals on which the family is based. A copy came into the hands of a Columbia, Missouri, editor whose knowledge — by common repute—of the uses of alcohol was greater than his respect for academic pursuit of truth. Instantly the "sex questionnaire" was state-wide news. Editorials (except for the mature *St. Louis Post Dispatch*) viewed with alarm; the State Legislature, source of the University's funds, was in session; President Brooks, his own head ultimately to roll in the academic melee, called the questionnaire "sewer sociology", summoned the Executive Board of the Curators who forthwith suspended, and recommended dismissal of, two professors, one, the internationally known Max F. Meyer, my client, head of the Department of Psychology. The fat was in the fire.

It was the first three of ten questions — quaint enough in the 1970's — which created the 1929 furor in Missouri.

1. (a) If you were engaged to marry a man and suddenly learned that he had at some time indulged in illicit sexual relations, would you break the engagement?. . . . . . .(b) Would you break the engagement

if you learned that he had so indulged frequently and indiscriminately? ...... (c) And if, after marriage, you were to find that your husband was sexually unfaithful to you, would you terminate your relations with him? ....

2. (a) Would you quit associating with an unmarried woman on learning that she had at some time engaged in sexual irregularities? ... (b) On learning that she had so engaged often and promiscuously? ... (c) On learning that she had accepted money in return for her sexual favors? ... (d) Would you quit associating with a married woman on learning that she engaged in extra-marital sexual activities? ....

3. (a) Are your own relations with men restrained most by religious convictions, fear of social disapproval, physical repugnance, fear of pregnancy, lack of opportunity, fear of venereal diseases, or pride in your own ability to resist temptation? ..... (b) During your childhood, did you ever engage in mutual sexual play with another individual? .... (c) Since sexual maturity, have you ever engaged in specific sexual relations? ....

The document was addressed to "Dear University Student," and was identical for men and women, except for the necessary variations in gender. It began somewhat sophomorically,

> During the last several decades it has become increasingly apparent that there is something seriously wrong with the traditional system of marriage in this country. But, unfortunately, the whole matter has been so inextricably bound up with religious dogmas, moral sentiments, and all manner of prudish conventionalities as to make it exceedingly difficult to ascertain with any degree of accuracy the precise reasons for this situation. The present investigation represents an attempt on the part of this Bureau to discover, by the direct questioning of several hundred men and women, the real causal factors which lie back of the widespread dissatisfaction with the prevailing institution of marriage, and to determine, at least in part, those elements in the present social regime which are today so profoundly affecting the American family.

Several professors whose fields touched one or another aspect of the research saw the questionnaire in advance. One said subsequently that he recognized the pomposity of the introduction but did not wish to be didactic with a student who was engaged in a serious project, designed for his course in sociology, called The Family.

The students who were canvassed seemed to take the questionnaire seriously. So did some legislators and newspaper editors, the

Board of Curators, and some parents—but for differing reasons. As for the students, there was a mass meeting which filled Jesse Hall in protests against the dismissals. Several hundred of the questionnaires were returned promptly. One young woman student told her disturbed mother that there was nothing to worry about — "just some information a man needed for his thesis." Another testified that she and her fiancé completed their questionnaires together. Reporters for the student newspaper, published at a high professional level as a long established project of the University's distinguished School of Journalism, found students undisturbed, their morals professedly unimpaired by this somewhat amateurish and much abbreviated forerunner of the Kinsey investigations.

But about half the Missouri public, judging from newspaper reports, were disturbed, not to say outraged. Brooks and the Executive Board had charged, without releasing the questionnaire for publication, that it "tended to make students sexually immoral * * * was shocking, especially to women students * * * could not produce any scientifically valid conclusion * * * tended to create the condition that it is alleged to correct." If the whole professional career and thirty years of distinguished tenure of Dr. Meyer had not been involved, one would have smiled at the intellectual and emotional muddle exhibited by the last point. The questionnaire was not designed to correct a "condition". It was an early, albeit perhaps unsophisticated, poll, now quite commonplace in American life.

The public reaction was ambivalent. University alumni comments varied from deep concern for academic freedom to shocked surprise that students should be asked such intimate questions. Criticisms varied from cries of outrage to murmurs about bad taste. Federal Judge Merrill E. Otis, University alumnus and student of Meyer, took a classical pen in hand; wrote the *Kansas City Star:* "that the questionnaire presented questions to those who received it which they had not heard of before is scarcely thinkable"; compared Meyer to Socrates; and suggested that the suspended professor was no more corrupting the morals of the youth of Columbia, called the "Athens of Missouri," than had Socrates in the original city of that name.

The contest of opinions fitted the mood of the 1920's. The

decade opened with woman suffrage and prohibition, neither of which produced the expected results. It was prohibition spawned gangsterism—not feminine influence—which reached its tentacles up to the very pinnacles of politics. The mountainous labors of the feminists delivered a mouse at the ballot box. But there were other consequences. Women, having gained the political rights of men, set forth to look like men, emphasizing their legs, de-emphasizing their breasts with boy-form brassieres, and bobbing their hair. And they wanted to talk-talk about everything, anything, and with men. A wit from Arkansas, addressing the Kansas City Bar Association in a summary of post-World War I changes, put it this way, "And then the clock struck sex (sic) and the American public finding they could talk about anything talked of nothing else." But he was only partly right.

There were limits, certainly in Missouri, certainly for a considerable portion of the population. Chivalry, the conspiracy of silence about reproduction, delusions of total sex ignorance in the young, the heritage of erotic shame—strangely persistent in the Western World and peculiar to it—none had wholly disappeared in the 1920's, nor have they even today. They made for disturbed excitement about the sex questionnaire at the University. Tensions call for action. Vague fears are insistent in their claims for reassurance. No one was providing that assurance—not President Brooks, whose duty it was; not the Curators, whose knowledge was inadequate; not the newspapers, none of which so much as printed the questionnaire so that the public might have had the facts rather than innuendo. Only the *St. Louis Post Dispatch* said that there was nothing to get excited about, and *that* assurance was not enough.

The public was waiting for the University's full Board of Curators to act, and most of the public expected blood. Whose blood the public really did not know. The Executive Board had nominated for the purge Meyer and a junior faculty member, Harmon O. DeGraff, in whose course on the family the student Mowrer had originated the fateful project. The case originated in mid-March—the Ides, Dr. Meyer later called the bitter event. The full Board set its meeting for April 6, 1929.

I do not know exactly why I volunteered for the case. Whittier has some advice which goes, "Young man, if you would get on in the world, select some worthy but unpopular cause and espouse it with all thine heart." I may have thought of that. Judge Otis' appeal was strong and he himself could not actively engage in the fray. A judge, certainly one of his stature, must stand aloof. My wife, Mary, then head of a private school for girls, in a newspaper interview had called the dismissal "a mistake", decrying the loss of two faculty members to the University "because of the puritanical resistance of its president and board of curators to intelligent psychological study." Certainly all these influences operated. But more potently, I think, my respect for teachers moved me. I had recently read Hendrik Van Loon's *Tolerance*. If a new martyr was coming up I wanted to know why. I soon found out.

Max Meyer was alone in his bleak laboratory on an upper floor of Jesse Hall, the principal University building, built in 1895. I had not been a student of Dr. Meyer and was meeting him for the first time. Judge Otis had written him a letter commending me as one in whom he could place his trust. My first impression was of a man, shy but unafraid; surprised at the furor; distressed that academic work had been so ignorantly misrepresented. He was a good client.

He avoided general questions: How will it come out? Will we win? Am I in trouble? An engineer can give categorical opinions: "The bridge as I build it will stand." With rare exceptions it does. Or the doctor: "You will not die of this"; or sadly "You have six months to live." But when an issue is to be decided by judges, juries, or anybody with the power of decision, the lawyer can only say, "You must let me try the case as I see best; the outcome cannot be predicted with certainty." Lawyers often say, "Every lawsuit is a horse race."

Dr. Meyer seemed to have no principal confidant on the faculty. But there was a vigorous committee made up of the cream of the senior faculty, ready to plan, testify, do whatever could be done. From this committee James Harvey Rogers, an economist whose brilliant book, *America Weighs Her Gold,* influenced American depression policies a few years later, had come for me in Kansas City. He had briefed me as rapidly as possible as we drove the 120 miles to Columbia.

E. J. McCaustland, Dean of the School of Engineering, and Professor Scott, whose The *Cultural Significance of Accounts* is a classic, were members of the faculty committee. I mention them because practical men of affairs such as those of the Board of Curators tended in those days—even today—to regard sociologists, psychologists, biologists, even historians and law teachers, as impractical and visionary. But an engineer and an accountant ready to stand up and be counted in support of Meyer arrested the Board's attention. As I review the committee names—men of the University's golden age, for some of whom campus buildings are now named—I am abashed to think that I may have treated them cavalierly in the tensions of those early April days in 1929.

Max Meyer's connection with the sex questionnaire, even if it had been reprehensible, was too slight to justify the dismissal which the Executive Board had recommended. Other faculty members of equal rank, if not equal distinction, Wrench (history) and Bauder (economics), had seen the questionnaire in advance. They were merely censored. There had to be some additional facts on which the Executive Board rested its harsh decision as to Meyer. There *were* such facts and they became the heart of the case.

Running throughout Missouri with the speed of all news unfit to print was the report that Dr. Meyer was teaching one of his classes the techniques of sexual intercourse. Now a lawyer accepts the representation of a client with an open mind, which is to say he is at once trustful and skeptical. A client often will withhold certain facts, sometimes innocently, believing them irrelevant; sometimes dishonestly, hoping that some magic of his lawyer will avoid the need of confession. So it is that a lawyer in preparing his case, whether a civil or a criminal one, must probe for the facts with a vigor little less than that required in police investigation. Nothing is so devastating in the courtroom as surprise; and nothing so disgusts a lawyer as when his client says, after the damage is done, "Oh! I didn't think it was important to tell you that."

One reason the client cannot do well for himself in a judicial proceeding is his incapacity to appraise the social significance of the facts he has made. Whether the person in trouble is an antisocial juvenile, paranoid and vicious, or a church-going businessman afoul of some trade regulation, the case is the same. He has acted according to some personal, professional, or special code and thereby is incapable of knowing why or how deeply he has offended society, its taboos, its prejudices, its moralities, or its laws. Some intermediary is required — usually a lawyer when a hearing and a decision-making body are involved.

I very quickly got all the facts from Dr. Meyer. A native of Danzig, he had taken his doctor's degree at the University of Berlin after extensive studies in mathematics under Max Planck (quantum theory) and research in the theory of hearing under Carl Stumpf, psychologist and philosopher (sensation of tone and other aspects of the psychology of music). In the long list of Meyer's publications in the learned journals, most frequently one finds him writing on the psychology of sound. In 1950 he published the then result of his lifetime studies in *How We Hear* (Boston, Mass., Charles T. Branford Company).

In Meyer's impoverished youth in Germany he had hoped to be a theologian but found "no tolerance of thought in the Lutheran State Church." Turning to philosophy he was again frustrated, finding it had "no relation to the biological necessities of the human race." In what we now call reflex psychology (he always was a stout non-Freudian) he found his métier. Hugo Münsterberg, then making his colorful career at Harvard, noticed the young Meyer's publications and, without promise of a job, suggested that he come to America.

All of that was thirty years before the April 5, 1929, on which I sat with Meyer preparing for our ordeal with the Curators on the following day. But I had his motive, and that was of immense importance. He was interested in the biological necessities of mankind. Whatever the facts, once a lawyer knows the motive, he can measure the degree of hope or depth of despair in the case.

Meyer taught an advanced course in social psychology. It was small—usually a dozen students who were preparing themselves for social work. For a textbook he employed Dunlap's *Social Psychology,* which treated of the civic, the marital, the reproductive, the religious, and other functions of mankind from the point of view of the biological possibilities of social organization. Meyer said that a scientific comprehension of human reproduction was impossible without a knowledge of the reflexes, not specifically human but essentially the same in all mammalian species which bring about the insemination of the female. But, he continued, such information cannot easily be given in a printed textbook because of federal laws which might be interpreted to exclude such a book from the mails.

He was right about the mails. A federal statute provided that, "Every obscene, lewd, lascivious, and every filthy book * * * is hereby declared to be nonmailable * * *." Periodically a controversy arises over the interpretation of the statute. The issue always is: What is art, literature, or science on the one hand and what is pornography on the other? The fighting words are always the same. Opponents of the subject always speak in terms of protection of the public against indecency, and critics of the particular enforcement always cry censorship and usually allege that by such standards (those employed by some harried postal official) much of the King James version of the Bible and much of Shakespeare could not go through the mails.

At the very time in 1929 when Professor Max Meyer was explaining to me his reasons for what came to be known as the "Sex Lecture", the famous Mary Ware Dennett case was working its way through the federal courts. Mother of two boys, ages eleven and fourteen, Mrs. Dennett had examined some dozens of publications on instruction about sex for the young and found them all wanting. She had then prepared a pamphlet, called the *Sex Side of Life,* of which 25,000 copies had been distributed to individuals and through institutions such as the Y.M.C.A. Her pamphlet was "far more specific than most information written for young people," employing "the proper terminology for the sex organs and functions," and emphasizing "our unlikeness to plants and animals." Mrs. Dennett was convicted of salacity in a New York federal court but on appeal to the Second Circuit she was acquitted.

In the opinion supporting the decision of Mrs. Dennett's acquittal, Judge Augustus Hand assumed "that any article dealing with the sex side of life and explaining the functions of the sex organs is capable in some circumstances of arousing lust," but that "risk", he concluded, did not outweigh "the disadvantages of leaving them (the young) to grope about in mystery and morbid curiosity***." He concluded that, "While it may be thought by some that portions of the tract go into unnecessary details," yet "the curiosity of many adolescents would not be satisfied without full explanation***."

Max Meyer's purposes in the "Sex Lecture" were comparable to Mrs. Dennett's but with a different objective. She was writing for the young, he for mature students training for social work. Why such material for them? Three reasons, this teacher of thirty years gave me. An unmarried woman engaged in social work must be able first to teach an inexperienced young girl how to protect herself from "ruining her whole life. And this she can no longer do by kneeling and praying with her or by threatening her with hell-fire***." First point.

Second point: "The social worker must be able to meet a professional prostitute in a dignified manner" but she cannot do that if the prostitute thinks of her "as a sort of idiot who does not have the faintest idea of what prostitution consists in." And finally—"perhaps the most important of these three requisites of the social worker—she must have an infinite amount of pity for the girl who is an expectant unmarried mother or who already has a legally fatherless child." It all sounds anachronistic now but it was heady business then.

Dr. Meyer assumed that the male members of his class had the requisite information but, he said, "What could I do to give the female members of my little class that biological information?" He solved his problem by the ruse of announcing on a given day that the class would not meet at its next scheduled time. Then he told each of the women that she might come to a special session if she wished. When the women met he gave them a paper, mimeographed by his own hand, setting forth a "tabulation of all the reflexes that enter into the sex act of mammalian animals from the remote beginning, that is, a mere distant vision of an animal by another of the same species, to the consummation, the insemination."

I interviewed all of the women who had taken the course and who were available on the campus. There had been a total of twenty of them in the four times the course had been taught. They were a somber lot, as social workers are likely to be. All affirmed an understanding of the reasons for the so-called Sex Lecture and all were willing to testify on behalf of Dr. Meyer. Of witnesses I had plenty—professors from every discipline of the curriculum, students of the accused professor. But I finished my preparations in mood of great doubt. Social work was as new as the mysteries of sex were old. I was sure that, with one possible exception, my court, the Board of Curators, had never heard of Jane Addams.

She did not publish her *Second Twenty Years at Hull House* until 1930. As late as 1920 there were only thirty-two Community Chests in the United States; there are well over 2,000 today. Clearly, training for professional social work would not, in the minds of the Curators, justify violation of the sex taboo.

As for the professors they would be treated with that mock deference — barely concealed patronage — which is still typically American, except for teachers in the physical sciences. Winterton C. Curtis, the zoologist—of Scopes Trial fame—might well testify that Meyer's "Sex Lecture" was ordinary, indisputable biology and physiology which any qualified professor in any academically respectable institution might teach as a qualified professor might teach mathematics or astronomy.

But the reality of the case was that three of the nine members of the Board were themselves on trial. Three weeks prior to the full Board hearing they, the Executive Board, had conducted a star chamber proceeding, had called Meyer at past nine o'clock in the night, his bed time. Dismissing the stenographers, the Chairman of the Executive Board, a lawyer and born prosecutor, had waved the sex reflex tabulation, procured by him from Brooks, at Meyer demanding that he admit either to having given instruction in how to, or how not to (the prosecutor made no distinction), conduct sexual intercourse. The Executive Board had recommended dismissal. Their colleagues would think twice before reversing them.

The measure of the disturbance one of the Executive Board had suffered was shown at the hearing when he said, concerning the tabulation, "This sheet says on its very top that it is to be given to females and not to males. Now when a thing is so vile that it would not even be given to men, what a veritable crime to give it to women." Obviously I had to find a way around *him,* just as I had to find a way around the absurd but vicious rumor that Meyer had participated in the Sex Questionnaire to get a list of easy girls.

I went to bed that night before the hearing full of doubts and with the key to my defense not yet apparent. In a trial it is always possible to employ worthy and professionally impeccable techniques: call witnesses, adduce testimony, ask the right questions, make the right arguments. But all that is seldom enough. The trial lawyer must pick the key adverse witness, and if he suspects him of perjury or error, must utterly destroy him. Or he must select the favorable witness, sometimes the accused, and know how to handle him so that the court will be moved to empathy.

I have been blessed with the ability to sleep under most of the stresses which have beset my life. Seldom have professional problems kept me awake in bed. What my subconscious has wrestled with in the nighttime is another matter. In any case, I awoke on the morning of the hearing knowing the key to Max Meyer's defense. It was *he*. I would have him deliver the "Sex Lecture" before the Board and in the presence of the women who had been and were his students. I would not produce this drama at the outset. I would proceed in a low key. I would keep the Curators waiting, wondering what could be done in what they would consider my client's desperate situation.

The hearing lasted from 9:00 in the morning until 2:15 the next morning. The lecture came about nine in the evening. The young women entered the room, one a cripple on crutches. The lawyers on the Board, four of them, knew what I was doing. Two showed well restrained approval. Two were unhappy. There was tense silence. I announced that Dr. Meyer would deliver the "Sex Lecture" and that I would ask his students whether he had faithfully reproduced the text and manner of the class proceedings.

As I summarize now the tabulation of reflexes and Dr. Meyer's accompanying lecture, I can only hope that my readers will see the picture of a tall, spare professor of fifty-nine, not on the defensive, in full command of the scene, making a classroom of his courtroom, students of his accusers. I shall not be able to put on paper his high pitched but not unpleasant voice, or the character of that voice, which made of every taboo word a sharp cutting tool to excise mystery from the subject and to expose the clean, bare bone of scientific fact.

He said that we were considering two main sources of group life: the individual's need for food, which leads to the finding of a specialized job in society; the need of the race for the sexual union of two individuals, which leads to a family and children. Eleven reflexes serve the latter need. But only three of them are truly sexual; those which precede seem innocent but constitute the danger which only full and accurate information can counteract. Dr. Meyer's analysis:

Hormones from testicles, ovaries cause forward locomotion (restlessness) as in the case of lack of food.

Signaling of another animal by odors, sounds, sights cause a "turning toward" by which identity of species becomes known.

Close view of features produces contraction of exterior muscles which stretch a limb or several limbs toward the other animal—petting, which may be homosexual or heterosexual. At this point Dr. Meyer interrupts the tabulation of the reflexes to warn, "Staying exposed to popular view is the sure protection" against the ensuing reflexes.

Having become a teacher myself, now over thirty years later, I see numerous cases on the campus lawns, benches, and in the public lounges which have progressed through the third and the next (fourth) reflex. One is inclined to feel a bit annoyed, even embarrassed, to see students of his, male head in female lap, a certain amount of stroking and fondling in progress. But by Dr. Meyer's analysis this public petting is safe and probably permissible, since, as he affirms, "It is normal to be social." Perhaps the same conclusion may be reached concerning the frequent occlusion of female passenger to male driver one sees in automobiles on the public highways—hazardous driving perhaps, but biologically harmless because it occurs in public.

The fourth reflex: sensory excitation by touch of palms or inner sides of arms or legs causes flexor muscles of arms and legs to contract—mutual grasping, pressing of the other against self.

After the fifth of the series Dr. Meyer observes that, "For 'reflexes' never practiced before there can be no habits of stopping them." Clothing does not protect, he says, "since everybody has (for washing, etc.) the habit of removing it."

After the sixth reflex (arching of the bodies, as in the case of a cat when one strokes its back or belly) there is no turning back. Dr. Meyer says that "since in young and virginal people this occurs for the first time in life no habits can stop the ensuing reflexes." He mentions St. Augustine's defense of Christian nuns "wrongly denounced by pagan soldiers—who had raped them—as hypocrites because they had co-operated yieldingly and even eagerly with their captors." Precept is no protection against reflex.

As Dr. Meyer proceeded in a cool monotone through the seventh, eighth, ninth reflex to the climactic tenth, the drama in the hearing room mounted with the reflexes. The women students sat impassive, showing by their faces that this was classroom subject matter which they had heard before. It was scarcely necessary for me to ask each of them at the close, as I did, if this was the class proceeding exactly as Dr. Meyer had conducted it. They all said yes!

Fortunately, two of the three members of the Executive Board, who had recommended dismissal, were lawyers. I saw that they would have stopped the proceedings, but they knew they could not. Seven centuries—since the barons wrested from King John in the meadow of Runnymede the right of due process at law—stood in their way. They had had the "Sex Lecture" in hand when they suspended Meyer three weeks earlier. They had inflamed the people of Missouri without telling them all the facts. Now when those facts fell from the serene lips of the accused, they sat abashed. Where was the indecency, the unspeakable vileness? Had their own pitiable inadequacy supplied it? In any case the lawyers, all of them, knew that no one dare deny me the right to have my client repeat at the hearing the very matter for which he was on trial.

Dr. Meyer had reached the eleventh reflex. "The body muscles relax. The relaxing womb sucks into itself the seminal fluid deposited in its mouth. Both animals relax their mutual grasp, fall apart, sleep." There was a hush which I did not hasten to break. One of the Curators had a back as stiff and straight as that of his fellow Missourian, John J. Pershing. Presently he fixed me with a fiery, frustrated eye, and said, nodding in the direction of the students, "Mr. Hazard, I will never cross-examine a woman on this subject." I waited. No other Curator spoke. The women students filed from the room. Chivalry for the ladies. Would there be justice for my client?

The hearing adjourned at 2:15 A.M. The session had begun at 9:00 the previous morning—the longest continuous hearing in my now almost fifty years of law practice. There was much more testimony available from students and faculty. But I had to think of the Curators' patience—men of affairs who might resent being held to another day of testimony. The lawyer must always make such judgments. When to stop—that is ever the question. Max Meyer's rendition of the "Sex Lecture" was the high point. I must stake everything on that, and I did. The Board adjourned until the next day, Sunday, when it would go into executive session.

On the day following the hearing the Curators refused to dismiss Dr. Meyer, as recommended by their Executive Board, but suspended him for one year without pay. The result was considered a victory. Judge Otis and former Missouri President A. Ross Hill were pleased. But none of us knew the deep sense of injustice which Max Meyer suffered silently. The economic penalty was heavy and it came at a time when his five children were in the most expensive period of their education. He spent part of the year at the University of Chile, where rumor circulated that he was teaching birth control—in a Catholic country. Everywhere he was associated with the Sex Questionnaire.

At the end of the year he was honored by the faculty of the University of Missouri: The Southern Society for Philosophy and Psychology made him its president. The American Association of University Professors in February of 1930, after an exhaustive investigation, had castigated Brooks and the Curators for failure to support him in the perennial "conflict between science and traditional taboos." Brooks had been fired for unstated reasons but everyone knew that part of the reason was his crude and dishonest handling of the Sex Questionnaire.

But Max Meyer's hurt was too deep for silence. In his presidential address to the society which had honored him, he related the whole case. The Curators felt that he had unnecessarily revived a closed issue and in a manner hurtful to the University.

There was a second hearing. The issue was insubordination so far as any issue could be abstracted from the confusion. Those who were unhappy about the earlier result saw a chance to do him in completely. I represented him a second time. Again he was close to dismissal. A committee of the faculty worked out a compromise. Meyer became Professor of Research Psychology on leave without pay. He pursued his work in the teaching of the deaf at the Central Institute for the Deaf in St. Louis for a time. Then he spent the remainder of his teaching years at the University of Miami. These were the years of the Great Depression. Fortunately the compromise saved him his meager Carnegie pension, which would have been lost if he had been dismissed in either of the bouts with the Curators.

The lesser known martyrs are nonetheless noble. Mary and I visited Dr. Meyer a few years before his death and found him in firm possession of his bodily and mental faculties, concerned to republish his book on *hearing* because one chapter needed revision; annoyed that he could not at once remember the technical name of a plant in his meager garden. He quickly found it with his glasses off in the fine print of a lexicon. Later he wrote to me in a steady hand, and sometimes on his own typewriter—a man in his 90th year, he once wrote, "You are my oldest friend." (Judge Otis had died at age sixty.)

His publications on the theory of hearing continued almost to the end. When he died he was the oldest member of the American Psychological Society.* History is hard on the teachers who challenge its taboos. There have been only a few of them in all time. Max Meyer was one.

It all seems long, long ago—and curious, now that women's campus dormitories are the assignation places—not secret—for the premarital coitus which Max Meyer thought should be avoided, and could be avoided, by better knowledge of the inexorable sequence of the reflexes.

The Money Maker

Elmer Rhoden began making money as a student on the campus at the University of Nebraska and he has never stopped making money to this day. His principal field when he was my client was motion pictures—the exhibition of them, not the production. He has held high offices in the Twentieth Century Fox complex, but at heart he was, and is, an entrepreneur—one who knows an opportunity when he sees it, will take whatever risks are involved, and—in his case—is almost invariably successful. He is a big man of fine physique and a smooth, candid face, who has lived by the swimming pool and Adelle Davis' cook book—healthily health-conscious. He is a lifelong ethical paragon, invaluable in an industry

---

*The University of Missouri has established the Max Meyer Memorial Museum, which houses antique equipment, much of it created by Professor Meyer. It includes a quarter tone organ especially built for experiments in the psychology of music. The Museum opened in 1972 on the 100th anniversary of Dr. Meyer's birth.

peopled with sharp-witted fast-buck artists. Elmer Rhoden never told me and I never asked him, but I suspect he has always been a latter-day Puritan who believes it is better for people to go to the movies than to do something worse.

In the 1920's the "movies" were becoming "talkies." The nickelodeon was graduating to ten cents, fifteen cents, a quarter, and more. Furthermore, toward the end of the second decade and early in the third, air conditioning was developing for suitably large areas such as a theatre. People would go to the motion picture theatre just to cool off in the torrid Midwest summer—quite often a better reason than the picture.

The two technologies, sound synchronized with film and air conditioning, coincided and called for large investments in a business which had previously been rather easy to enter. Elmer Rhoden's procedure was to acquire at a fair price—he was always reasonable in an industry beset with sharp traders—well established but declining theatres, close them for rehabilitation, install modern sound and projection equipment, new seats, and air conditioning. Then there would be a gala opening, attended by Rhoden and the principals of his staff and often by me.

Originally, I encountered Elmer Rhoden under Maurice Winger's aegis. Soon I noticed that he was calling me directly and then instructing his staff to call me. I always kept Maurice Winger advised. He never showed any sign of jealousy. Elmer Rhoden, even in his early thirties, was the dean of the Kansas City motion picture exhibitors, a lot of fierce competitors. A theatre of any kind is a cash business which closes its books every day. The customers either come or do not come and the day is done for better or for worse. There is nothing to carry over as in the case of a merchant with an inventory. The inexorable necessity to "make it every day" breeds a hard-bitten type of businessman, suspicious, vindictive, and cunning. Soon they began coming to me—Rhoden's competitors, whether because of the magic of his name or because he sent them, I do not know.

Their interests were often in conflict with his. But it is typical of the motion picture trade that its members will commercially knife each other, employing the most lethal practices and epithets, and then, on confrontation, embrace like brothers. Often I would not take their business without speaking first to Rhoden. That was all right with the "independents" because they thought I had influence with "Rhoden," who would always say, "Go ahead, Leland. If you don't represent them somebody worse will." So it was that at one time or another I represented about all of Kansas City's locally owned motion picture theatres and at times literally all of them. To this day when I go back to Kansas City, over three decades later, some old friend, in introducing me to the current generation, will say, "He was Elmer Rhoden's lawyer."

The industry-wide confidence I enjoyed among all the theatre owners, great and small, fetched me an experience at once rewarding and awkward. The first talking movies involved crude devices for synchronizing with the film picture the sound which came from a disk essentially the same as the phonograph disk. The cumbersome operation required two operators in the projection booth, one for the film and one for the sound.

No. sooner had the theatre owners invested in this makeshift equipment than better devices were developed so that the sound was put on a track of the film strip itself. The theatre owners had to scrap their first investments, sometimes even their second investments, in order to modernize their booths. Yet the powerful operators' union demanded and forced the retention of two men in the booth. I use the word "forced" advisedly because, as in much of Kansas City's business activity of the late 1920's and early 30's, gangsterism was standing by, literally armed for action. A theatre owner who refused to sign up on the union's terms could expect a stink bomb in his theatre and, of course, irreparable damage to his trade.

Motion picture exhibitors have a sense of the dramatic. They would come to my office to describe their plight: business was not good (that was true; the Great Depression was on us); the second operator in the booth got more pay than they, the owners, could take out of the business. "Prove it for yourself," they would say: "Go past the union hall and see the new Buicks lined up. Then come down to 'film row' any morning where we go to lease our pictures and see the old Fords lined up." I did just that without saying so and the superficial sights were as the owners described them. Indeed there was a reason for the Buicks. One particular agency for that car was favored by the Pendergast-Lazia-McElroy underworld establishment, and its beneficiaries—in this case the booth operators' union—were required to buy Buicks from that particular source. McElroy and the underworld ruled the city ruthlessly with only rare exceptions when they encountered Judge Otis—and in this case, me.

I had often said to the small theatre owners when they would describe in moving terms their plight, "Why don't you combine to produce a city-wide lockout and keep your theatres closed until the union agrees to eliminate the unneeded second man from the booth? A stink bomb can't hurt a closed theatre." The reply was always the same: some *so and so* would agree to close and then open his theatre to make a "fast buck" at the expense of the others. That was the attitude among the "independents"; and as between them and the big owners such as Rhoden, Dubinsky, Paramount, there was such distrust, suspicion, and general paranoia that a comprehensive agreement was unthinkable.

Finally Elmer Rhoden told me that I had sufficient confidence throughout the industry that he would like me to try for a binding agreement. I prepared a uniform document under which I became the agent of all the signatories to bargain with the union and to close the theatres when I deemed it necessary. The agreement provided a penalty of $1,000 for breach by an independent and a larger penalty for the "majors." We bargained with the operators for days. The union was adamant. There must be two men in the booth. I prolonged the negotiations purposely so that the public could be fully aware of the issues. Then I closed all the theatres in Kansas City with one or two trivial exceptions and every owner kept his agreement.

"The theatres are closed." That quotation from my announcement the newspapers headlined on front pages. They quoted my expressed regret for all of the people who would be out of work and my hopes that the union of projectionists would reconsider. Of course I was staying close to Elmer Rhoden and a small group of "independents" headed by Jay Means. But so far as the public and the union and its allies in the underworld could see, it was I who had done it to them.

The theatres closed, the town quickly seemed to have died. Peripheral businesses, large and small, suffered. I had counted on that for pressure on City-Manager McElroy. Only he, supported by Lazia's gangs, could tell the union what to do. I had put together a power of boycott to which neither the union nor McElroy was accustomed. Days passed. The theatres remained closed. Then Elmer Rhoden called me to say that City Manager McElroy had asked for a committee to see him, but I must not be included. "Shall we see him?" Elmer asked me. "Of course," I replied, knowing that we had won. McElroy never talked if he could act. He knew that my clients, by combining, had put themselves beyond the goons to whom he often committed the community interests.

In short order our principal demand to eliminate the unneeded second man in the booth was conceded. There were other items in the settlement and I had the job of convincing the independents, who now were relishing a taste of power, to accept the settlement. The theatres were opened when I said so.

Then shortly a call came from the business agent of the union asking if I would come to the headquarters to clean up some details of the settlement agreement. Rhoden said I should go and Jay Means went along in case there were technical points. The business was short and unimportant. As Means and I left to pass down a long wide corridor, by then filled with people, men with drawn guns took us in charge. Jay Means, a big flabby man, made a brave move to help me. I saw the gun in his back which stopped him. I broke loose to run to the business agent's office, only to find the door locked. Then I submitted.

The plot was simple enough. The gangsters disrobed me, substituting for my clothes a woman's dress of which I never had a view because I was blindfolded. To this day I do not know how well it fitted. One of them said softly, "We are not going to hurt you." But a gun was constantly nudging me in the back. They led me to a car and shortly I was put out, as it developed later, at the Harzfeld corner of 11th and Main, the heart of the then fashionable center for women shoppers. My bundled clothes were tossed to the sidewalk. Some kind person led me into a dressing room on the first floor of Harzfeld's.

I changed to my normal male attire. A policeman and police car were waiting to conduct me to police headquarters, then known to be run by the gangster Lazia. Of course Jay Means had sent out the alarm. Private agencies, not part of the gangster administration, were looking for me. Elmer Rhoden and his associates were at police headquarters by the time I arrived. One of Elmer's fiery associates was kicking the union business agent on the shins. The stage was set for a donnybrook. But I said to the chief of police, "I make no complaint. Let us treat this as a prank." Of course, there had been a technical kidnapping, but it could not have occurred without the prior approval of all law enforcement agencies. The plan was to hurt me by keeping the silly episode in the newspapers. The chief of police looked at me with mingled admiration and disappointment and then brusquely said to the filled room, "Get out of here, all of you." My refusal to make a charge was featured in the *Kansas City Star*. Cyrus Crane said to me at a Bar association meeting, in the presence of other lawyers, a few days later, "Never have I been so proud of a member of our profession." He knew that I had frustrated a juvenile scheme, triggered by amazement and anger that a lawyer's plan had undone brute force in a corrupt city. The *Kansas City Star* expressed concern that a citizen could be treated as I had been and agreed with me editorially that the "second man in the booth" was an unconscionable condition.

One aspect of the case provided what we lawyers call negative proof. The union *did* have contracts with the theatre owners. When I closed the theatres those contracts were technically broken. But a contract obtained under force and duress is no contract. There was so much evidence of gang-play in the so-called contract negotiations that I believed the union would never raise the question of its contract rights. I was correct. The union fulminated ineffectually, but there was never a suggestion of going to court. My clients, even those known to be chiselers, paid my fees promptly and fully.

A few years later, in 1933, Mary McElroy, disturbed daughter of the City Manager, was kidnapped for sure. McElroy ordered the city police to keep hands off and turned the investigation over to the gangster, John Lazia, and his underworld. They turned her up, soon enough, at a ransom of $30,000, which rumor said was requisitioned from the illegal slot machines which pervaded the town. I did not write him a note of sympathy. When McElroy, heavy with the disgraces of his evil days, summoned before a grand jury which had figures indicating income tax violation by him, conveniently died, I did not attend his funeral.

Truman and the Pendergast Machine

I was invited to serve on the board of directors of the Kansas City Public Service Institute, later known as Civic Research Institute and headed professionally by Walter Matscheck. An able and courageous expert in public administration, Walter Matscheck kept the ideal of efficient public administration and good government alive during the dark days of the Pendergast-McElroy-Lazia underworld dominance in Kansas City. Harry Truman was then a member of the County Court, not a judicial but an administrative body governing Jackson County, in which Kansas City is located. He was, although little known, considered one of the few respectable personalities in the Pendergast administration. Walter Matscheck would often consult with him about the feasibility of our proposals and would report to us that Harry Truman could always be depended upon to give a forthright and unequivocal answer. Truman would say, "No, that is not politically possible," or he would say, "Well, if you made this change and that change, it might be worth trying." On our Board at the Civic Research Institute, we considered Harry Truman our only approach to the all-powerful machine. The Institute was not a crusading organization. It was a research organization, and our only interest was to get accepted through whatever government existed, whatever its nature, proposals for better government and more efficient use of tax dollars.

There is a story about the man who was to become President of the United States and who was to make great decisions in momentous times. It is possibly apocryphal, certainly I have never found it documented, albeit the story is widely known, and seldom do I try it out on a person of Kansas City, and of that era, who has not heard some version of it. After Judge Truman had finished his admirable administration of the County Court, during which roads had been built, honestly designed and correctly laid—with Pendergast concrete, of course—he was out of a job. The story is that he went to Tom Pendergast's headquarters on the second floor at 1908 Main Street, in a commercial slum area, by appointment (anyone arriving without an appointment was subject to physical expulsion by the guard at the top of the steps). Truman said, "Mr. Pendergast, as you know, I have finished my term on the County Court. I have tried to do a good job; and now I would like to be

County Collector," a fee job, and one of the best in the county, then paying about $20,000 a year. Pendergast replied, "I can't give it to you, Harry. I have promised it to Harrington, and you know I always keep my word." (That seemed to be true in political matters.) "But," continued Pendergast, "I have a place for you, Harry. I want you to go to the United States Senate." Truman gulped and blurted out, "But, Mr. Pendergast, do you think I am qualified?" (James A. Reed had set a very high standard of personal charisma of the type which Truman then thought, and others thought, he did not then possess.) The story closes with Pendergast's answer, "What in the hell does that have to do with it?"

In any case, *Senator* Truman emerged from the interview. He combined, almost uniquely, personal independence with political loyalty. It was charged in the senatorial campaign that he would be a stooge for the "Boss," but despite the ultimate record which showed Pendergast to be utterly corrupt, there is nothing in Senator Truman's record to negate his public statement that Pendergast never asked him to do a dishonest thing. As Vice President of the United States, he attended the funeral of Tom Pendergast, although that erstwhile epitome of bossism had been convicted of income tax violation in the midst of devastating disclosure of machine corruption and massive vote frauds and had served a term in the penitentiary. Judge Otis delivered the sentence: 15 months in Federal prison and a $10,000 fine; three years on another count with probation for five years on condition that Pendergast refrain from all political activity. This was in effect a life sentence.

Throughout the 1930's most of the business leaders, good and pious citizens of Kansas City, were wont to view with concern our gang-ruled city but to exonerate Pendergast, as just a strong political leader who could not be responsible for everything that went wrong—so they said. It was not uncommon for a leading citizen to go to the Boss for permission to do this or that—some important matter, perfectly proper; but so blurred had become the line between the underworld, where force and gunfire ruled, and the upper-world, where regulation and law should have ruled, that our most Christian gentlemen, from the greatest established wealth and business to the newest climbing parvenu, would consult Pendergast rather than their lawyers, knowing how complete his per-

Joseph C. Fennelly who led the
Youth Movement that began the
destruction of the Pendergast
machine in Kansas City, Missouri.

Judge Merrill E. Otis who gave
Pendergast a federal prison term
followed by a probation of
political death. *Courtesy of
Kansas City Star.*

Kansas City Lawyers in retreat at Lake of the Ozarks, Missouri.
Left to right: Edgar Shook, Jack Murray, Carl Crocker,
Leland Hazard (sole survivor), Bill Kemp, Dupuy Warrick, Lynn Webb.
We called ourselves "The Academy". The institution still survives.

John Lazia — gangster — in his day Kansas City's real chief of police. *Courtesy of Kansas City Star.*

Pendergast at his daughter's wedding. *Courtesy, Kansas City Star.*

sonal control over legislative, executive, and judicial functions in Kansas City had become.

Judge Merrill Otis knew history and he knew that the whole political economy in Kansas City would be as sound or as rotten as the man who pretended to government by men; hence, his ingenious probation of Pendergast, relieving him of an additional three years in prison on condition that he stay utterly out of politics. Judge Otis was criticized for the lightness of the sentence. Few understood the astute device by which he grubbed out the root of Kansas City's cancer. Pendergast scrupulously observed the probation, but he made a determined appeal to Judge Otis for repeal of his political exile. His petition was "recommended by a group of prominent citizens, including the town's leading banker, its foremost real estate man, a Protestant minister and a Catholic priest." The quotation is from William M. Reddig's book, *Tom's Town,* not because I need him for the facts but to show that he, a not unworthy successor to Lincoln Steffens, withholds, as I do, the names of those "prominent citizens." What insidious hold did the Pendergast system have on such men? They were not just prominent. Anyone can be that. They were at the top of the Kansas City social and business community. Yet after twelve years of disclosures — 1932 to 1943 — during which every political crime, from 60,000 "ghost" registrations and votes to bribery and admitted income tax violations, was traced directly to the Boss— after all *that* our best citizens asked Judge Otis to return him to political power. The judge refused.

History will probably accord President Truman greatness in the sense that he did not flinch when historic decisions were to be made: dropping the bomb or removing MacArthur from the Korean command or integrating the armed services, for examples. But *Senator* Truman had one benighted day in the United States Senate when, in the midst of the disclosures of ubiquitous vote frauds and multifarious corruption in Kansas City, he made a direct attack upon Judge Albert L. Reeves and Judge Otis, who were presiding over grand juries and trials in Kansas City which were disclosing the depth of the community and personal corruption of the Pendergast regime.

Humble beginnings have never detracted from greatness. But were President Truman's beginnings really humble? He came up in a municipal political system, the corruption of which only the blind or the stupid would miss. After utterly conclusive proof, Truman, neither blind nor stupid, did not repudiate the system. He probably could not. The Kansas City record is a blot on his escutcheon with which he and his place in history must live. One wonders whether, if President Truman had come up by way of political *thinking,* rather than in the municipal arena of political *action,* he would have dropped the bomb.

Significantly, Truman's defense of his Hiroshima decision was of the same character as that of Pendergast's final defense of himself. Truman pleaded and, in his distinguished television defense of his decision more than 15 years later, continued to insist that dropping the bomb saved the lives of a million American boys. Yet he made us the only nation in history to make the ultimate use of the fire which Prometheus gave man from the gods; and he caused us to use it, not against our white brothers, the Germans, but against our brown brothers, the Japanese. History will struggle with that decision for a long, long time.

Pendergast, usually taciturn, delivered his swan song to a reporter for the *St. Louis Star-Times* (the *Kansas City Star* having at long last ended its Olympian tolerance of his misdeeds) at age 72. He said, "I've done a lot for Kansas City—for the poor of Kansas City. I've done more for them than all the big shots and bankers, all of them put together. We used to take care of our poor, with coal and wood and food and rent; and we helped them in their trouble. We never asked the poor about their politics." Truman's million American boys; Pendergast's poor—the justifications are of a piece in which there is political acumen—but not enough to achieve the elusive ideal of good government or the ancient dream of world peace.

I Become a Political Counsellor

I always thought of myself as an observer of public affairs, never imagining a participating role. When in early 1932 Rabbi Samuel S. Mayerberg lashed out against the "Machine," then at the peak of its power, I was incredulous but vaguely hopeful. He was rabbi of the distinguished congregation of the reformed Jewish Temple B'Nai Jehudah. He was young and handsome of body and face— the male beauty of a Michelangelo's David.

The Rabbi picked a strange time, with McElroy out of the city, only the routines of corruption and gangsterism in progress, and the next election two years off. But he proceeded in the best traditions of solo reformers, Carry Nation, for example. Just as she personally entered saloons with her hatchet, he in due course confronted McElroy in his own office; forced an appearance before City Council; demanded to see the pay rolls, which years later were found to be just as padded as he suspected; inveighed against the ex-criminals on the police force; and shamed his own ministerial colleagues to speak up from their pulpits. It was a disorderly crusade and at its height, he called me for advice. I supposed that his telephone line was tapped, but I counselled with him nevertheless. His move was abortive—too far removed from any election date. There was little likelihood of sustaining high fervor for two years until the next election. There was no feasible procedure for a recall election. Even so, his vast energy, his brilliant oratory, straight out of the tradition of Old Testament prophets, and the depth of the corruption which he sensed might have carried him through to a victory over the machine—a victory which did not come for another eight years and was then not his.

He did a curious thing. There were rumors that the Board of his Synagogue demanded that he soft-pedal his crusade (this would have been in the then prevailing best-citizen tradition); that he had been framed or in some way compromised (he was equivocal about that when I asked him two years later). In any case, to my surprise and dismay, he took a trip to the West Coast for a month at the very height of the storm he was brewing. That was the end of Mayerberg's abortive crusade. But a cloud in the Machine's sky—the size of a man's hand—had appeared.

I suppose that Rabbi Mayerberg came to me because of the Max Meyer case in which my name necessarily appeared repeatedly on the front pages of the State's newspapers. He was one of the very few ministers who spoke out in support of Max Meyer in Kansas City, he and Burris Jenkins, magnificent preacher whose Community Church was packed every Sunday, and L. M. Birkhead, the minister of our Unitarian Church, where Judge Otis was a member.

After the collapse of the Mayerberg effort, I began to hear of a somewhat mysterious activity called "National Youth Movement."

122

I did not know any of the principals in this Movement. It turned out that my University of Missouri friends and contemporaries, Edgar Shook, William E. Kemp, both of whom were products of the University of Missouri Law School, and Prewitt B. Turner, a graduate of the School of Agriculture at the University of Missouri, were advisors to the Movement. I have never been very alert to what was going on. Events and opportunities always seemed to come to me, and to come as a surprise. I am not proud of this record. It seems to me to indicate a certain element of fortuitous circumstance in my life, rather than a design or a plan.

The president of the Youth Movement was Joseph C. Fennelly, a young man in his early thirties, son of a distinguished Kansas City father and of a mother who retained her gracious charm into an advanced age. He was of erect carriage, of a handsome physiognomy, and with a twanging, intense, but pleasant voice.

Joe Fennelly said that the object of the young men's Movement in Kansas City was to analyze the set-up of our American cities; to encourage a better type of American citizen to take part in political work; and to safeguard the interest of the public in more efficient and economic government. These, of course, were obvious ideals. I found, however, that the young men associated with Joe Fennelly knew their Lincoln Steffens and were under no illusions; they were quite practical reformers. They were conservatives, concerned about mortgaging the young man's future to municipal bond issues which would be wasted in inefficiency and graft.

These young men were of Kansas City's oldest and best families. They had access to any door. No citizen however financially or otherwise powerful would deny them an audience. Yet, hear Joe Fennelly's account of the early responses which he and his associates encountered: "Young man, if you expect to make a success of business in this city, you must cultivate the friendship of the powers that be." (This meant the Pendergast machine.) "I am all for you but you know I can't make my stand public, nor can I donate any money to your cause." Again, "I believe in boss control; of course, there may be some graft and corruption but that can be easily overlooked in return for the favors I have received."

The admirable thing about Joe Fennelly and the close social friends whom he inspired was that in a truly scientific spirit they entered the most hallowed halls in Kansas City and said very simply, "We think the town is ruled by gangsters and corrupt politicians and we think that condition ought to be changed. What do you think?"

One day in 1933 Joe Fennelly came into my office and said that the National Youth Movement would like me to become its legal and political advisor. This was a surprise to me. My dear friend, William E. Kemp, was known to be interested in politics. He was then a junior member of a law firm, whose head was a respected and powerful figure in the Democratic party. Edgar Shook was known to be interested in politics. He had been general counsel to the Highway Commission, a position which could not be held without some political stature. We were all about forty. Both Kemp and Shook became very significant political figures in Kansas City later, but this was in 1933, when the Machine was at the apex of its arrogant corruption and power, and, for better or for worse, I accepted the assignment. Of course it was uncompensated public work. Therefore there was no necessity of consulting Maurice Winger who, I must say, belonged to that great majority of leading citizens who felt that Machine rule for Kansas City was inevitable.

Joe Fennelly's program in Kansas City had certain astute aspects. First, there was secrecy. No one knew exactly what the movement was about. The obscurity of purpose and method was disturbing to the Machine. Rabbi Mayerberg had been open and oratorical. Joe Fennelly was no orator; his appeal was direct, conservative, and practical. Young people would ultimately have to pay the cost of corruption and gangsterism, and, therefore, they should nip blight in the bud. The movement was conservative, but it was not puritanical. Its proponents were not after Utopia; they were after the dollars wasted in municipal corruption.

It was after the Movement had reached a membership of some 6,000 and was definitely becoming a factor in the oncoming 1934 election that I became its legal advisor. At first the young men had protested that they did not themselves wish to go into politics; that they did not wish to become candidates. This was a delusion which they speedily abandoned.

Until late in 1933, the Youth Movement had not even held meetings in its own right. Its speakers delivered their messages to church groups, luncheon clubs, and other organizations. In

September 1933, the Movement, in its own name, announced a meeting. Prominent men and women, both Republicans and Democrats, were invited to attend. The response was quite remarkable. The meeting hall had a capacity of only a thousand, and long before the time when the speakers were to begin their oratory the hall was filled to overflowing, and the faces of prominent older men and women of Kansas City were numerous in the audience. This meeting was the first step in the formation of a citizens' or fusion ticket.

I shared the platform with Joe Fennelly and Webster Townley, Secretary of the Movement, and poked fun at the Machine, pointing out, among other jibes, that we ought to have some minimum standards for selection of members of our police force other than prior criminal records. A policeman had recently testified that he had never seen a slot machine on his beat — one which was known to be cluttered with slot machines. So I suggested that we introduce eye examinations for policemen. The next day an emissary from the Machine called Elmer Rhoden and asked if he couldn't stop his lawyer from making fun of the city administration. Elmer reported the call to me — noncommittally.

We set out to form a fusion ticket, meaning a ticket composed of non-machine Democrats and Republicans. The Republican organization was either impotent or actually aligned with the so-called Democratic machine. We got over the nonsense, including my own, that we could be a moral force without being a political force. We must form a Fusion Party with the Republicans, whose legal status we needed in order to get on the ballot in the forthcoming 1934 election. Yet we used unconventional methods in putting together a ticket for mayor, eight councilmen, and two municipal court judges. Over 400 letters were sent out to business, civic, religious, and cultural groups, regardless of party, asking for suggestions for the ticket. It was something of a miracle that such neophytes could form a ticket. Many of our meetings were held in the University Club — as to place, a political innovation.

Among the dissident Democrats was my friend, W. E. (Bill) Kemp, ultimately Mayor of Kansas City. He was a man of distinguished appearance, mellifluent voice, honest and politically ambitious. He indicated some displeasure that the Youth Movement had come to me for legal guidance, but we were friends from

University of Missouri days and my preferment did not dampen his ardor for the Movement. Another man Mary and I loved was Edgar Shook. He had a crisp voice, hypnotic eye, impeccable manners, and a puritanical conscience in public affairs. Ultimately he served on the Kansas City Election Board, appointed by a reform Governor of Missouri, Lloyd Stark, elected with Machine support, but turned independent in office ("ingrate", the Machine called him). This was the election board which, with the help of federal prosecutions under Judge Otis and Judge Reeves, purged the Kansas City election rolls of 60,000 fictitious names.

The issue on forming the ticket came over the selection of the mayor. The two most prominent possibilities were A. Ross Hill, former president of the University of Missouri, a conservative, and manager of his wife's very substantial real estate holdings in Kansas City; the other was Frederick E. Whitten, a big brusque, bombastic man — a rough phrase-maker, with great personal appeal. Whitten *did* become the anti-machine candidate four years later — and lost. We selected Dr. Hill for the 1934 effort. He was not without qualifications in politics. In his best days at the University of Missouri he could bring to the campus such men as the great but controversial Thorstein Veblen and the young, untried Manley O. Hudson, and Winterton C. Curtis, the zoologist of Scope Trial fame, and still handle the mostly rural Missouri legislature to produce the money for a golden age at our state university. He *did* represent the conservative respectability of the Youth Movement. He was considered aloof and was, of course, no youth. One day at a ticket-forming meeting it was one of my assignments to take aside a hardy character from the Kansas City stockyards, one of the few places where McElroy and the Machine were not supreme, and persuade him to support Hill. After ten minutes of argument, during which my prospect was constantly, silently nodding his head in seeming assent, I stopped for his answer, which was, "You're absolutely right. He (Hill) won't do." That episode I have always considered my most complete failure as a pleader.

When we selected Hill to head the ticket, he asked me to be his campaign manager. He was a difficult candidate. Tall, distinguished — his intellectuality apparent at every turn — his greatest handicap was his brisk manner of speech. None of us could say, "slow down, and produce some oratorical pauses." I hit on a feasible device — possible because I was writing all of his speeches. I caused the typist to use only capital letters, with each word separated by an extra horizontal space and each line separated by three vertical spaces. This mechanical scheme produced remarkable improvement in his delivery.

McElroy promptly called Hill a "squaw man," referring, of course, to the wealth of his wife, Vassie. This blast came at noon and Prewitt Turner, a walking encyclopedia of the Machine's skull-duggery, and Joe Fennelly were in my office by 2:00 p.m. with enough stored up political filth to fill three columns of the *Star* the next morning, headlined, "Hill Slashes Back." I put it all in that verbal order which the Youth Movement expected of me — ability to dictate on the spot a political retort, or a complicated business agreement, in the presence of others, whether in my own office, the office of a country lawyer in the Kansas "dust bowl," in a New York, London, or Paris hotel suite, or in an airplane, or in my own automobile. This book has given me much greater pain than other writings ever gave me.

The 1934 election day was bloody. Four men were shot to death—none of them our people. The fervor our campaign aroused had caused some internecine feuds to surface within the machine itself. All day long, however, our people came into our headquarters, some with bandaged heads, to report rough treatment at the polls. We had no police protection.

We knew that the election rolls were padded, we thought by 50,000 fictitious names. But our surveys indicated that we might win even over that handicap. By nine o'clock that night we conceded. I advised Dr. Hill not to congratuate the usurpers of office in a stolen election. He said quietly, "I will not congratulate them." Some leading citizens were ashamed of the display of brute force. Maurice Winger said to me somberly, "Leland, it's a shame."

We did not really lose in 1934. The vote was: Hill, 81,677; the Machine, 141,338; the difference, slightly more than 60,000, turned out to be the number on the padded registration rolls and the number, incredible as it may seem, of the ghost votes which the Machine could, and did, produce. We had underestimated the padded rolls by 10,000. The *Kansas City Star* had preserved a benign disinvolvement in its news coverage of the campaign, but the *Star* did editorially opt for the Fusion Ticket at the last minute, saying that our case had been well stated. That pleased me. Furthermore the *Star's* distinguished editor, Henry J. Haskell, who had himself driven in the big black car out among the polling places, got roughed up. That helped later.

The 1934 election was the beginning of Kansas City's redemption. Within four years Edgar Shook and his colleagues on the Election Board had cleaned off the 60,000 ghost votes—the unbelievable number added fraudulently to a total valid electorate of only about 175,000. (I had gone to Pittsburgh, Pennsylvania, as my readers will soon know, before final success came.) By 1940 a form of coalition of four Republicans and five non-machine Democrats led first by a homespun, cattle raising lawyer, John B. Gage, a Democrat who had not helped us in 1934, but who changed to become an effective reform mayor, and then by Bill Kemp, who consolidated the reform and set the patterns by which Kansas City gained good government. Before becoming mayor, Kemp was City Attorney, and he had to sue one of the most prestigious banks in Kansas City to recover funds which McElroy had diverted by such crude methods that the front citizens who were officers of the bank must have knowingly acquiesced in the fraud on the public.

The collapse of the Machine turned into general rout. If all of the disgraces, convictions, disappearances, resignations, suicides, and miscellaneous deaths could have been put on the stage in one scene it would have rivaled the dénouement in Hamlet.

Father was Right

One day my indispensable secretary, Essie L. Ellis, told me on the telephone that I had an interesting letter from Arthur Van Buskirk. He had proposed me to Pittsburgh Plate Glass Company, an old, big, and rather stodgy industrial firm, for general counsel. My father had several times told me that I would be called away from Kansas City, and so it turned out.

The decision was difficult. Within the year I had opened my own law office after an amicable separation from Maurice Winger. Mary would have to leave her significant post as head of a school which had gained a national reputation in progressive education. I would have to leave clients toward whom I felt loyal and grateful.

I would quit public work which even the *Kansas City Star* had editorially approved: criminal law reforms and a plan for taking judicial selections out of politics. Kenneth Teasdale and I had labored to form the Missouri Institute for the Administration of Justice, which ultimately achieved the "Missouri Plan" by which in effect judges are nominated by their legal peers, not by politics. Teasdale became a president of the Missouri Bar Association and a leading St. Louis lawyer.

I did not relish leaving Judge Otis. There was nobility in his courage. I would miss his wit, too. One day a juryman asked to be excused, saying, "My wife is about to become pregnant." Of course, there was a titter in the courtroom. A lawyer arose to say, "Your honor, the juryman must mean that his wife is about to be delivered of a child." Judge Otis said from the Bench, "In either case I think the juryman should be at home."

Elmer Rhoden said, "Leland, you will never like yourself unless you try it out." So Mary and I went to Pittsburgh and its Golden Triangle. (1938).

PART III
In the Trying

Big Business

We came to Pittsburgh; and it was dark at noontime—black and yellow with smoke and acrid with sulphur smell; and the ladies at cocktail parties said, "We love the smoke and the smell," adding, "There was good air in Pittsburgh during the Depression but no business in the mills. We like it this way."

Pittsburgh is a city of industrial managers. But there are always controlling interests back of managers. If a large block of stock is owned by a single family, then whoever speaks for that block of stock—family member, lawyer, banker, advisor—will be an inevitable power, whoever occupies the office of president or chairman. It was into such a situation that I came in 1938. The family were Philadelphia based—three sons and a daughter of John Pitcairn, founder in 1873, with a certain Captain Ford of river steamboat background, of the first plate glass plant in America. Considerable vision and courage were needed for this venture in a heavy and capital-intensive technology, first located some 25 miles from Pittsburgh at Creighton, Pennsylvania. The plant still stands—now one of some 42 domestic and 27 foreign plants producing the diversified products of the presently named PPG Industries, a company which stands in the top ten *per cent* in the ranking by *Fortune Magazine* of America's 500 largest corporations.

It is exceptional that a single family should own (1938) approximately one-third of the stock of a large corporation, such as Pittsburgh Plate Glass Company, as the name stood when I came. The next sizeable block of stock, much smaller, was owned by the Mellon family. After that, percentage holdings are quite small. Corporate officers of most corporations own mere fractional percentage points of total shares. Often they refer to themselves—not derisively—as hired men.

A Certain Rich Man and a Lawyer

John Pitcairn's first and only full-time lawyer was Clarence Brown. The young graduate of the University of Pennsylvania Law School had guided his client through a break with Captain Ford and into what became control of the first American plate glass enterprise. Clarence Brown was seventy when he approved me to organize a law department at Pittsburgh for the legal controls which circumstances had made difficult from his seat in Philadelphia.

The circumstances were the Depression-born New Deal legislation which ran the gamut of business, economic, and social controls and concerns—from the price of gold, the price of labor, the size of business to the length of human life. On the last point the Social Security Act of 1935 had launched the welfare state in America (more tolerant critics of that era said, "state of welfare for Americans"). The process continues today, who knows to what end.

In the American Great Depression of the 1930's, Franklin Roosevelt and his brilliant brain trust transferred responsibility for the fallen sparrow from God to government. Adam Smith's *laissez faire* had failed. Herbert Joseph Davenport had taught me 20 years earlier that it would fail. St. Paul's God had failed. Never again would a Christian say with the great salesman of Christianity, "If a man will not work, neither shall he eat." Puritanism had ended. It would be no more that a man must find work; rather that the system, whatever it was to become, must provide work, and failing in that must care for the man—man, woman, and child.

I am not certain whether Clarence Brown knew all that had happened to the American business and social world. He told me from behind the sparkling lenses of his *pince-nez* that it might take 20 years for the country to get straightened out, meaning, to recover from the New Deal. Meantime he had bought real estate mortgage bonds at such low depression prices that his own substantial fortune was assured. What he did know was that a spate of new laws was controlling literally every aspect of business and industrial activity and that he was 70 and I was not yet 45—in 1938. He had remained alert in mind and lithe of body—an ardent Arthur Murray dancer. He was a bon vivant but with a Philadelphia sense of economy and restraint. He wore blue shirts with white collars. That way the cuffs might be good for two or three days so that only the collars would place a burden on the laundry.

In any case he knew and I knew that a new day had come for lawyers.

Just as in the early days of the Depression, bankruptcy and insolvency greatly enhanced the need for lawyers' services, so the New Deal laws, controlling the stock market; sale of securities; labor-management relations; minimum wages; maximum hours; trade practices of almost every kind—these new and detailed controls also called for lawyers. Ultimately many of the new restraints were worked into the warp and woof of corporate administration but the laws were new, traumatically new, not to say "socialistic". Worse than that, the United States Supreme Court by the late 1930's had approved all of the major New Deal legislation with the single principal exception of the National Industrial Recovery Act. That bureaucratic complex which brought to the United States Supreme Court the question whether a chicken had been legally butchered was too much even for a frightened court majority. Moreover, the Court which, for the greater part, gave its constitutional blessing to the New Deal was still composed of Drew Pearson's "Nine Old Men," Charles Evans Hughes usually casting a deciding vote in favor of Franklin Roosevelt's "forgotten man." By the time I came to Pittsburgh it was common talk that F.D.R., who began his campaign for the presidency on issues of economy and efficiency in government, had in fact carried out the platform of Norman Thomas' Socialist Party.

In a true revolution, as in the 1917 communist seizure of power in Russia, lawyers are the first to go. In drastic evolution, which seems to many to change the system, but does not involve violence and usurpation, lawyers are the first to be called in. Such was the situation at the mid-point of Franklin Roosevelt's second term. Clarence Brown, a lawyer himself, had decided to "call in" a lawyer. He held the unqualified confidence of the two brothers, sons of John Pitcairn, who managed the family's undisputed control of the business, now grown to both plate and window glass (a good business even in the Depression, because glass breaks) and other products such as paints; alkalis (for rayon); and chlorine (for water purification, and incongruously, as modern chemistry goes, for making plastic substitutes for leather). My client was Clarence Brown in Philadelphia but I must have rapport with the officers and executives who carried on the daily work of producing and selling the company's rapidly expanding complex of products.

Some Kind of Saint

The elder of the two Pitcairn brothers, both active as directors in the business, was Raymond. He and his brother, Harold, were faithful attendants at all meetings of the Board. A third brother, Theodore, was devoting himself to a European ministry in the Swedenborgian Church at the time of my advent. Most American Pitcairns were and are devoted adherents to one branch or another of that Swedenborgian religion known as The Church of the New Jerusalem.

In business Raymond and Harold acted for the family, which included a sister and many children and grandchildren, sons and daughters-in-law, and cousins, nephews, nieces, and aunts. Swedenborgians, although Swedenborg himself was never married, believe in large families. Raymond once said to me of his wife, Mildred, "She is never so well or so beautiful as when she is carrying a child." An assembly of the entire Pitcairn clan would fill a sizeable hall even when I first arrived. The family fortune stood high on the list of America's "Sixty Families" but they lived in almost complete obscurity at Bryn Athyn in Montgomery County, Pennsylvania, whose serene hills made the setting for their estates —all commanded from the highest point by Raymond's castle.

Over the years the stationery on which letters from Raymond came would sometimes read, "Raymond Pitcairn, Attorney at Law," if it came from his office in Philadelphia or, it would read, "Bryn Athyn, Studios of Building & Architectural Arts," if the letter came from the castle, which had a noble tower of Norman-Romanesque feeling. I use the word, "feeling," not knowing whether Raymond, who died in 1966, would approve even that slight suggestion of his borrowing from any established form. Raymond was the architect for his castle.

The lines of the upward thrust of the tower are noticeably concave. Thus he seems to have made a virtue out of the ocular phenomenon that a vertically straight architectural line becomes concave—something the classical builders corrected by giving the line a slight convexity, called entasis. Raymond called his upward lines "free", and was pleased with the zenith reaching sweeps, as he was with the individual stones in his manor house. He would pat a fat stone, chiseled to such a texture that all hardness was gone, saying where his personal explorations had found it and giving the life history of the workman who had shaped it. He would caress a bronze latch of elegant amplitude, designed by him, and relate how, in the presence of the artisan who had fashioned it, he had once told a visitor that the exquisite piece came out of a Sears-Roebuck catalogue. Humor was rare with Raymond, although, except when he was temporarily distressed or momentarily asleep at Board meetings, there was an enigmatic smile on his face. The great tower is integral to the castle, whose vast hall, vaulted and ribbed, has accommodated the Philadelphia Symphony for a special concert and the community for the occasion of a visit by Dwight and Mamie Eisenhower to Raymond and Mildred.

When Raymond conducted a tour of the castle he waxed eloquent not so much about the overpowering Gothic greatness of the hall and its adjuncts and its art-filled niches—one with a 12th century Virgin in stone—as about the Swedenborgian inscriptions which make the friezes of the upper rooms: library, lounges, bedrooms, and balconies. He would hold his visitors immobile while he read aloud from the boldly and beautifully lettered words—one long excerpt to the room—of Swedenborg's "Writings", which rank with the Scriptures in the New Church, as it is sometimes called. To Raymond a precept was a reality. That it was not real to all men left him sad but all the more determined to work and contribute for the election of Republicans at every opportunity, local, state, or national.

The castle was built during the depth of the Depression. Raymond called it his personal social security program. It stands on ground in the Bryn Athyn Swedenborgian complex higher than the Cathedral which the New Church began under the architectural guidance of Ralph Adams Cram, well known for redesigning the Cathedral of St. John the Divine in New York City from its original Romanesque to the Gothic style. Despite Cram's eminence in Gothic architecture, Raymond broke with him and finished the most impressive of the New Church structures according to his own knowledge and taste. An accomplished violinist, Raymond thought of himself—as Beethoven of himself in music—as a liberating influence in architecture.

For me a cathedral—any cathedral—is not so much a religious symbol as the concrete expression of man's need to know the infinite. I should not try to say it in words better than those of Henry Adams in *Mont-Saint-Michel et Chartres:* in the cathedral, man flings his passion against the sky. There isn't a cathedral I wouldn't enter no matter where it rises.

Raymond's cathedral does not have as awesome and black an interior as that at Cahors in France. It is not as huge as Strasbourg, with all the apostles in full figure above the portals. It is not as rich with embellishment as Chartres or as spectacular in landscape setting as Salisbury. All of this is only to say that each cathedral has its own particular charm or grandeur: Tarragona in Spain and its alabaster altar, Leon with its vast expanses of glass; Aix-la-Chapelle and its sculptured doors, precious and protected behind stout wooden coverings, and its aging portal Virgin Mary (forty, if a day), who was saved from vandalism in the French Revolution with a man's hat jammed on her sacred head.

I know that my traveled readers will protest that I have omitted this or that cathedral, each the greatest of them all: Aachen; or Rouen; or Albi. Raymond's cathedral has one thing in common with them all—distinctiveness. It lacks a great portal facade, un-needed, perhaps, because the location is in the countryside, not in the course of urban movements. Yet there *is* an adequate entrance into the nave, opposite the chancel, of course. Then there is a cloistered entrance which leads into the front pews from a path which descends from the castle. The interior is luminous. The acoustics are excellent, as they would be, because some members of Raymond's clan will always be singing or playing some instrument in the choir. One has the feeling of architectural restraint in favor of function but equally of pure and knowledgeable expression of early Gothic forms.

Those who have founded a church on Swedenborg's detailed accounts of his religious experiences believe that he affirmed instantaneous resurrection and eternal life—and in a literal sense. Mildred, fragile and beautiful as fine porcelain, Raymond's wife, once spoke to me of an elderly blind man, widely revered in their community, who had just died. She rejoiced for him, "Because now he can see." She was reflecting Swedenborg's concept of death: that *continuation* of life, which is death, is in the human form with the important exception that there is bodily perfection —all imperfections, impairments, and illnesses spent. I could not see that Raymond's own death shook Mildred's faith.

The Right Rev. George de Charms, former Bishop at the Cathedral, conducted the final services for Raymond, saying, "We can hardly imagine his delight as he awakens, as if from sleep, to find himself in that new and wonderful world—his glad reunion with the beloved relatives and friends who have gone before—his eager search for the special place prepared of God where he may enter into the heavenly use for which his life on earth has prepared him."

After the Cathedral services we went up the path to the castle. Mildred sat serene at the center of the circle of big leather chairs, which for many years I had always thought incongruous in the great hall. The eldest son Nathan introduced two sons-in-law, Robert Junge and Willard Pendleton, both ministers of the New Church, the latter Bishop at the Cathedral. Both spoke well and with complete composure, Robert affectionately of "Daddy"; Willard of Raymond, the "man of affairs in the world of business, a gifted musician, a member of the legal profession, a man who loved the beauty of nature, and an inspired builder and architect." Then there were tables of wine (Raymond was an ardent and effective anti-prohibitionist, although he himself always had only one drink) and Mamie Eisenhower and the Richard Nixons were there, and everyone spoke to Mildred, and looked again at the stones and the high vaults, and I wondered why Jesus Christ had seemed to say, by the analogy of the camel and needle's eye, that a rich man could not enter the Kingdom of Heaven. Once I took Beardsley Ruml to the Castle for some professional conferences. On the train back to New York he said of Raymond, "Surely, he is some kind of saint."

Functions in Big Business

If Clarence Brown was my client, Raymond was his client, and they both firmly approved me. Therefore I set about with considerable confidence in 1938 to do what I later realized was quite difficult. There are certain functions in an industrial corporation which are inevitable, whether or not they are cleary identified. The product must be produced. This function is called "Production," and is carried on by engineers, civil, mechanical, chemical, electrical, electronic, or by scientists—or by technicians who may have simply grown up in the art of producing the product. These men are tight-minded and often are poor dinner companions. Yet, when one finds the exception he will be well-grounded in whatever subject he is willing to discuss.

The product must be sold. This function is called "Sales", and it is performed by men who even today cannot be trained, at least the great ones, as a welder or a bricklayer can be trained. The question, "Who could have trained Shakespeare?" would not seem hyperbole to a great salesman. The idea of training a successor would be nonsense. Whether he knows it or not, the salesman practices the Christian concept of the worth of every individual. Everyone he meets, and he is zealous about meeting people, is a potential friend and customer, and he makes no distinction between friend and customer.

We had such a superb salesman when I came to Pittsburgh. Frank Judson was reputed to know more people than anyone else in the United States—outside of politics. Occasionally there would be a need for him to know someone whom, in fact, he did not know. In such an extremity he would pick up the telephone, get the tycoon on the line, and in three minutes have the victim apologizing for not remembering Judson. Frank Judson worked his magic almost until his death. Yet there was something poignant about a man whose only resource was in his friends and customers. Arthur Miller caught the poignancy in the less fortunate Willy Lohman—friends gone and times changed, then comes the death of a salesman.

When one leaves the clearly identified functions of production and sales, the lines of demarcation become rapidly less clear. Historically, the treasurer is next in order of respected functions because he receives the fruits of the sales and pays out the costs of the production. In modern times, however, even higher in the hierarchy is the controller who keeps the accounts by which business has known how it was doing since the Italians invented double entry bookkeeping to account for the trade of their merchants in the 14th and 15th centuries. Nowadays there is likely to be a vice-president of finance who has jurisdiction over both the treasurer and the comptroller. This function is called Finance.

The law function is much newer in big business. It arose clearly in the late 19th century when, after the "trust form" of big business, pioneered by John D. Rockefeller, had been denied legal sanction by the Ohio courts, the State of New Jersey stepped forward with a highly flexible corporation law. In these days when everybody from Paul Getty to the man and woman on any street corner buys corporation stocks—in these days of "People's Capitalism" it will seem strange that within the lifetime of many living persons a corporation, which is always the creature of legislative law, had limited, if any, rights to own even land, much less the stock of other corporations.

Other states quickly followed New Jersey: Delaware, Maine, West Virginia; finally, in every state in the union in one way or another a corporation may do almost anything a natural person may do and, in many cases, more—subject, of course, to the maze of governmental regulations which makes the lawyer necessary and his life rewarding. When, at the turn of the century, J. P. Morgan the Elder made Judge Elbert H. Gary the first president of the then largest corporation in the history of the world, United States Steel Corporation, composed of ten existing giant corporations, the business world knew that the law and lawyers had a place in big business.

On another point, Thorstein Veblen, my teacher, was wont to inveigh against banker-manipulated consolidations and mergers. He would point out, as others have done, that the bankers' fees for putting together U.S. Steel were 60 million, of which Morgan had 12 million—and for what service Veblen would ask. It has been said that the original stock of U.S. Steel was not even water; it was air. But, it is not a perfect world. Veblen urged technocracy and forecast a managerial revolution which did not come off. He did not know enough politics or psychology. U.S. Steel has been a major factor in the growth of the American economy. Its former chairman, Roger Blough, with whom I have often discussed questions of public concern, is a lawyer.

Whether or not a particular function is clearly identified and assigned to a functionary in a corporation, nevertheless the need for the function exists. Someone will attempt to satisfy the need. That there is no law department does not mean that there are no law questions. They arise every day and must be dealt with for better or for worse. Non-lawyers throughout the organization build up limited reputations for expertise in making contracts, handling taxes, real estate, labor laws, and many affairs which involve law. Frequently they do very well over a long period of time. Early in my tenure an old and beloved purchasing agent came to me and said, "Mr. Hazard, a survey team from the controller's office says I ought to have more conditions in my form of purchase contract." "Let me see it," I requested. The form was indeed devoid of sophistication. But I asked if he had ever had any trouble with a supplier under his standard form. "No," he said, "not since 1896. I don't know whether or not my predecessor had any trouble." So the form was a half-century old, but I left it untouched for the moment. The purchasing agent's character and his knowledge of the character of sellers were a reasonable substitute for a tighter contract, which, of course, we produced after the good man laid down his responsibilities.

Some legal mistakes of laymen, which a lawyer of even reasonable competence would avoid, get buried—and in rather shallow graves. I was told that a fine piece of property in Pittsburgh's East End had been bought as the site for the Company's own building, the plans for which had been drawn by a distinguished architect, Benno Janssen. Why the project never went forward was never precisely stated—not even by Harry Wherrett, a president whose cool deliberate mind never lacked clarity. One day I came on to a policy of title insurance covering that intended office building site. The title was insured right enough, but subject to the *city zoning* which *forbade business* in that area. Some non-lawyer never read the policy. The title was insured, wasn't it? Such mistakes help to identify the law function.

The fact that law functions are being exercised all around the organization by non-lawyers makes a heavy risk for a newcomer. The network of alliances, friendships, obligations, and reciprocities is thick and intricate. One never knows how a necessary and correct decision on a law point, communicated to a minor executive, will be reported to a head of some department as an unnecessary and arrogant change. What is really bothering him is that decisions which he formerly made on a non-technical basis, such as "fairness," or "equity," or "good citizenship," or "mother love," are now subjected to more refined analysis. And, more than that, his area of usefulness—and therefore claim to compensation—is reduced, so he thinks. Actually, such is not the case. He is really freed to do what he knows how to do. In the transition period, however, he does not know that, and he reacts defensively. I saw such forces at work. Fortunately for me I was never the victim of them because part of the time I was gentle, and when I was not gentle, the firm resolve of Clarence Brown and Raymond Pitcairn to support the law function stood me in good stead.

Help from the New Deal

There was a third factor, perhaps more potent than gentleness or high level support, which enabled me to survive the initial venture and build an organization of lawyers. On several fronts, particularly in labor-management relations and in antitrust enforcement, big business was getting a baptism of fire in the late 1930's. The fire continues but the baptism was new when I arrived on the scene.

In 1937 the United States Supreme Court had sustained the National Labor Relations Act, passed by the Congress two years earlier. This Act was the first affirmative intervention by the American Government in the long American struggle between management and labor. Earlier interventions such as the Norris-LaGuardia Act had been negative—court injunctions against strikes having been prohibited in 1932. But the Wagner Act, as the new law was called, established the right of workers to have unions of their own choosing; provided procedures for fixing the units of industrial workers in which the union elections could be held; and required management to bargain with the winning union, which, having won, had the legal right to represent all the employees in the unit. All of this was a vast change from the early 19th century, when it was a criminal conspiracy even to form a union, and a sudden change within a brief four years from the 1933 bloodshed in the coal mines and steel mills of Western Pennsylvania.

An era—a long era—had ended. An aspect of history which began with the slavery of human beings—a concept which Spengler suggests came with the domestication (enslavement) of animals—had moved 90 degrees. It was not that the ancient master-servant relationship was reversed, but rather that the master must now bargain with the servant. Endless complexities would ensue, but I had the advantage of a pragmatic attitude. There was no time to be lost in fulmination. Many "black tie" lawyers quoting Latin maxims before the "revolutionary" National Labor Relations Board were doomed to frustration and failure. I had a certain amount of understanding of workers' needs and management's insensitivity. I also had a lawyer's understanding of the importance of what John Kenneth Galbraith came to call "countervailing power" in the new management-labor dichotomy. A lawyer tends to believe in orderly controversy as a good method for achieving justice. My views in that regard have changed in some degree as the reader will presently discover. The Wagner Act provided serious penalties, some monetary and some penal, and management for a time went into a funk. One of my early insights was management's need for restored confidence in itself in labor matters.

A contemporaneous new law was the Federal Wage and Hour Law, the purpose of which was to put a ceiling, finally 40 hours, on the work-week, all hours beyond being subject to overtime at one and a half times the hourly rate. The law also contained minimum wage provisions, prohibitions about child labor, and exceptions as important as the law. The permutations and combinations could approach astronomical complexity. "Two ducks before two ducks; two ducks behind two ducks; two ducks beside two ducks: how many ducks?" The answer to an apparently complicated question was often as simple as in the duck case. But it was laborious business reading the fine print of the deluge of regulations which emerged from the United States Department of Labor. Again there were no patterns; again the civil and criminal penalties were severe; again a lawyer needed to protect the executive against indiscriminate collapse. The rain of regulation was falling hard and I added my first associate in the Law Department.

Building a Law Department

Joseph T. Owens had a good record at Harvard Law School, where it is easy to have a bad record. He had come from a provincial community and provincial schools in Kansas, from which he brought the teetotalism which he has endured to this day. I had happily engaged him for our big and growing law firm in Kansas City. Now a bare ten years later his name came first to my mind when I needed an associate in my new venture. Lawyers seldom refer to another lawyer as an employee, even if that is in technical fact the relationship. The youngest lawyer, the most recently out of law school, knows something, has some skill, some bent of mind which the most senior and seasoned practitioner needs. So it is customary to treat a junior lawyer as a professional colleague and to refer to him as an associate—not as an assistant. This mode may have an American democratic flavor. Anyone who knows Gilbert and Sullivan's *Trial by Jury* or Charles Dickens' *Bleakhouse* will recall the low estate of the British law clerk, pronounced "clark," but that is not the American mode.

Before I came to Pittsburgh, Joe Owens had left us in Kansas City to accept an important legal post in the Federal Reserve System in Washington. So I had to disengage him from a government position and a pleasant residential community in a Washington suburb. He knew at once that the opportunity was good, but he could see for himself, when he visited Pittsburgh for the necessary interviews, that the grit and grime of the town might not attract a wife who remembered the clean wheat fields of Kansas and the geometric perfection of the tennis courts of Washington's suburbia. This problem he solved by devising a route into Pittsburgh an hour or so longer than necessary so that he could carry his wife, Ella, by devious ways through the remnants of Penn's Woods which have survived industrialism. Being unfamiliar with normal routes of travel into Pittsburgh, the dear lady was none-the-wiser until the next morning.

Joe Owens had, in good measure, the ability to bore into the "fine print" of the "regulations" in whatever field, except taxes— a highly specialized area. His experience in the bureaucracy of the largest central banking system in the world stood him in good stead. He had another aptitude, not at first fully expected by me. He quickly proved himself the ideal "organization man." He quit tennis, a necessarily competitive game in which the opponents must be individualistic and are in direct confrontation, and betook himself avidly to learn golf, a game which, he said, he understood big business men played. He became speedily proficient, an achievement which had always eluded me by very wide margins.

The law department grew very rapidly and always by the same process: new and specialized needs arising for the greater part out of the impact of federal and state governments upon big business or by reason of better internal identification of legal questions or, quite simply, because, after the Great Depression, everything in America began getting bigger.

I Begin to Make Policy

One of my earliest memories is of some men digging a trench in our front yard in Kansas City, Missouri. Suddenly Father appeared on the scene and discharged one of them—the one who had interested me more than the others because he was jovial and talkative. Later that evening Father explained to me that the fellow had been talking unionism rather than digging in the trench. That episode occurred around the Century's turn some 35 years before the Wagner Act, which made it an offense to discharge any employee for union activity. Of course the Wagner Act applies only to employers in interstate commerce; so Father and his front yard trench would have been immune even today; not so with my client in 1940 whose many plants and establishments reached from coast to coast with employees numbered in the thousands.

Even five years after the Wagner Act the majority of American managers thought of unions as fraternal orders of a sort, to which their *disloyal* employees belonged, but not their *loyal* employees. Although the Wagner Act had established a national policy which introduced unionism into that part of industrialism which involves manual work, skilled and unskilled, and some orders of mental work, management was not yet fully aware of what had happened. Early unions themselves had fostered the idea of their own preciousness. For example, in 1878 the Knights of Labor (the very title was drawn from the medieval elite) restricted its membership against "lawyers (sic), bankers, stock brokers, professional gamblers and anybody who had anything to do with the sale of intoxicating beverages." Gambling and drinking per se were not proscribed. It was rather that the line was drawn between professionalism and enterprise on the one hand and labor on the other hand.

It was, I think, not unreasonable that management's attitude toward unionism in the early days of Wagner Act administration was one of skepticism and hostility. Unions had helped to foment the idea of hostility by such slogans as "An injury to one is the concern of all." The old school manager who knew his employees by their first names, knew the wives and children, sent turkeys to all at Thanksgiving and Christmas, was openly and honestly paternalistic—he was to suffer an acute trauma. Witness a case reported by Clinton S. Golden in the book, *Dynamics of Industrial Democracy*. A meeting of workers was called at a plant in the Pittsburgh area where wages and working conditions were widely known to be excellent. Nevertheless 1,000 workers attended. One attractive girl summed up the general sentiment: "It's about time something like this happened. We have got to stand on our own feet. They do everything for you but provide a husband, and I even know girls who they got a husband for. And them who ain't got time to get pregnant, they get foster kids for." When I first read this charming and, I then thought, profound bit it seemed to me a revelation: people must have some power of their own; they were not to be well-off as a matter of good-will or grace or even law but as a matter of guarantee by reason of their own collective power —unionism.

I did not then see unionism as one of the prices of an undisciplined—the nice word is pluralistic—society, in which direct action and force, economic, sometimes physical, are the tools for compelling "social justice" for one group or another. I did not see unionism as the forerunner of "black power" and a host of intervening power assemblages. I did not foresee that Negroes would have to organize in power groups to compel unions to give them the opportunity to work; or that jurisdictional disputes among unions would victimize employers and consumers; or that craft unions would use accumulated dues from hod and other craft carriers' unions to invade and destroy professionalism in education and make Luddites of teachers; or that Ludditism would drive American newspapers out of publication and American ships off the seas and out of our ports. Of all this more later. I make the confession now only to add that if I had foreseen all those excesses my contribution to one aspect of unionism in the early 1940's would nevertheless have been the same.

Union leaders employed in those days—even to some extent today—the pretenses of young national regimes such as huge Communist Russia or tiny Communist Cuba; some greater power is planning or seeking destruction of our nation—or in this case, our union. Union leaders were, and are, very clever about tactics. In any controversy it is always the employer who is "Unfair to Organized Labor." The issue may be whether the employer was right in discharging a kleptomaniac, but if the union needs for its purposes to take the position that the discharge was an injury to one which is the concern of all the picket signs never read "Was John Doe Improperly Accused by Acme Corporation of Kleptomania," and therefore wrongfully discharged? Nothing so precise and explanatory as that would ever be employed—no, the picket sign will read simply, "Unfair to Organized Labor." Union members are conditioned almost as animals are conditioned in an experimental laboratory to respond to signals. A picket sign is a signal.

The unions in 1940 were saying that they were insecure because not all of the workers in the plant belonged and many of those who did belong failed to pay dues. Management laughed silently up its sleeve—so the unions are not so strong; we *do* have loyal employees, management chuckled to itself. Yet the unions had a point. Any union which at some time gained over fifty per cent of employees in the plant or other unit had the obligation under the Wagner Act to represent *all* the employees. It was a well known phenomenon that union membership and dues payments would go up when a wage increase or other vital issue was up. Then the issue having been resolved, to the satisfaction of some workers and the dissatisfaction of others, membership and dues payments would decline—among both the satisfied and the dissatisfied. Management would say, "See! There is no honor among these people," meaning union members; "they are purely opportunistic, without loyalty even to their own union."

Thus it was that when, in the early 1940's, unions began to "dues picket" at plant gates, management was understandably enraged. Dues picketing meant that "loyal unionists" appeared in sufficient numbers to prevent erstwhile union members who had not paid their dues from entering the plant. Management asked, "Is it right that a union can close our plant because some of its own members are disloyal to the union?" The phrase "close the plant" was no exaggeration—nor would it be today. Since the flowering of the Industrial Revolution in the 18th Century mass production has been a process of many specialities. If there is a crew of eight men and one is stopped at the gate, it may be impossible for the seven to do their work. If in an electrical power plant or a water pumping department, both utterly critical to the whole

plant and either involving relatively few specialized workmen—
if those workmen are stopped at the gate, the whole plant goes
down.

When the "dues picketing" was brought to my attention by Fred
Keightley, Director of our company's Labor Relations, I watched
the process for some weeks and concluded that on any given day
10 per cent of any work force could either close a plant or render
its operations utterly inefficient. Fred Keightley had come up
through the ranks of iron and steel workers. He was a big, overweight man, engaged for that very reason by then Vice-President
Robert L. Claus, who noted that many union leaders were overweight and who had, so he told me, the idea of matching avoirdupois with avoirdupois. This was a novel selection method, but in
1935, with the just passed Wagner Act opening a whole new era
of management-labor confrontations, perhaps as good as any.

Fred Keightley knew the bitterness between loyal dues-paying
union members and the non-paying members. He convinced me
that we could get harmony in the plants if the Company adopted
a policy requiring all employees to pay dues to the established
union in whatever manufacturing operation. I agreed but with an
important reservation: we would discharge an employee only for
failure to pay a reasonable initiation fee and reasonable dues, the
amounts of which we would bargain out with the unions. We
would *not* discharge an employee for "bad standing" in the union.
I knew too many cases in which union management had declared
members in bad standing for a speech on the union floor or some
other cause unrelated to his work. We refused the conventional
"union shop" contract but we began carefully to work out what
I finally called the "dues shop". We refused indiscriminate union
security but allowed "financial union security." In other words,
we agreed that the unions had responsibilities; that it costs money
to run a union; that our Company's efficiency would increase if
we laid to rest the internecine warfare between the dues-paying
members and the "free riders", as the non-paying workers were
called; but we refused to turn over to the unions the power of discharge as would be the case under a conventional union shop
contract.

Even so, it was a hard pill for our management to swallow. Our
gentle but firm minded president, Harry Wherrett, was still con-

cerned about the "loyal employees." He was also concerned about what has come to be called "the right to work," meaning that it seems wrong that a man or woman must pay a tax (dues) to a union in order to hold a job. An important minority of states still have laws forbidding either the "union shop" or the "dues shop." It was not perceived, however — not at first — that the Wagner Act had made unions of the employees' own choosing instrumentalities of industrial government. If a majority of employees chose a union, then the minority must take the bitter (dues) with the sweet (constantly increasing wages and improving working conditions).

I convinced Harry Wherrett to abandon his concern for employees whose loyalty I doubted more than he. Fred Keightley spread my careful documentation into the operating echelons, some of whom were relieved to be rid of dues picketing; others were sure the company had capitulated. It took about five years to get the policy firmly established at the foreman level. A time lag of that duration is not unusual in big business. Even the clearest directive from top management, if the subject matter is controversial, will be discounted among some of the managerial rank and file. Surprisingly, they will assume that the policy declaration from on high is for public consumption only, or for some ulterior purpose; or, in any case, the subordinate will reason: "I don't care what the boss said; I know what he thinks."

Senator Robert A. Taft Agreed

The whole matter was laid at rest in the Taft-Hartley Act of 1947 and I played a role in that legislation. Senator Taft, one of the finest minds ever in Washington, knew that there must be some discrete withdrawals from the advance positions which had been staked out by the National Labor Relations Board and some federal courts under the Wagner Act. He was certain that the "closed shop," which gives the employer no right to select his own employees, must be barred, and it was barred. Senator Taft was not sure about the "union shop", which permits the employer to select his employees but they must join the union within 30 days or less, and the employer must discharge any employee certified by the union as in "bad standing" for any cause, for example: being a Jehovah's Witness; having red hair; or calling the union president "stupid".

I traveled to Washington and camped there to urge the "dues shop." By this time several lawyers had been added to my department. One of them accompanied me on this important mission, Donald J. Sherbondy, an engaging young man, hale, hearty, and lusty—not overweight. I had selected him in 1945 to deal with the problems of labor law and labor relations. (Much later he became vice-president in charge of all industrial relations.) A graduate in law from George Washington University, he knew his way around Washington—down the back stairs in the dark, as the saying goes. We caught Senator Taft, sometimes in his office, sometimes on the go. He quickly understood the difference between the union shop and the dues shop and opted for the latter. We worked out the language with Thomas E. Shroyer, a legal advisor to Senator Taft, and today the "dues shop," now officially called the agency shop, is the only legal form under federal law. A union which has the power of hiring, as in the closed shop, and of firing, as in the union shop, has too much power. On the other hand, it is not unreasonable to require every employee to pay his reasonable share of the costs of many important services which the union renders to all employees, once a majority of them have chosen the union.

Quid Pro Quo

Once unions were recognized and had gained financial security, management could then make its own demands. One of the demands I pressed was for security of the company against little strikes during the term of the contract. For example, a dispute arises in some corner of a plant of 3 or 4,000 workers. It may involve only a few men, often only one man. Words pass; tempers rise. There are orderly procedures for handling grievances but these are forgotten in the heat of the moment. Soon a few men walk off the job, rumor spreads, and the whole plant goes down. This is called a quickie or unauthorized or wildcat strike, as distinguished from a big and often prolonged strike when an old contract has expired and the terms of a new one cannot be agreed upon. Successions of wildcat strikes can be just as costly as a big strike—costly to consumers and the public. Unless strikes utterly destroy an employer he will pass the cost of them right on to consumers. There is no other place to put costs once the profit is driven to the vanishing point.

I was an early proponent of union contracts of more than one year—first two- and then three-year contracts with reopenings on wages only or with wage increments settled for the whole period, but only if we could get company security against wildcat strikes. I had resistance both from the union and from management. Union officers knew that they could not always control their members and therefore hesitated to contract against wildcat strikes. Management, on the other hand, said that a union's word is no good anyway, so what is the use of a contract. My position was that with financial security union treasuries were becoming sizeable and union officers would not risk the liability for damages—very heavy damages indeed, if employees stopped the plant in violation of the contract. Management persistently countered with its low opinion of the veracity of union officers. "These wildcat strikes are all really authorized," our executives, high and low, said, adding, "Union officers disavow them for public consumption and foment them for union membership action."

The solution turned out to be quite simple. The conventional no-strike clause pledged the union against strikes and any form of work stoppage during the contract. I proposed a provision that if any employee or group of employees violated the no-strike contract, union officers would disavow the violation in writing to be delivered to the company and published to the employees. This seemingly mild provision could be quite potent. If the union disavowed, the company could discipline the dissident employees; if the union failed to disavow or supported the dissident employees, then it would be in default under its contract and its treasury would be liable for the company's damages in very large amounts or would be subject to court injunction to cease its support of the dissident employees.

Creeping Confidence

George W. Taylor* was chairman of the War Labor Board in World War II. He is known throughout the whole of management and labor in America as "Dr. Taylor" rather than by the more familiar "George". In addition to his long and distinguished career at Wharton School of Finance and Commerce, he has served five

---

*Dr. Taylor died on December 15, 1972, at his home in Philadelphia, Pa.

presidents of the United States in various high-level capacities. I first encountered Dr. Taylor when I appeared before him to support World War II wage controls. The formula, which he had created, was known as the "Little Steel Formula," and was designed to hold the line on wages just as the line on prices was being held under Leon Henderson's Office of Price Administration. Labor had attacked the formula and I was among the defenders.

One of my associates in the law department was an economist, F. Taylor Ostrander, graduate of Williams College. During his tenure with me he added greatly to my ability to deal with macroeconomics. Thus it was that in my presentation to Dr. Taylor and his colleagues on the War Labor Board, I tackled problems of national fiscal and budgetary significance with confidence – in Ostrander's substance and in my own articulation. We won our case in the sense that we gave the Board some additional, solidly stated material to support a wage holding policy to which the War Labor Board and the government were strongly inclined and in which my client had a stake. At the close of the hearing Dr. Taylor sent Frank Graham, a Board colleague, over to my part of the big hearing room to say, "You have been burning the midnight oil."

George Taylor: Practicing Labor Philosopher

Dr. Taylor has always said that there are four ways in which wages may be set: (1) by management; (2) by union; (3) by government; (4) by collective bargaining. For most of history, government has indeed set the wage for the simple reason that slavery was the mode of getting society's work done. All of the vast physical works of man's 6,000 years of history, except in very recent times, have been done by enforced labor: Pyramids, Parthenon, Pantheon. In a sense even the cathedrals of our own Western World 12th, 13th, and 14th centuries were built on governmentally fixed conditions: the "just wage" was the prevailing concept of both church and state; and the just wage was the amount necessary for subsistence of the worker, which is the equivalent of the cost of maintaining a slave. Finally, in totalitarian countries, in which the majority of the world's people live today, the wage is fixed by government, and the restriction of freedom of workers to change jobs is a form of slavery. We do not like this record of slavery and governmental control of workers and their rewards, but if one looks at the long record or at most of the world today he reads and sees the un-welcome facts. Even in nations where democracy prevails military service is enforced and the wage for fighting and for the support-ing services to front-line soldiers is fixed by government. I saw all of this for the first time in the early 1940's when my big business client thrust me into negotiations with big labor. Unionism is the ultimate antislavery movement. Yet to run an enterprise, or con-duct a symphony, or sail a ship, command is essential. How to keep command from being tyranny—that was one of the problems I worked on for 25 years—I was not the first, nor will I be the last to grasp that nettle.

George Taylor has been a practitioner of what he teaches—the religion of collective bargaining. He pursued his crowded schedule of teaching and consulting right into academic retirement. He has recently aided Governor Nelson Rockefeller in devising the New York law legalizing unionism of government employees, the "Taylor Law." His almost unbounded faith in collective bargain-ing has never faltered. What can be agreed upon between manage-ment and union will work—nothing else. He has a remarkable ability to articulate his sometimes unwelcome pragmatism. In one national labor crisis he was charged on national television by his opponents with getting bogged down in specifics. His reply was, "Let us not get bogged down in generalities." He had a way under stress of seeming to draw his neck into his rotund body, his big eyes smiling through heavy glasses, his round head cocked for the verbal fray. He spent his earlier years as an arbitrator in the gar-ments makers' unions, where the minds and tongues are as sharp as the needles.

George Taylor always said that there are things worse than a strike; a strike may be the necessary end of collective bargaining; a strike is the way things get settled. I agreed 20 years ago. I em-ployed that philosophy in two great strikes in the industry where I had some immediate responsibility. Each of them was 13 weeks long.

The first occurred in 1945. The union's wage demand was high. We expected to pay an increase but we wanted something in return. Usually a wage demand—after the preliminary sparring—should be treated as an opportunity to gain some condition which manage-ment needs. In 1945 we needed from the union an agreement not to strike during the term of the contract—3 years. The 3-year contract was an innovation which came in during the 1940's. One cannot emphasize sufficiently that so-called "quickie strikes" during the term of a contract are extremely costly to heavy technology, which is utterly dependent for efficiency upon long cycles of continuous operation.

Of course, if the union agrees not to strike, management must agree to arbitrate the numerous misunderstandings which occur in daily operations. I had difficulty in persuading my client to give up the power to say, "No", in exchange for the union's agreement not to strike. The union did not like either "no-strike" or arbitration. We stood fast and the strike came. Both sides knew it would be long, as it was. Finally, after 13 weeks both sides agreed to submit to arbitration the issue whether our contract should contain "no-strike" and arbitration. The arbitrator held that it should, and thus the no-strike clause I have described earlier became a reality—not a theory. But what a costly way to reach agreement. The workers would never regain the lost wages and the company would reap the fruits of its victory only at the cost of millions of lost production and sales.

Thirteen years later in 1958 another strike came—on issues not unlike those of the first: higher wages for the workers offset by management's demand for correction of costly seniority practices. One illustration: the union had gained over the years plant-wide seniority, which meant that if a vacancy occurred in an operation involving a dozen men in one corner of the plant the oldest worker in point of service among 4,000 in the whole plant could claim the job and, if not qualified, must be trained at the company's expense. This was called by the union—quite frankly—preference "for the man with the whiskers." (Now that youthful beards are the mode the symbol is no longer applicable.) The issue, which I have just simplistically illustrated, was a hard one: human concern for the older worker versus the employer's need for the efficiency of assigning the most immediately ready and competent workman. The same issue in another application is acute today (1972) with respect to black workers, who demand jobs if they are "qualifiable" without regard to their existing competence.

In 1958—a depression year—we finally challenged the practice of plant-wide seniority. A strike over such a deeply ingrained practice is taken deliberately—seldom in anger. Union leaders often fully understand the company's problem but they are elected and must often follow, not lead, their constituents. Sometimes the workers' practices are so costly as to price the workers out of jobs. Recently (1971), I. W. Abel, President of the United States Steel Workers, made a historical call on his constituents for more productivity so that the American steel industry could compete with Japanese and Benelux steel. Such frankness can cost any labor leader his job. At the close of our 1958 strike of 13 weeks the union got higher pay and we got far-reaching, cost-saving modifications of seniority practices—but again at great cost.

My philosophy is: so long as society has no better way than the strike to resolve conflicting needs of management and labor, never have a little strike. If, on contract termination, you *have* a strike, let it be big and long—long enough for someone, management or union, usually both, to get hurt. Strikes should not occur if the issue is not fundamental. A management which gives up after a short strike was not sincere about the issue. My formula was: after a strike over a new contract, management should not talk for about three weeks; from three to six weeks, conversations should begin; if a settlement cannot be reached in about 3 months there must be two explanations: (1) something wrong with management or (2) a "phony" strike because workers had gotten temporary-permanent jobs elsewhere and therefore could allow union leaders the luxury of jousting with management for the satisfaction of the ego.

Strikes and Slavery

The strike in its noblest aspect is an antislavery declaration by a concert of workers. It is an assertion that men will not work except on terms which they themselves have exacted from whatever institution is to pay the wage and provide the conditions of employment. The conditions may cover the gamut from provision of adequate toilets for men and women, and time off to attend them, through maternity leaves; pay for jury duty; paid time-off for funerals, weddings, and holidays of all religions; extended vacations up to four months every three years; increased pensions for widows of deceased former employees.

Some of the conditions, but only some, would seem so obviously proper that one wonders why workers would have had to demand them. We forget, however, that it was the last and degenerate stages of Puritanism which produced the English-American "factory-system" during the half century from 1825 to 1875. The rationale was, as Calvin had taught, that men were by nature debased—except the few of God's (self appointed) "elect"—and the way to prevent their self-condemnation to hell was to keep them in grueling factory labor. Incredible? Yes, but that is the record. I am sure that a kind of class memory about such cruelty persists. I have seen it in the faces of workers sitting across the bargaining table.

Over 25 years ago I was attending a collective bargaining session at a paint plant in Detroit. There was a uniform wage of one dollar per hour throughout the big plant, despite the fact that jobs ranged in skills from the grubby work of kettle washing to the high skilled work of tinting, in which the expert eye and hand must produce just the right red for a barn or just the perfect pastel for milady's boudoir. Just across the table from me sat a giant Negro with huge, beautiful hands—a kettle washer. "Mr. Hazard," he said, "who are you going to elevate? the man who works with his hands or the man who works with his head?" Elevate was pronounced *eleate,* and head was rendered *haid,* and the great hands were lifted and extended toward me not in threat but in poignant emphasis of his part in the eternal dialogue between the gods and the giants. Of course, the uniform wage did not last. The tinters in the end saw to that. But for a time workers subordinated self in a dramatic show of determination to have their own scheme of things.

Friendly Critics

By the early 1950's my associates in the law department were well seasoned. They left me with time for thinking about our life and times. I was writing and speaking a great deal, but I would not have thought of major publication except for Lawrence C. Woods (Pete Woods), an original and literate Pittsburgher. He actually *read* my speeches in full, even though he had previously heard them or had seen accounts in the newspapers. Pete Woods sent off to the Editor of the *Atlantic Monthly* a batch of my writings. He read them, made discriminating comments, some favorable, and said that the *Atlantic* would consider submissions for publication.

Furthermore, it was not only that I had time for thinking and writing at the very height of my corporate career and that I had discriminating friends but also I had Mary, whose eye for a dangling participle and such like has always been as keen as the scent of the hound for the fox—and no less avid. Her procedure was, and is, to read first for sense. She has never permitted me the pride of authorship. "I am," she would say, "a person of average intelligence (actually a vast understatement) and if it is not clear to me it will not be clear to others." On one occasion I was involved with several other lawyers in construction of a most important law brief. Our lead writer was George Nebolsine, a charming and somewhat imperious friend-at-law, who possessed more confidence than patience about his writing. I asked Mary to read the finally printed product, and she guided me in preparing 20 pages delineating errors which ranged from lack of parallelism in the table of contents to points of legal substance. I have learned from Mary that bad writing and bad thinking are but the two sides of the same coin. We reprinted the brief with Mary's corrections. John Cahill, who was George Nebolsine's senior Wall Street partner, told me that George, who was the son of a Russian admiral, was all but incoherent—even in Russian—with rage. He had not learned to sit quietly, as I had, when Mary took a sentence or paragraph apart. Nevertheless, my writings have all been my own. I have never had a ghost writer. Even when Mary spotted the defects, it usually would be I who supplied the corrective words.

My first *Atlantic Monthly* piece was about the guaranteed annual wage. It was published in 1955, a year in which Walter Reuther was pressing that demand. He got from the automotive manufacturers a form of supplementation to governmental unemployment compensation. That was all—nothing to approach the concept of employment of workers by the year at a guaranteed amount of money for the year. That concept, so different from actual practice in industry, is a sleeping, not a dead, issue.

Since the Industrial Revolution of the 18th century—a tick of the second hand in the total span of man's life on earth—many men have been required to work in collaboration with machines. This has been an unequal partnership because the machine, once in motion, goes rhythmically on at its own mechanical pace—not at the human pace, which is erratic and whimsical. To understand this fact of the machine age one must see Charlie Chaplin's "Modern Times," one of the great satires by pantomime from the era of the silent screen. In lieu of seeing "Modern Times," visit a zoo where there is a good collection of caged simians—chimpanzees, gorillas, orangutans, or gibbons. The casual, unprogrammed conduct of these primates gives us the clue to our natural equipment, which is not made for the regularity of the machine but for the irregularity of nature's behavior in a total environment of unpredictability. Man's biology seems to be against his technology.

The machine when running is a man-pacer. Yet another of the aspects of the machine's dominance in the machine-man collaboration is that man can work only when the machine can work. There is nothing a man can do when his machine-companion is doing nothing. The machine may do nothing for a number of reasons: failure of its mechanism; failure of its fuel supply, as when a severe winter requires diversion of natural gas from industry to home heating; failure of its raw material supply, as when strikes, war, or disasters interrupt the flow; or failure of demand for the machine's products, as when men in simian-like whim decide not to buy new cars, or not to wear hats or garters, or women decide to wear no skirts—the euphemism in 1967 and later was "mini-skirt."

There are other factors in addition to the machine which make for irregularity of work opportunities. Construction of housing and commercial buildings is governed in seasonal climates by weather; construction of ocean vessels goes ship by ship not year by year; construction of munitions of war is interrupted by peace; and the making of things for peace is interrupted by war. Although the virtue of machine production is continuity, yet the system is subject to many interacting factors which compel both short and long stoppages.

Hence most industrial workers have employment only by the hour, and in consequence labor contracts reflect the fact that men are to be employed by the hour and disemployed instantly when a particular job is no longer needed—for whatever cause. This fact of job uncertainty has resulted in many deeply vested conditions for protection of the job. Seniority, as I have said, is one of them. If a plant has 4,000 jobs and 2,000 of them end, either temporarily or permanently, the older workers are entitled to the remaining

2,000 jobs. The illustration is over-simplified, as any worker, or union leader, or labor expert knows, but in general there must be major reshuffling of work assignments.

Union contracts create a kind of title to a job—just as one might own a house and lot or a piece of jewelry. Why not? The worker is an industrial citizen employed by the hour and therefore he protects every last hour of work opportunity with a veritable complex of rules and regulations as impenetrable as the fires which Wotan set about Brünnehilde. Seldom, if ever, does a managerial Siegfried penetrate the flaming wall which protects the worker's job.

There are exceptions. For example, the rate at which people consume, and therefore buy, shoes, soap (detergents), and meat is relatively uniform and the technology is not so heavy as in steel, glass, or machine tools. Therefore it is no accident that over thirty years ago Nunn Bush Shoe Company, Procter and Gamble Company, and George A. Hormel and Company tried out with some success their separate plans of guaranteed annual wage; but their workers relaxed many of the rigidities applicable to hourly work in exchange for relatively constant annual earnings.

The key to any such plan is regularity of production—avoidance of peaks and valleys. To achieve that result would call for some changes in management and consumer attitudes. Often management says piously that the customer is king—how can we level off production when the buying habits of customers are uneven? Few production managers would have the courage to suggest to an elated sales manager with some big orders in hand that he might have urged his customers to think ahead and fit their buying to a production schedule. If they all stopped to think about it—and they do at times—the corporation president, the sales manager, the production manager, and the customer would all be ashamed of their assumption that labor must always be waiting in the wings ready to rush onto the scene whenever demand takes a seat and claps its hands.

It all comes down to this: steadier industrial production would produce steadier work on an annual basis, if top management, production engineers, and sales executives would convert customers to the habit of more level buying and if unions and workers would agree with management to convert work and pay rules from an hourly to an annual basis. Many if's, of course. Computers are helping to predict demand and to schedule production more tightly to demand. If the several factors did combine to achieve level annual production, then the question of the guaranteed annual wage would become moot. Uneven production makes uneven pay. The worker asks, shall I buy a house, a car, an encyclopedia, a season ticket for the symphony, or plan a vacation trip? Asks whom? The production manager will tell him to ask the sales manager, and the sales manager will tell him to ask the customers. But the worker wonders whether a system which he fundamentally respects has to be quite so casual about his quest for security.

If production were stabilized fewer workers would be needed for the reason that more workers would do more things around the calendar. As practices now go, more men are on call than are needed. That is the consequence of tightly defined jobs paid for by the hour. Fewer men doing more things, paid by the year, would provide more certainty of income for those on the job; more variety of work, and, therefore, more interest and greater sense of participation; lower cost of the product, and, therefore, lower prices to consumers.

Change comes slowly, but it will come to the hourly concept of industrial work. When we move to stabilized buying, selling, and production, fully half the grievances which now beset management and labor will pass away. The processing of grievances in industrial plants is a costly aspect of mass production. When the housewife buys a toothbrush or toilet paper or the husband a trailer for the family vacation or for following jobs from place to place, some portion of the cost is for the processing of grievances: X was promoted instead of Y; Z was discharged because a foreman wrongfully charged him with drunkenness on the job. The names of the workers who complain would exhaust the alphabet and the categories of grievances beggar imagination and confound logic. It is all very human.

Yet, of the whole industrial world, we Americans have almost blind faith in collective bargaining.

Collective bargaining to the rank and file of workers means personal participation. A labor contract is usually printed and given wide distribution. Workers put their own interpretations on words and phrases. If management differs, then the reaction is extreme. Any idea that the contract might have been inadequately written, or that changed circumstances have rendered a provision obsolete, or that a clause relevant to an originally valid purpose is being tortured to cover another purpose irrelevant to the original intent—all such discriminations are swept aside. If management raises such a point, the charge hurled across the bargaining table will be, "You're trying to tear up our contract." The reverence for the contract as the rank and file understand it is as if the document were something apart from the human beings who originally wrote it. It is held in animistic awe.

On one occasion I appeared for management before a panel of the World War II War Labor Board. The labor issue was important. The usual gallery of union members was present, occupying prime seats, to watch their entirely competent lawyer, William T. Lewis, handle their case, which had bogged down on a trivial point of procedure. Union leaders and union lawyers cultivate great patience. They will tolerate the most patent nonsense on the part of workers because they know it is sincere and serious and that the price of too hasty correction will be loss of confidence. In this particular situation my patience gave. Members of my staff were present, other corporate officers were waiting to be witnesses; war was waging; the nation was in jeopardy—the absurdity of the situation with so many people immobilized and the important issue not being reached suddenly overwhelmed me. I said to the judge, "If you will suspend this formal hearing for 5 minutes, Mr. Lewis and I can dispose of this little preliminary matter by agreement and then we can all get on with the case." A worker in the gallery arose and said, "Mr. Hazard, you and Mr. Lewis probably could, but that would not be collective bargaining." No facile-minded lawyer he, yet unashamed and unabashed he made it plain, and with dignity, that the proceedings must go at his pace, not at mine.

No Pot of Gold

The price of any product is determined by the cost of making it. The cost includes the rental value of the land for the factory; the cost of the building and machinery divided by the number of years they will respectively last; the cost of repairs and maintenance; the cost of supplies, materials, labor, and management. There are many ancillaries to these costs and many refinements of what accountants call them and how they classify them. What I have said will do for our purposes.

The manufacturer must sell the product for more than the total of his costs. That is a fundamental. To sell for less than the total cost may delight the buyer but will confound the seller—and, if the practice is continued long enough, it will lead to the seller's ruin. Business does not do well on losses. That method has been tried out many times and it does not work, as the records of the bankruptcy courts attest.

It might be superficially supposed that questions of cost and selling price are the concern of the businessman. Why should the reader bother? The answer lies in the inevitable effect on costs of what the reader's society does in the field of social welfare. When society legislates minimum wages, limits hours, requires overtime pay above those hours, requires collective bargaining, provides unemployment compensation and pensions after some chronological age—the manufacturer's portion of the costs of those humanitarian benefits must be added to all the other costs of the product and so the price of the product goes up. It matters not whether the manufacturer incurs these social costs directly, as in the case of collective bargaining on trivia in the episode I have related a few moments past, or by taxation, as in the case of unemployment compensation. The costs, direct or indirect, increase the price.

There is a widespread, persistent, and erroneous idea that corporations could absorb the welfare costs if they only would. The costs of labor are usually the major portion of the product cost. Anything which bears on that cost, either to increase it or decrease it, has a major effect on the price. There is no corporate pot of gold to dig into. During World War II Franklin Roosevelt foolishly proposed limiting all incomes to $25,000 per annum. Not even labor liked the idea. Some union officers would have had to cut their hard earned salaries. President Roosevelt's abortive proposal (Congress quickly rejected his plan) prompted me to make some calculations about confiscations. I took the extreme figure $10,000 and assumed that all incomes over that amount would be confiscated; furthermore I seized all dividends to stockholders and all earnings retained by corporations—by these confiscations I created the mythical pot of gold and divided it up among all people earning less than $10,000 per annum. Result: about $500 per person—and in one year only. Never again. Our system of enterprise would be ruined. Executives, corporate or labor, would not work under such restrictions, stockholders would not invest without dividends; and without retained earnings for plant expansions, enterprise would die on the vine. I have often published and spoken of my hypothetical confiscations. No one ever questions the data; yet, there is a persistent and potent folk-thought that management need not increase prices just because costs go up. Parkinson in his dour charm tells us that we are always voting taxes to be paid by somebody else—mentally blocked, as if we were all fit subjects in delusion and dream for Doctor Freud, from seeing that the tax shifts to the prices of goods we all live by.

How the Costs Go Up

Let me take a case out of my own experience. In one large metropolitan area the union membership of a construction craft was maintained by the union at about three times the total requirements for the particular type of craftsman. The union management rotated its membership around the available jobs according to a scheme as precise as clockwork so that two-thirds of them—in numbers, not the same persons—were routinely drawing unemployment compensation. The employer's cost for premiums on the legally required unemployment compensation varied, as it still does in some states, according to his unemployment experience: the higher the employer's unemployment the higher his premiums. The union practice made it appear that the employer had two-thirds of his force unemployed and hence entitled to unemployment compensation. The fact was that the union compelled the employer to keep on his rolls three times the number he needed. The employer's insurance cost was therefore three times what it should have been and the price of his product and service was higher by that amount.

Multiply this type of case by hundreds of variations and project the case I have given as essentially typical throughout industry—with notable exceptions, of course—and you have the problem. It is called cost-push inflation, which means that prices rise because costs rise. This is not to say that all the onus falls on unions or on anybody, for that matter. Union leaders are not always statesmen anymore than business leaders are statesmen. The short-run view is compelled by strong forces operating on both management and labor. Management must look to its immediate profit. I call this compulsion "the quarter-annual psychology"; union leaders must look to constituencies with pluralistic and sometimes disparate demands; either can be ousted—management by directors, unionists by workers; both know the truth of what John Maynard Keynes said, "In the long run we are all dead."

Should the Strike Go the Way of the Duel?

I went to Arden House in the fall of 1966. It is the seat of E. H. Harriman's mountain mansion up the Hudson above New York. Given to Columbia University by the son, Averell Harriman, it houses periodically the American Assembly of sixty participants, who can be housed, slept, and fed for three days of discussions and resolutions on public issues. I have participated several times. The subject on this occasion was "Collective Bargaining." There had been an airplane strike which had immobilized 60 per cent of air transit facilities. Not even the President of the United States and the president of the union together could settle that one. The airlines workers, particularly the mechanics, revolted and the strike went on while stranded passengers all over the world huddled, some ill, in airports. The misery was both human and economic: florists who could not get supplies; operators of airport restaurants and bars; cab drivers and porters without customers and tips, a whole galaxy of satellites, large and small, from adjacent motels to automatic vendors. Secretary of Labor Wirtz called all of these agonies "inconveniences".

There had been other revolts. In 1964 Walter Reuther had wrested from the Big Three "the best contract the UAW has ever negotiated"; yet his constituents at GM called a strike which lasted six weeks. In January of the next year Longshoremen's president, Thomas Gleason, announced "the best contract ever." But the longshoremen struck nevertheless, at a cost of $67 million a day in the export and import business alone. In 1968 Big Steel did reach an agreement without a strike—without, contrary to precedent in that industry, an intervention by a president of the United States. But some of the results of the threat of the strike were comparable to the case of a strike itself. When a strike threatens, customers, large and small, overbuy in anticipation of the strike; then, the strike not having occurred, they don't buy while they use up the oversupply. Hence steel mills, for example, curtail production, and steelworkers are out of work and draw partial compensation from the unemployment insurance, and the cost of all that irregularity goes into the price of a ton of steel and ends up in the higher price of beams for bridges, binders for boutonnières—not to mention the price of beer cans, boats, and barbers' shears. Then everyone but the "hippies" complains about the price of haircuts. The smite of a single stone on the economic waters sends perturbation to distant shores. No part of modern mass production is independent of the whole. Steel, glass, aluminum, or chlorine (building block of the synthetics) sneezes, and dozens of dependent industries come down with pneumonia.

At Arden House in November of 1966 I proposed a general suspension of the right to strike until a federal industrial peace commission, appointed by the President with the advice and consent of the Senate, had investigated and made a proposal for settlement. Then, if management rejected the proposal, the strike could occur. If management accepted, then the proposal would go to the workers for a vote of all the workers eligible to vote, not just the usual 10 per cent who attend union meetings. Arthur Burns, the dean of American conservative economists, liked my plan for an IPC, and pleased me by saying so to the Arden House conference, calling my piece "crisply stated." Curiously, when the returns were all in, it was not so much labor but rather professional arbitrators such as John Dunlop, Theodore Kheel, and William Simkin, head of United States Conciliation Service, who objected. Kheel thought we would have to accompany IPC with federal price controls. I do not think so, because I would not abolish the strike (not in one stroke; that is not politically feasible); I simply would require, as a start, more worker and public attention to the issues before the strike could occur. Let the reader consult his memory concerning the issues in any strike he can recall. It will be blank. How many people know what A. H. Raskin of *The New York Times,* a respected member of the old guard of labor philosophers, reported six months ahead of me in *The Atlantic?* When the New York subway union called the big strike of 1966, "it still had on the negotiating table as its only formal position a demand for a package pay increase twenty times as large as it had ever got before." I say that bluff, threat, and crisis are no longer tolerable; and advocates of collective bargaining *as is* will lose all unless they realize that times change. Dunlop proposed more powers of intervention by the President on an *ad hoc* crisis basis. Simpkin thought a certain amount of bluster and bluff in midnight sessions in smoke-filled rooms was not a bad way to reach labor-management agreements. Indeed, some labor writers will frankly say that the result of a labor negotiation will depend in the end on the relative stamina of the parties.

Noble concepts such as that embedded in our federal law that the labor of an individual shall not be an article of commerce can become as much a fetish as the honor which for some centuries until recent times was supposed to justify killing in a duel. There is an uncomfortable parallel between the justification of the duel and the justification of the strike or the collectively bargained settlement, regardless of public interest. The mystique for the duel as for the earlier trial by combat was that the loser but suffered the judgment of God. So in modern times there is a mystique that if labor and management reach a bargain in a smoke-filled room in the early morning hours, so be it, and let God take care of the public as best He can.

There must be a better way. I do not think there are demons or devils in any camp. There is no scapegoat. What we lack is adequate institutionalism. It will come—slowly; I hope not out of mass frustration as in fascism. But it must come as institutions have always come to help man out of his mystiques. The strike is as anachronistic as the duel. It is not true that collective bargaining is useless if the right to strike is subjected to procedural limitations as I propose. We curtail the strike in wartime, but why are the emergencies of peace any less than those of war? The untamed strike is the modern counterpart of the six-shooter of our untamed west of a hundred years ago. The strike will be replaced as the six-shooter was replaced by more mature methods for achieving order and justice in the economy by which we *all* live.

In October, 1970, Victor Riesel, a conservative labor writer, blinded some years ago by acid-throwing goons, reported cautious probings by AFL-CIO head, George Meany, toward "voluntary arbitration instead of voluntary civil war." Some discussions were put in motion by Donald Straus, President of American Arbitration Association. The Riesel syndicated report from Washington is headed, "Toward a Strikeless Society." In my writings and in my capacity in the American Arbitration Association, I try to speed the day. An industrial state can no more tolerate constant civil war than can a political state. There is a happy straw in the wind. United States Steel Corporation and United Steel Workers have agreed to arbitrate the terms of new contracts. If this is a trend, it is a favorable one.

Peppercorn

In 1949 I had lived in Pittsburgh a full ten years. On arrival, Mary and I had purchased an apartment in Park Mansions, a name she disliked. We thought apartment living would be temporary but we are in the same quarters over 30 years later—except for week-ends at Peppercorn, an hour and a half from Pittsburgh in the Ligonier Valley, which lies between the first and second mountain ridges of the Alleghenies. We got the name Peppercorn for our 70 acres of field and woods from a defect in the title—an old mortgage of 1790 to secure a debt of 7 pounds 10 shillings. The mortgage was in the form of a lease reserving an annual rental of one peppercorn. Our landscape architect, Ralph Griswold, who has been the designer for archaeological reconstruction several places in the world (the Agora at Athens, for instance), said, "Waive the title defect because in that you have the name for your country place, Peppercorn."

From Park Mansions we look over the campus of Carnegie-Mellon University and beyond to the 42-story Cathedral of Learning of the University of Pittsburgh, the Mellon Institute of Industrial Research, and up the towering hill on whose side perch the hospitals which have made Pittsburgh a medical and psychiatric center of national prominence. The scene, especially with the lights of the night, is as spectacular as any in San Francisco or Lisbon.

From Peppercorn we look some seven miles distant across dogwood and crab in the foreground to oaks, maples, tulip poplars, and locusts in a woodland view of Laurel Mountain unblemished by human construction. There are in fact many country residences not far from Peppercorn. It is just that the mountain contours pro-

The house at Peppercorn.

The fireplace at Peppercorn.

The cook at Peppercorn.

vide us a box seat from which we are aware only of the diurnal drama on the huge woodland stage.

One who owns a country residence in the Ligonier Valley usually belongs to Rolling Rock Club, which was the original shooting, hunting, and fishing lodge of R. B. Mellon, son of the patriarchal Thomas and brother of the better known A. W. Mellon, secretary of the treasury under Harding and Hoover, and then ambassador to Britain. Arthur Van Buskirk arranged our membership in the Club, now grown to a vast complex of activities from trout fishing to trap shooting; bridge to beagling; golf shooting to grouse shooting; comings-out to cocktails; fox hunting to flower arrangements. All has been possible by the generosity of the late R. K. Mellon and his sister, Sarah Mellon Scaife, also now deceased. R. K. revered his father, who loved the Valley, as the son did for the 70 years of his useful life. The Club is much used by executives of the industrial empire over which R. K. actively presided even in his advancing days. He told me some years ago that he had spent 120 nights of the year in Pullman cars. We were standing on the railroad platform at Greensburg waiting for the "Pittsburgher", famous overnight shuttle between Pittsburgh and New York.

Mary and I are not good club members. We do none of the things which other members do—not golf, nor fishing, nor riding. On Peppercorn we walk the paths which criss-cross our woods; scent the pink crab and sight the white dogwood in the spring; watch the pines and spruces send up their bizarre finials and stretch out their soft paws for a vernal handshake. Throughout the summer we hurry the corn, beans, and squash from the garden to the pot while the vitamins and flavor are intact, and in early fall, when the frosts of our short season threaten, we cover the ripening tomatoes and bring in the butternut squash for Thanksgiving and Christmas pies.

From spring to fall on a sunny morning following a wet night Mary goes for mushrooms—often "to one of my secret places." Her knowledge of the science and art of identification is extensive. On an occasion when G. David Thompson, Pittsburgh's famous modern art collector, brought Alfred Barr, then head of New York's Museum of Modern Art, to Peppercorn the conversation went to mushrooms. "Her enthusiasm is absolutely authentic,"

Alfred Barr told Dave Thompson later. We eat some 25 varieties on Mary's identification and live to tell the tale.

When winter comes, the breezeway and overhung areas of the house are stacked with wood for the fireplaces. On the distant mountainside the massed, bare branches of the crab stand out in ghostly gray; and in the foreground the pepperidge, maples, and oaks present their naked beauty. Evergreens are not indigenous to Ligonier Valley but in the early days Mr. R. B. Mellon brought them in by the train load and started nurseries of them under Ralph Griswold's advice. Many of ours at Peppercorn are gifts from the Rolling Rock nurseries. They and the laurel and the rhododendron make pompons of a wet snow. Yet it is in summer, with the towering pines and spruce, which we transplanted when they were in the human scale—it is then that we know that time does pass. Even so we plant the spent garden with winter rye to keep the soil good and mulch the asparagus bed and protect in the tool shed—against mice—the seeds which will be needed when spring comes again.

One day when we were building the house at Peppercorn, Charlie Hays came by and just stood for an hour as the early work progressed. Finally he asked if there would be any common labor he could do. The contractor was Norman Schultz, a country carpenter, but one who could read the plans of our patient architect, Robert W. Schmertz. Norm once told Marion Humfeld, a childhood friend of Mary's and an artist who did a mural for Peppercorn, that the house was his masterpiece. We hired Charlie Hays, who abides with us yet—now into the third decade. He is a mountain man, bred to the axe and the shovel, only imperfectly adapted to machinery, but what has been done on Peppercorn is for the most part his handiwork. He calls me Leland and Mary, Mary, and unless the doors are bolted against his keys, he will walk right into the living room, whatever guest is there, with three days' stubble on his face and a wad of tobacco in his cheek, and say, "Leland, the tractor has stopped." Then I inquire what he was trying to do with the tractor, and if I think it is an emergency, he abandons the machine and gets a cart or barrow and does it by sheer strength and awkwardness. Charlie must have deeply suppressed aggressions. I never knew him to open a conversation—short of an emergency, but he will lie in wait for a snake, or track a groundhog to his hole, or burn out a hornet's nest with obvious joy. "I got him," he will tell me with a bright light in his otherwise sad eyes. If he is told there is an acute need, nothing will stop him. Once when I had told him several days in advance that we must come to Peppercorn on a certain occasion, I found a cut in a snow drift 50 feet long and as deep as the car was high—done by his hand. When Mary and I arrived and I commented on the huge labor, he replied, "You said you was cumin." That was all.

Charlie must be very lonesome. If another workman comes I have to separate them to get any work done. Who knows what happens, or doesn't happen, if I am not there? If I say, "Charlie, we are going to have company next week-end," he will appear shaved and in a clean, drab gray shirt. If Mary or I introduce him to a guest and some pleasantry is expressed he will emit an irrelevant, cackling laugh so gauche that the episode ends. I always give him a good, big Christmas present of money and he never thanks me until I have thanked him for some rather good utilitarian piece which he has obviously acquired for me with trading stamps. Then he will say, "I thank you for yours." I do not really know Charlie and, of course, never will.

When Norm Schultz was finishing the house at Peppercorn, he invited all the workmen and Mary and me to a "first fire." Everyone had been forbidden to burn anything in the principal fireplace with its big hood of standing seam copper. Twenty-two craftsmen came, dressed in their best, trying to stay in the kitchen rather than come into the living room where the ceremonies were to occur. With some drinks and under the guise of getting help to pass the food, Mary got them in for the occasion.

Norm Schultz called upon the stonemason, DePollo, who had been the object of many mock questions about whether the chimney would draw, to strike the first fire. The old man, then in his 76th year, first explained in technical detail why the chimney would inevitably draw—a fact which seemed to be in some way related to DePollo's having finished it himself on a high scaffold on a bitterly cold day, while his young assistant—plainly considered the weaker of the two—remained below. Then he crossed the room, as Duse the stage, and with a gesture suggestive of incantation, struck the match and touched the tinder. The smoke curled, up and up and out—success.

That was far from all. DePollo then delivered a lecture against unionism and inflation which would have done credit to his countryman, Pareto; the painter, Egner, looking pensively out through the great glass window over the seven-mile view, spoke of the beauty of the Ligonier Valley and the sterling qualities of its indigenous people, allowing at the end, nevertheless, that Mr. and Mrs. Hazard were welcome; the electrician, Shadron, a young man who had not been quite acceptable to Norm Schultz because of his inexperience, made an unintentionally moving speech about how much he had learned from me and all the older people on the job. There was much more. Finally I was called upon by Norm Schultz and said a little about the house we had built in Kansas City, but mostly I said that no one man alone builds a house—a house is the product of many skills and much mutual respect among all the builders. Finally, it was over and everyone seemed pleased, and the electrician, Shadron, allowed in parting that there ought to be more "first fires".

Norm Schultz told me a most useful story about William Hoffman, a distinguished contractor, now deceased, who for many years owned a noble point of land not far from Peppercorn. I seldom employ a joke in a speech, but in negotiations, particularly when they are tense, or in meaningful conversation, the joke is often an important mode of communication, as in the case of this one. Hoffman asked an applicant for work, "Are you a finished carpenter?", a term of art importing a certain degree of competence. "Yes!", said the applicant. "Did you ever make a mistake?", asked Hoffman. "No, sir." "Well then," said Hoffman, "I don't want you, because without any experience in mistakes, if you did happen to make one, you wouldn't know what to do about it." What better description of the difference between the theoretical and the empirical could one encounter?

I had a sadness about Mary which beset me almost as soon as we arrived in Pittsburgh. In Kansas City she had been head of a nationally known school of progressive education. When she left, the *Kansas City Star* acclaimed her achievements and extolled her gracious personality. In Pittsburgh no one thought to engage her talents. Despite the fact that Arthur Van Buskirk made a considerable point of my addition to the Pittsburgh community, recognition for Mary did not come until later.

I never mentioned this unhappiness to Mary. There was nothing I could do about it. So Mary corrected me when she read this portion of the book. "I was not unhappy in those early years. It was a relief to go out on the streets without being stopped by some fond parent inquiring about a child in my school. Furthermore we lived within walking distance of the superb Carnegie Library, where I read widely in fact and fiction about Pittsburgh. Pittsburgh was an adventure—like a trip. It never occurred to me that I was unnoticed." I would have saved myself much pain many times if I had been able to talk about my feelings.

Pittsburgh is a man's town to a somewhat greater extent than is the whole of America a man's society. In our city of corporate headquarters, executives' wives are to join the Twentieth Century Club and attend the Monday morning lectures, or wait a long time and be invited to join one of the garden clubs, or one of the older social agencies. But to be considered a person in her own right is more than Pittsburgh will generally accord a woman.

Few, if any, are the women on the boards of public institutions such as the University of Pittsburgh or Carnegie-Mellon University. In the case of one important women's school, Chatham College, the board is male-dominated and on one of the school's epic occasions all the speakers were men. The school is upwards of a hundred years old. One would suppose that out of a body of alumnae of such an era more women would have been found. But no!

Mary resumed her piano in our early days in Pittsburgh. Bach, of course. She would intrigue me with the intricate left hand melodies. But then her hands were not up to the execution which her head understood. She pursued graduate work in her field of psychology at the University of Pittsburgh, became a member of the faculty, and all of this led to becoming Assistant Director of the Veterans Guidance Center, where she counselled hundreds of World War II veterans in the use of their G. I. benefits.

Gradually, Mary's reputation spread. She served on important boards where her expertise counted, such as United Mental Health and Family and Children's Services. Finally, and not because of any move from the establishment, she became a member of the Pittsburgh Board of Public Education. This Board, appointed by the judges of the Court of Common Pleas—not elected

—occupied her vigorous talents for fifteen years. She knew a budget from a blackboard and she also understood the blackboard. The staff were delighted and accepted her as a professional and the male chairman of the board would take her to lunch to get himself oriented. My male friends would tell me that she was "the best man on the board." Today (1972) Mary is selective about her boards but there are enough of them to keep our schedules complicated. Carnegie-Mellon University gave her an honorary doctorate concurrently with mine. In the fall of 1973 Mary was made a Distinguished Daughter of Pennsylvania.

Pearl Harbor and After

For the first ten years in Pittsburgh I attended strictly to corporate knitting, except for the speaking and writing I have mentioned. Mary and I were in New York on December 7, 1941. We had spent the day in the museums of art, and were having dinner at the old Lafayette Hotel when the voice of Fiorello La Guardia on the radio broke into our consciousness. He was urging calm and only then, hours after the event, did we learn of Pearl Harbor.

I was due in Washington the next day because, long before Pearl Harbor, American industry knew what the American people would not yet concede, that we must supply the equipment and ultimately the military strength to stop the Hitlerean bid for global power and domination. For five years, the first half of the 1940's, I traveled constantly to Washington and learned about the inevitable bureaucracy which war brings.

The most visual aspect of a bureaucracy is acres of clerks. The hidden fact about bureaucracy is that the affairs at hand are so great that the administration of them requires rules and regulations, ever and ever more refined, detailed, inconsistent, contradictory, and frustrating to the activist. I say this in sympathy, and with some understanding. Nevertheless, it was my role in the World War II years, in behalf of a large private enterprise building huge plants for critically needed war materials, to deal with the Washington bureaucracy. Often I had occasion to think of Elsa Maxwell's line, "There is less in Washington than meets the eye." One day, we, a group with common public interests, were conferring in the Carlton House when John D. Biggers entered the room. He was the long-time president of a large company; his record was one of public service; for example, he conducted the first statistical survey of unemployment in Franklin Roosevelt's efforts to discover just what the Great Depression had done to us. At one time he was Minister to Britain, a special office created pro tem to honor him at the end of his Washington service.

Jack Biggers' purpose in entering our meeting was to see what we might do to untangle a pending bureaucratic snarl. He described the depth of the problem by defining the fragmented responsibilities at the highest levels. Then someone asked, "What does the President do?" One of our Pittsburgh lawyers, John Frazer, answered, "Why, he heads up the confusion."

Often the bureaucrat himself, at an intermediate or lower level, is glad enough to have a sympathetic ear. I encountered such a one at Philadelphia in the very earliest days of World War II wage and salary controls. He had been precipitously transferred from his long-time happy lot at a Washington desk. He had been residentially ensconced in a pleasant Washington suburb. Now war had interfered with his placid estate. His Philadelphia offices were disordered because there had been no time to order them. He would never have been a good military field commander because the battle front would never be tidy enough for him. He had not found a residence for his family in Philadelphia, and government regulations in his branch of the civil service did not make adequate allowance for the extraordinary expenses entailed in a sudden move. I listened for a full two hours, from ten to noon, presenting such a sympathetic physiognomy as I could devise with my somewhat contemptuous facial muscles. After all we *were* at war and men *were* dying at the front. Noon came and I invited him to lunch. He refused rather unctuously, and asked me to return at 3:00 that afternoon. My carefully prepared and voluminous document lay on his desk scarcely noticed, its purport and purpose but vaguely understood with what sketchy explanation I had been able to work in during his recital of how the war had disarranged his life.

The matter at hand was of great importance to my client. Wages and salaries had been frozen under the wartime powers of the federal government. For hourly workers their unions or employers could appear before the National War Labor Board for permission to make changes—a very necessary permission because manpower gets scarce in a war economy and, except for the draft, workers are free to move about in search of the best pay. For salaried workers —from the corporate president down to the janitor—pay could be increased only if there was within the company an established plan of classification of employees into salary grades with brackets of authorized pay within which increments of increase could be automatically made. Such a plan was called a *salary rate schedule*. My client, although standing high on the list of America's 500 largest corporations, had not yet gotten around to administrative modernity. It had no salary rate schedule. What to do? How would we hold all of our necessary several thousands of executive, administrative, and clerical employees against the competition for their services of companies equipped with long-established salary rate schedules and therefore the legal right to offer pay higher than my client could legally offer? Trouble of that sort usually comes to a lawyer.

There was a provision in the fine print of the federal salary-freeze regulations which permitted an employer to reduce existing salary administration practices to writing and if those historical practices met with the criteria of the regulations, then the writing would be accepted in lieu of a pre-existent salary rate schedule.

Men of action, whether in the grand affairs of history or the mundane business of fixing the salaries of secretaries, stenographers, clerks, and executives, act within a rationale of which they are unaware. Their actions will make a pattern. What is science but generalizations from the observed behavior of men or atoms? I guessed that my client had been acting as if there were a salary rate schedule and that reduction of actual practices to writing would reconcile fact and theory. The problem was to find the pattern in a maze of facts.

Stuart Campbell was our recently arrived controller. He understood. He produced from the historical payrolls the data from which the practices could be reduced to theory. We worked night and day.

Privately I called the schedule which Stuart Campbell and I constructed "A country lawyer's salary rate schedule." To call oneself a country lawyer, even on Wall Street, is a kind of immodesty, because the term imports a substantial measure of common sense coupled with a modicum of shrewdness. The document which lay on the Philadelphia desk of the unhappy bureaucrat was the fruit of common sense and a modicum of shrewdness. I returned at 3:00 P.M., the appointed hour. He handed me the document with an official approval stamp, duly initialed by him. With a minimum of amenities—albeit adequate—I left. Never stay around after the sale is made. That was a rule I learned in 1914 when selling the encyclopedia in St. Paul and Minneapolis. On my way out the secretary said, "It's too bad you had to come back this afternoon, Mr. Hazard. This morning we had not yet received our approval stamp from the stamp maker."

The word went around Pittsburgh of the "country lawyer's" salary rate schedule. Shortly, one of the Pittsburgh banks carried such a document to Philadelphia and was promptly turned down. One of my associates, David A. Cort, observed, "That just shows what happens to a country lawyer's salary rate schedule without a country lawyer." I think a more likely explanation was that in the meantime the bureaucrat had found a house for his family, although it is possible that the bank's representative did not trouble to learn the secretary's name.

Bureaucracy and Finesse

In World War II America had the best brains in the industrial establishment in Washington. Business executives once they go to government are more hard-nosed than regular bureaucrats. They know what to look for. It is at lower levels—seldom at the top—that a bureaucracy becomes heavy handed. Some of my friends were in the high echelons. Arthur Van Buskirk went to Lend-Lease in the State Department; John Fennelly, a scholarly Chicago investment banker, older brother of Joe, went to War Production Board, as did Frank Denton, then chief financial mentor of the vast Mellon interests, who employed his Washington experiences to bring, after the war, several military men to Pittsburgh to head leading corporations. Leon Henderson was the first to administer the Office of Price Administration. I engaged him a few years later as economist in an antitrust case. He told me that Franklin D. Roosevelt moved him into that man-killing job, after a series of government posts which he had held throughout the Great Depression, because, said Leon, "When he swore at me, I swore back at him."

John Fennelly wrote a book about his experiences, called

Memoirs of a Bureaucrat. As with many high ranking bureaucrats, John Fennelly had the onus of disappointing friend and foe alike. There were just not enough materials to go around. Some claimants were so egocentric as to demand what they wanted regardless of the war; but more often the claimants sincerely believed that in each particular situation the allowance of the supplies would win the war. There is a tinge of bitterness, tempered with humor, in John Fennelly's description of the partings at his Washington farewell dinner: "First came General Hopkins of the Air Force, who addressed me as follows: "I must tell you, John, that your greatest contribution to the war effort is your current resignation from the War Production Board.' "

"Next came Captain Small of the Navy. While shaking my hand he said: 'You will never realize, John, the hours I have spent pacing the floor at night, trying to figure out how I could get around that bastard, Fennelly.' "

"The finest compliment of all was reserved for the last. It came from a former associate of mine on the WPB staff, Dr. Melvin de Chazeau. His statement was: 'You know, John, I really hate to see you leave because you are the most successful son of a bitch I have ever seen in action.' "

I have learned in later years that my associates were afraid of me. This information comes from the distaff side. I take it with a grain of salt. But there is evidence that at one time Dave Cort may have suffered from my great self-confidence. He came in one day to say that he felt quite inadequate for the job and would like to quit. That meant he would go into the office of his father—a fine lawyer of modest achievement and Dave would follow in his footsteps. I said, "Dave, put on your hat and walk a dozen blocks or so; then please come back; I will see you whatever other pressures may be." He did just that. Upon his return, I said, "Now, Dave, we have all kinds of work here, some very hard, some much easier. You tell me what work you are willing to try and I will give you that work." He had made some mistakes. He knew it and I knew it; but he went back to his office and we never had to give him easier work. Today he travels the world on the most complicated legal problems.

Dave Cort was fundamentally a secure, not to say stubborn, person. He proved it once in a classic confrontation with one of our most prestigious executives, Edwin T. Asplundh—a Swedenborgian and therefore, a favorite of the Pitcairns, and a superior executive. (The Pitcairns did not generally practice nepotism.) One morning Ed Asplundh came into Dave Cort's office saying, "Dave, you can abolish the law department. I was in New York yesterday and made a deal in the Plaza Hotel with X. We wrote it out and here it is. Read it." Dave Cort read it. "Well," he said, apropos of the vital part of the writing, "it can mean *this* or it can mean *that*" —this and that making a precise polarity. Ed Asplundh was aghast and asserted that the bedroom document could mean only *this.* "Well," said Dave quietly, "let us call X and see what he says." Asplundh, a reasonable man, agreed; they called, and X said, "Why, of course, it means *that.*" When I heard the story I had only admiration for both Dave Cort, who had the courage to stand up against a high-powered executive, and Ed Asplundh, who had the character to say, "That's the end of my being my own lawyer."

Samuel Johnson Understood

"The lawyer does that for his client which the client would do for himself if he could." So spoke Boswell's Johnson—music enough to the lawyer's ear, not as pleasing to the client. Lawyers are troublesome to business executives, who have difficulty with postulates which may frustrate the main thrust of the proposed enterprise. Prolonged contract negotiations between two, or among more, big companies are often necessary; supplies, sales, patents are the subjects of long-term written commitments. Many contingencies must be taken into account. One of the possibilities which businessmen regard with incredulity, not to say short tempers, is that the other party will become unreasonable if an unexpected development creates a divergence of interests. They would much prefer to rely upon both, or all sides', being fair and equitable if trouble arises. It is hard to think through the disposition of a remote contingency. It is precisely because the untoward development is a remote possibility that the business man feels put upon by the "lawyer's technicalities."

How many times has a client said to me, "Oh, Leland, that will never happen!" Then I level with him and say, "Look, you don't need me to protect you against what is *going* to happen. You can do that yourself. You pay me to protect you against what *is not* going to happen." That usually settles the issue. I could learnedly tell him of all the actual cases which stick in my head, showing how honest men were forced to court because they did not adequately contemplate in advance the vagaries of commerce. Rather, what I suggest to the businessman is that he ought to get his money's worth.

Occasionally a lawyer will encounter a really churlish corporate official, who will have worked without legal counsel for weeks on a big deal and is sure he has reached a complete understanding with the other party. Then some superior officer will have said to him, apropos of his report of success in the negotiations, "Very well, it's time to call in the lawyers." He is unhappy about that, is afraid—and often with reason—that the deal, which is his pride and joy and possibly the basis of a salary increase, will be upset by some technical lawyer. Under such circumstances I have often been greeted with such sour comments as, "Now our deal will really get complicated." I was never one to tolerate such an attitude; rather more likely to reply at once, "You may be right; 'There are more things in heaven and earth than are dreamed of in your philosophy, Horatio.' " The executive will be vaguely aware that I have said more than he can identify, since more often than not he will be a product of that 20th century engineering or business education in which one may obtain a degree without knowing whether Shakespeare is the name of a poet or of that superior fishing reel called Shakespeare. Such an immediate confrontation is usually enough to induce a cool but candid attitude toward the lawyer.

If the hostility persists, then I have occasionally applied the sharp analogy of an experience related to me by an itinerant Baptist preacher, who was traveling by his own car through the unpaved streets of a Southern town. Coming to a mud hole, he paused to contemplate whether to go through or turn back. A small voice from the side warned, "You cain't go in dar, Mister"; but another voice asserted, "Yas he cain, but he cain't get out." I once used this technique with an unusually bumptious but bright executive in the Koppers Company. When we resumed the next morning he opened by saying, "I thought you won the round yesterday; let's get on."

The business executive is not invariably hostile to the lawyer—

far from it. After all, the general counsel of a large corporation usually occupies a high and special place on the organization chart. Normally he reports directly to the chairman or president, whoever is the chief executive officer, and frequently he enjoys the confidence of the controlling interests among the stockholders. A lawyer who can command alternatives will not have it otherwise. There is a case in point: William T. Gossett, a long time professional friend of mine, was for many years Vice President and General Counsel of Ford Motor Company. He reported directly to Henry Ford II. A reorganization of functions and authorities within the Company would have required him to report to an officer other than the head. He resigned and continued his distinguished career in another association. Later he became president of the American Bar Association, a distinction which would have been difficult to attain if he had continued to practice his profession for Ford only.

Occasionally a corporate head takes to the technicalities of the law with relish. Such a one I encountered in a long and difficult negotiation. He was W. Lester McKnight, then head of Minnesota Mining and Manufacturing Company—the 3-M of Scotch Tape fame. He immediately introduced his lawyers, Paul and Gilbert Carpenter, into the discussions but very soon it was apparent that he too was following our work, draft after draft, because Gilbert would frequently introduce a question or an idea and openly attribute it to Mr. McKnight. At long last the contract was completed and signed. Then came many months of experimenting by 3-M with my client's process, which turned out not to be economically feasible for 3-M purposes. Then we lawyers took out the contract and found that all the contingencies were provided for. The process in question was useful in certain industries, and valuable. 3-M had expended large sums to apply the process for its special purposes, all without success. Yet there were no claims, counter-claims, or recriminations. The contract had anticipated the worst as well as the best. Gilbert Carpenter said to me with sad satisfaction, "Well, we did not need to endow a chair in a law school to find out what our contract meant."

In Greek lore there is the case of a beautiful prostitute charged with impersonating Aphrodite. She must appear before the old men of the Areopagus where under the rules her lawyer could not speak. When she protested her inability to plead her innocence, he advised her to take her stand at the appointed place on that great rock platform below the Acropolis and midway to the Agora; then to unleash the single clasp which secured the folds of the Grecian gown and stand disrobed. The old men acquitted her on the ground that if she impersonated Aphrodite the act was justified. The folk tale exemplifies a widespread feeling about lawyers that if they would just keep quiet the facts would speak for themselves.

I once had occasion to suggest to a client a courtroom demeanor in a reverse situation to that of the impersonator of Aphrodite. My client was aging. She had gone almost through a fortune left her by a husband, deceased 20 years before, whose memory seemed to evoke the only gentleness of nature left to her. The remnant of the fortune was important and she must stand trial on a claim which, if allowed, would be ruinous. She had an uncontrollable temper and in a tantrum her grotesque hats, garish dresses, and embittered face all but deprived her of human appearance. On the merits her case could be won, but she would so alienate the jury that the merits would not matter.

I thought out a plan and asked her to come into the office several days before the trial. "Mrs. A.," I said, " you and I are about to defend property which belonged to your husband. You loved him, did you not?" Her face softened almost into beauty. "Oh, Mr. Hazard, I did!" I continued, "When we appear in court, I want you to feel and look as you did on the day you carried your husband to his grave. We must act in the courtroom as if he were watching, because only you and I can help him now."

On the appointed day she appeared in black with a chaste white band at her neck and just a touch of white on a tiny black hat. In court she was as a widow of one day—despite the 20 years—and the jury did her justice. Not all of a lawyer's work appears in his briefs. Although he lacks the independence of the surgeon or engineer, he can often get the right result by the techniques of the medicine man. With words I cast a spell over Mrs. A which lasted long enough for the desired and proper outcome.

Common Crooks

Lawyers who represent big business usually encounter an antitrust case at some time in their practice. There are not many big business lawyers and they are divided into two categories: those who practice for one client only, usually called general counsel; and those, usually in very large firms in major cities, who practice for many clients, although they are careful to avoid conflict of interest as between or among clients. When a corporation seeks to engage a New York, Chicago, or San Francisco law firm, the first intra-firm routine is to clear the central index of clients for conflicting interests as between an existing client and the proposed new client. During my tenure as a general counsel we organized an association of ourselves to meet twice a year for discussion of corporate law problems. The organization was small, even now including only about 65 out of the 500 corporations designated by *Fortune Magazine* as the "largest". On the contrary, an annual meeting of the American Bar Association will always fill a great hall. The number of lawyers who have been involved in an antitrust case, like the number who have ever appeared in the United States Supreme Court, is a small percentage of the whole.

The antitrust case which engaged a considerable portion of my time from 1940 to 1948 involved the flat glass industry. Glass is a common and necessary product. There is no substitute for it. Plastics have been tried but they abrade too easily. There is no foreseeable time when one will look inwardly at Macy's displays in New York or outwardly from a little gray home in the west except through glass. Therefore, if the price of glass is high, or the services of supply are bad, or the opportunity to enter such a stable business is restricted—the federal government, through the Antitrust Division of the Attorney General's office, stands ready to explore the causes and attack the malefactors. Yet the American preoccupation with the trust and the monopoly has probably passed the zenith. Theodore Roosevelt and Franklin Roosevelt both assumed the role of St. George against the big business dragon, but big business is big for so many reasons not understood by those two fundamentally conservative statesmen that their crusades suffered a collapse.

However all that may be, a businessman may go to the penitentiary for failing to compete or for having a monopoly, even innocently, and the laws which hang that sword of Damocles over him will not soon be altered. Competition, sometimes called free enterprise, is an American folkway.

John D. Rockefeller, Jr., son of the original Standard Oil monopolist, made the ultimate poetic defense of monopoly when he said, "The American Beauty Rose can be produced in its splendor and fragrance only by sacrificing the early buds which grow up around it." But Senator John Sherman of Ohio and the Congress were for the economic buds, however imperfect their preservation might render the full flower; and so in 1890 the Sherman Antitrust Act made conspiracies in restraint of trade and all monopolies, however attained by private owners, illegal—punishable as crimes and correctible by United States courts of equity. Thus I came to defend a possible corporate criminal, although the government in the first instance sought only to reduce disastrously the size of my client.

The antitrust laws in the United States were almost a dead letter from their establishment in the Sherman Act of 1890 until Theodore Roosevelt's "big stick" enforcement program was launched in the Northern Securities Company case in 1904. J. P. Morgan the Elder had put together one of the railroad empires, popular among the so-called "robber barons" of those times, and Roosevelt stimulated his attorney general to move against it. The United States Supreme Court held the combination illegal, but Justice O. W. Holmes dissented, and so ended a beautiful friendship between the Roosevelts and the Holmes. "I could carve a better judge out of a banana," snorted Roosevelt; "Let him get a better law," retorted the greatest of our American jurists, whose biographer, Catherine Drinker Bowen, in *Yankee From Olympus,* has produced one of the most poignant and prescient delineations of great character and great causes one could hope to read—or see in its stage version.

Mr. Morgan was deeply hurt. Why could the President not have approached him as one gentleman to another and made known the government's wishes, he complained, rather than sue him as a "common crook"? That question is on the lips of big businessmen to this very day. Of course the government does not answer, except in conventional and traditional anti-monopoly planks in party platforms. It is left to big business lawyers to explain to their clients that they can go to the penitentiary (the clients, not the lawyers) if they conspire about prices or get too big, especially by predatory methods, or engage in any one of scores of practices which might deprive people of the benefits of competition.

How could I explain to such good men as Raymond Pitcairn and his brother, Harold, or to Clarence Brown, a practicing Episcopal churchman, or to Harry Higgins, who shaved with an open blade, never having given in to the safety, much less to the electric, razor? He once told me, after the antitrust suit was filed, that he and his close associate, R. B. Tucker, whose brothers were Episcopal bishops, had looked back over their corporate lives and had concluded that if they had to do it all over again, they would do it just the same—every bit and piece of it. How could I explain that the company the Pitcairns owned in large part, and whose managers the Pitcairns had selected over many years, must now defend charges of illegal conduct for which, if proved, the company could be dismembered, and, in the end, individual officers could go to the penitentiary? I could not—not to their satisfaction; nor did I try. In an antitrust case the lawyers take over, just as the doctors do in a heart attack case.

In our case the government charged all the members of the flat glass industry, some nine companies and an equal number of company officers, with a long continued course of conduct over a period of 19 years which, said the government, added up to conspiracy of fixed prices, division of markets, and monopolization of the flat glass industry. One of the routines in such a case is an examination of the accused company's files—in our case, for an entire period of two decades, and, for some purposes, even farther back. The FBI participated in the file search, thus adding to the gloomy aura of criminality which enveloped the proceedings.

Thousands of letters, memoranda, and documents were examined. A careful record must be kept of everything the government examines. Officials high and low were disturbed; even clerks and stenographers wavered between resentment that the ethics of their company should be questioned and concern that the institution to which they had committed their lives might be, after all, in the wrong. How could they know, out of their experience with only segments of a great total enterprise, which included establishments of one sort or another in every state in the Union, and in 1940, some 30,000 employees? Not even I could know. The alleged conspiracy was supposed to have been initiated more than a decade before I arrived on the scene. Lawyers have a way of saying, "I didn't make the facts." That indeed is the exact circumstance—the lack of personal involvement—which gives the lawyer the objectivity essential to doing for the client what the client would do for himself if he could.

I issued instructions to the employees nationwide to treat the investigators courteously but to do or say nothing except on my advice—exactly what a lawyer tells a client in the police station. In my case, however, the advice was accompanied by a nicely printed legal document, which Joe Owens had prepared, clearly delineating the limitations on the powers of the American government to examine papers or people. A portion of my instructions directed employees to hand a copy of the document to the investigator, thus attesting the glory of a government of laws—not of men. The agents of the great United States could not examine the files or the people of my client without coming to me for agreement upon procedures. It was for such a government of law that the barons extracted Magna Charta at Runnymede in 1215. "Corny?" Yes, but true. Even more true, it was for such a government that the Puritans beheaded the saintly Charles I in 1649 and that his predecessor, King James I, was frustrated by Edward Coke, celebrated—and rightly so—by the deep scholarship and the rich writing of Catherine Drinker Bowen in *The Lion and The Throne*.

My widely published assurances that even in an antitrust case there could not occur in America the midnight knock on the door quieted the rank and file of the organization, but I was not universally popular in the upper echelons, and there were suggestions that in a case so fraught with horrendous consequences, the company should have special counsel. Clarence Brown and the Pitcairns stood firm. I was to "run the case"— in lawyer's vernacular —for our company. My client was the oldest and the largest in the industry and that meant a certain amount of leadership fell to me for the strategy of the whole case, but only a certain amount. Lawyers are not sheep. They will say with Rostand's Cyrano de Bergerac, "I do not follow." No lawyer worth his salt, and in our case of 18 defendants for the most part separately defended, the lawyers were worth their pay, which was high—no lawyer worth his salt will follow some other lawyer just because that lawyer's client is big.

Rule One

A wise lawyer, 20 years my senior, came to my rescue. Edwin J. Marshall was head of the largest law firm in Toledo, Ohio, which was the home office of my client's principal competitor—a competitor so skillful, under the leadership of John D. Biggers, that the plate glass business of America was all but divided between the two companies. Indeed, this fact was the basis for a large portion of the government's case. How could such a condition exist except by agreement between the two giants, asked the government. What the government overlooked was that when an irresistible force meets an immovable body the universe divides behind them, that competition as well as conspiracy can divide a market. The philosophers of antitrust suffer a real dilemma: if a competitor competes so hard that others are driven to ruin, then the successful one is a monopoly and must be broken into fragments. On the other hand, if a fragmented industry seems to represent a "live and let live" policy, then there *must* be a conspiracy which *must* be punished by penitentiary sentences or by the imposition of economic restraints. As O. W. Holmes once put it, men must compete but no one may win. The logical inconsistency has never been resolved. Businessmen are equally inconsistent. They believe in the antitrust laws because they represent a folkway business morality—but, as in the case of taxes, they ought to apply to somebody else.

Edwin J. Marshall was counsel to my client's largest competitor. As in my case, he had the confidence of the controlling stockholders. We both felt secure and neither of us suffered from a sense of inferiority. E.J. was a big man of loose-jointed frame and he carried no surplus fat in body or mind. He adopted a mucker pose to conceal a refined, sensitive, and honest nature. He curbed his arrogance with a genuine humility, so that he could rightfully say to me, "Hazard, never forget Rule One: don't take yourself seriously." By his own testimony, he was constantly driven by a fear of failure, but that testimony came only in the rare, serious moments. More often he would say, "I have to win this case so Mama can spend money." Mama was Helen Boardman of Boston—gay, sophisticated, ingenuous.

Mary and I were often guests of Helen and E.J. in Toledo and also at their fishing lodge near Grayling, Michigan—on the banks of the Au Sable, a wide, shallow, swift trout stream. Many of

Toledo's industrial elite had lodges on that stream. E.J. was contemptuous of outsiders who would find the stream, calling them "lily pickers." He was no democrat but his tastes were catholic. Mary would find him in the cool Michigan mornings on the screened porch—up early because he could not sleep—rereading Thomas Hardy's *Far From the Madding Crowd*. Then they would talk, E.J. for the moment a literary aesthete.

Rule One Continued

The ladies of the Maumee, a river flowing into Lake Erie, in the environs of Toledo, where the estates of the great industrialists stand on a wooded escarpment—those ladies called him Mr. Marshall. They were rich, sophisticated, and socially and economically powerful. They loved E.J. in some quite real sense over and above the love for a husband, but they called him "Mr. Marshall." Perhaps it was because he respected them. He regarded a dinner party or a cocktail hour with as much reverence as a business conference. One of his favorites, Emma MacNichol, wife of George P. of established industrial wealth, he called "Mrs. Emma." "I am going to see if Mrs. Emma will work on that," he would say to me. He was Freudian in a sense. Nothing that happened, or was said, or not said, escaped him. The tight little Toledo society knew that, and the ladies brought to him, sometimes through his wife, Helen, their opinions and discoveries like children—with confidence that he would know what to do with the treasure-trove.

Unlike William Jennings Bryan or Hubert Humphrey, E.J. did not have a magnificent eye. The iris had no distinguished pigmentation nor indeed clear separation from the pupil. There was nothing hard or piercing as in the eye of most salesmen and many executives. One could not face him down because one could never be sure he had E.J.'s eye. E.J. communicated in words, tone of voice, and by subtle movements of hands and body rather than with the eyes. E.J. was capable of great hatreds, one of which he heartily entertained for a little man who was president of a great corporation. He would say, "Hazard, that man***," and then he would shake his great frame so eloquently that one could all but see the lice popping off.

E.J. smoked a pipe and, as with all habitual pipe smokers, he used the pipe and its incessant lighting for theatrical effects, espe-

Helen Marshall.

E. J. Marshall
at Grayling.

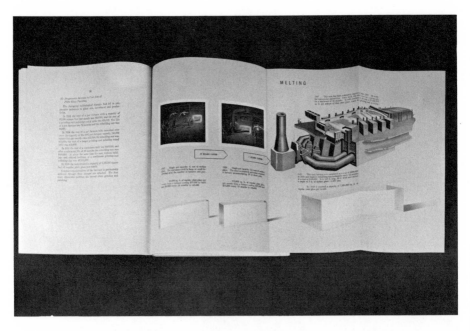

From the teaching brief in the Antitrust Case.

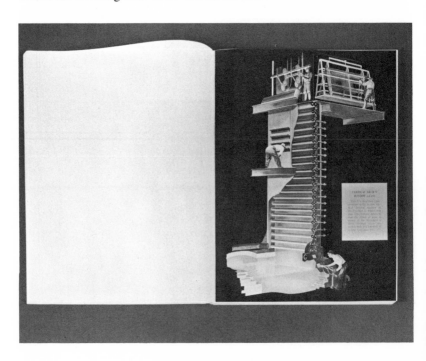

cially in tense moments when he needed time to think. His language was colorful. "Hazard, that man is so ignorant he does not know whether Christ was crucified on Calvary or shot at Bunker Hill." His illustrations, like those of Lincoln, were often salacious. Yet, at Grayling, he would have Mary read him poetry: "In Zanadu did Kubla Khan a stately pleasure dome decree***." On his estate in the suburbs of Toledo he raised daffodils. I often came with him from a hard day at the office and he would at once begin pouring over huge antique volumes about varieties of the narcissus, known affectionately, among many variations of the word, as daffadilly. I watched him in silence pour over his books for daffodil lore and poems about the narcissus. He would share his finds with me, and with Mary when she was there. I think there can be no greater assurance of friendship than when a friend pursues his interests in the presence of a friend. Mary and I agree that we could have eaten a peck of salt with E.J. He published a little monograph, "Daffodils on the Marshall Farm." It was all his, but the putative author was his landscape gardener.

He despised the New Deal and its high priests, Frankfurter, Landis, Hopkins, Eleanor, and he always found a way to dramatize his feelings, as in an episode when I wished to walk over the 20-acre grass meadow which lay in front of the Toledo house. "Very well," he said, "and if you need more exercise just stop and pull up the dock whenever you see it." Every gardener knows that the pestiferous dock cannot be pulled up by hand; it must be grubbed. "Now, Hazard," E.J. continued, "I'll tell you how I do it. When I come upon a plant of dock I give it the name of one of the New Dealers. Then my strength is tripled and I pull it out with ease." Of course, it was sheer poetry—his way of saying that our society needed to be exorcised of the evil spirit of the New Deal. I did not always agree with E.J.'s political, social, and economic philosophy. I did not agree with his unqualified condemnation of Franklin Roosevelt or his contempt for the "brain trust." But this difference of opinion did not diminish my delight in his extravagances. Apparently E.J. told his formula for dock removal to Grove Patterson, the great editor of the *Toledo Blade,* who put it into an editorial which began, "The other day I met on the street one of the wisest men I know***."

He was a modest, arrogant, devious, whimsical man—a legal and business statesman to his admirers, the majority; a manipulator and fixer to his detractors, the minority.

The government's antitrust case against our flat glass industry, launched in 1940, had gone into abeyance during World War II. Antitrust is a semi-luxury in the American way of life. It yields to war and depression. The Sherman Act was suspended during the ·Great Depression of the 1930's in order that business might rationalize itself in favor of profits. Franklin Roosevelt's economic advisors explained to him that there must be a bottom to wages, to prices, to competition. A bitter story made the point. A tenant says to his landlord, "I must move." "No," says the landlord, "I know your salary has been cut, perhaps more than once. I will cut your rent in half." This confrontation of landlord and tenant is repeated at intervals, as the depression deepens, until the landlord invites the tenant to occupy the premises, rent free, admitting that he could not find another tenant and that a vacant property would be simply vandalized. Then the tenant comes again and announces that he must move. The landlord enraged, says, "Why! You must have a roof over your family of wife and four children. Where will you get rent for less than nothing?" The tenant replied, "I know, but I can get a bigger house on the same terms." No doctor of economics could do better in explaining how evil competition can be when the conditions are right for it to do its worst, as they were in the 1930's. So it is that a nation, suffering loss of profits, the stuff of enterprise, or loss of peace, the condition of security, suspends its ideologies and puts first things first.

Then came the Normandy invasion; the capture of Berlin; the suicide of Hitler; and then Hiroshima—the dawn of the atomic era —and antitrust as usual. We had made, E.J. and I, vigorous efforts to settle the litigation. Our attitude was that of J. P. Morgan: let the government tell us what was desired and we would discuss the problems like gentlemen. But to no avail. The lawyer of the Antitrust Division who was in charge of the case thought he had a great case. There is a folkway in the Antitrust Division which makes for a powerful incentive. A lawyer who wins a big case for the government will certainly be offered a very good position with a large firm in Wall Street or may, as in the case of Thurman Arnold, who was head of the Division during the early stages of our case, form his own law firm and enjoy a justifiably lucrative practice. It is hard to settle an antitrust case with a government lawyer who has his eye on the ultimate professional reward—employment as counsel to defend the interests which, as counsel for government, he has attacked. I see no wrong in this. The administration of justice under any law is more likely to be served by a good, healthy, selfish motive than by ideological zealotry—certainly so in a government of law, not of men. Justice under law is done when two sides are represented by highly motivated advocates of comparable competence.

World War II Ends—Another Begins

An antitrust case is like war. When at last the case was launched in 1945 I had to build up my forces just as a peaceful nation does when international war rears its ugly head. I had already engaged George P. Cheney in 1940 because he had a hypnotic eye and a firm voice. He was one of the original government investigators who searched our files, and so I went to Thurman Arnold, head of the government's Antitrust Division, and said that I needed George Cheney for work with local tax officials throughout the nation, and we had no intention of using him in the antitrust case. We could pay more than the government, and Thurman Arnold, from behind a huge desk in one of those great rectangular offices which high-level government officials occupy, said, "Why, of course; if you have a better job for him, why not?" George Cheney showed great aptitude in dealing with governments at all levels and grew into an important role in the company's public affairs activities.

I mentioned the hypnotic eye to make fun of myself because I must make fun of Harry Wherrett, our president, in the selection of Nicholas R. Criss, a law graduate of the University of Pittsburgh. Harry Wherrett was an excellent executive of the old school —before scientific methods were employed in selection of personnel. When I proposed the employment of Nick Criss, just out of law school, Harry Wherrett disapproved, saying, "I don't like his eye." But Nick had a good record in law school and Harry Wherrett graciously bowed to my judgment. So George came because of his eye, and Nick in spite of his eye. Harry Wherrett and I were equally unscientific. George and Nick were equally successful— Nick, after yeoman service in the antitrust case, as our principal labor lawyer, in which field his eye or mind or character was so assuring that, once an oral agreement had been reached, no union, despite traditional union suspicion of lawyers, ever doubted that Nick would put it in writing just as it was.

Within two weeks after the antitrust case was filed I engaged two lawyers, different as day and night. Maurice W. Hibschman (Hibby) came first in November 1945, a lawyer from George Washington University and a graduate of the United States Naval Academy, with a high ranking naval record in the war just closing. Tense, sensitive, intelligent perhaps beyond any of my other associates, he could interpret a legal concept unerringly—and after only a minimum of conversation. In draftsmanship he was superb. Only one who has prepared a complex legal document can know the anguish of the work. One must remember the provisions on page 10 in what he writes on page 60. It is possible to produce the most absurd consequences unless one has a mental grasp of the whole and all of its parts. In this regard Hibby had no peer.

So exacting is the process of legal draftsmanship that I imposed the task upon myself occasionally—at least once a year—to determine the state of my own mental competence, and I have continued this self discipline to the moment. Although I occupied an executive position in which I might have divested myself of all technical work, I always chose to do enough so that my associates would know that they were not asked to do what I could not do myself. The rewards have been high. Now that I am an elder statesman in public affairs, I can still draft with my own two hands the resolution or the document which produces, at the least, a majority consensus for action. Competence is maintained by performance.

Cyrus V. Anderson came two weeks after Hibby. A lawyer from Washington and Lee, he came from the Antitrust Division of the Department of Justice. He had, and has, a real respect for the philosophy of competition. His skepticism about his client knew no bounds. If he had been a physicist or chemist, he would certainly have devised an experiment to unsettle the status quo of some long accepted propositions. Facts, facts, facts—for nothing else had he any respect. What an executive said left him utterly cold; what he did or the consequences of what he did—that was the grist for Anderson's mill. He knew everyone of the more than 7,000 documents in our case. They were organized, indexed, cross-referenced, and rated as to significance. Bright, stable as a butcher, he was all lawyer and a yard wide, and, in addition, an extrovert so engaging that he could make any price-fixing salesman believe, "There must be a better way."

Cy Anderson gained an unusual professional distinction which left him quite independent of my praises. The antitrust bar is, as I have said, small. It is correspondingly elite—a high priesthood whose analytic refinements and esoteric distinctions would be worthy of the ancient Sanhedrin. The number of that august body, which was dissolved with the fall of Jerusalem in A.D., was 71— approximately the number of first-rate antitrust lawyers in America today. What a Hebrew could do on his Sunday and what an American big businessman can do in his five days in the market place —both call for great and proud learning; the one of the ancient Torah, the other in the equally elusive vagaries of American antitrust laws. Corporation lawyers who practice for one client—not in general practice—are usually not invited into the inner councils of lawyers' associations. Anderson was, and is, an exception. He was a member of Attorney General Brownell's National Committee to Study the Antitrust Laws. He worked his way up through the committees of the American Bar Association. He was Co-Chairman with Whitney North Seymour, a New York lawyer at the very pinnacle of prestige, of a national committee to deal with the complexities of litigations which involve many parties and several jurisdictions. He became, and continues to be, a peer among the highest.

Hitler married his long time mistress, Eva Braun, on April 29, 1945, and committed suicide with her the next day in the underground shelter beneath the Berlin chancellery; the United States brought its antitrust suit against my client and other members of the flat glass industry on May 23. I began my endless treks to Toledo and New York for conferences with lawyers, of whom there were for all defendants a total of 55 in various and several capacities.

Follow the Leader

The first problem E.J. set for himself was to dominate the selection of Toledo trial lawyers for each of the defendants. I put it that way because that is the way it was. E.J. knew the importance of harmony among lawyers. He knew Toledo lawyers like the back of his aging hand and he wanted lawyers he could influence—who would respect his judgment. I agreed. We had both seen two famous antitrust cases end disastrously: Socony-Vacuum Oil Co. and Hartford-Empire Company. We knew that in these cases the lawyers were not organized or led and that often in the courtroom the ball had fallen between players. A trial is a drama of a sort and all the rehearsals should occur out of the sight and hearing of the one-man audience, the federal judge.

In our case the judge was Frank L. Kloeb, who had presided over the Hartford-Empire case. An appointee of Franklin Roosevelt, Judge Kloeb was thought of as a "New Deal Judge." It was widely thought that his decision in the Hartford-Empire case, which ended a technological monopoly in glass bottle and container making, had been harsh. In our case it was supposed that the Government, which can bring an antitrust case almost anywhere it wishes because big business has corporate residence in many places, had selected Judge Kloeb for his supposed anti-big-business bias. E.J. and I did not share those views. We knew some of the weaknesses in the Hartford case and, particularly, we had little admiration, despite the eminence of its several lawyers, for their failure to organize for a smooth courtroom procedure.

Furthermore we knew what most experienced lawyers know—that a judge, whatever his origins and original orientation, soon becomes objective and truly judicial—not always but more often than not. We knew also the important mundane fact that to some considerable extent judges try the lawyers as well as the issues of the case. We needed a cast of lawyer-actors, who would eschew competition among themselves—in our planning, a virtue which was the exact vice with which our clients were charged. Although businessmen must compete, once they are sued for default in that regard, their lawyers may lawfully collaborate closely in the defense.

"If you don't agree with me, I'm going to agree with you." That was the way E.J. put it to me time and again—a disarming method of causing me to try very hard to agree with him. We were completely of one mind about a generalissimo to lead all the legal forces. We must subordinate ourselves and, by example, ask other lawyers to do likewise, in order to secure internal consistency in the defense preparation and in the courtroom performance. The range of choice for such a leader is not wide. He must come from one of the large firms in New York or Chicago or San Francisco. In our case the geography dictated New York, where one would find in any given decade not over a dozen men of requisite stature. He must be supported by a large and existing organization, experienced in antitrust litigation because the logistical problems, quite aside from the legal problems, of marshaling facts and witnesses are quite comparable to those of warfare.

Our choice was an engaging Irishman, product of Harvard Law School, a former United States District Attorney, and a Democrat in his mid-forties. Everyone of his qualifications was important, his relative youth not the least, because litigation, like a labor negotiation, is an endurance test. Stamina is not a substitute for intelligence, but in litigation intelligence without stamina will usually not be adequate. John T. Cahill had both. He was head of his firm, which was rooted in the great old Cotton and Franklin of Wall Street fame. Great law firms almost never die. Sometimes even the original name persists for generations after the founders have died.

Now the time came for me to test E.J.'s formulation about who would agree with whom. He had parceled out the Toledo lawyers to the several defendants except for my client. It is a well-founded custom that when a lawyer enters the court of a jurisdiction other than that of his residence, he is accompanied by "local counsel." There are important reasons for the custom, which often rests upon a mandatory rule of the local court. Resident lawyers know the judge, the clerk of the court, the reporters, the marshals. At a minimum the sponsorship of a local lawyer is a needed amenity; at best he may prove to be a tower of strength.

Furthermore, when the case is big and the fees will be large and the community is of moderate size like Toledo, failure of an important party to the litigation to engage a prestigious member of the bar may have repercussions. John Cahill, whose realism was as hearty and unashamed as that of E.J., explained the problem. When a big lawsuit lands in town the lawyers' wives all arrange in their minds the employment of their husbands long in advance of any decision by the clients. Then they buy new hats and otherwise spend some of the expected fees forthwith. Now, if some important lawyer is left out, his wife, who has confidantes, talks about it and her unhappiness spreads and the reasons for it grow and become distorted, and presently and before you know it, an aura of inequity, or unfairness, or unreasonableness has worked its way into high places.

Ross W. Shumaker was one eminent Toledo lawyer whom E.J. intended should have no place in the case. Ross had been a younger lawyer in E.J.'s firm and had withdrawn to form his own firm and, of course, to take some business with him. I have seldom seen such deep-seated animosity. Occasionally, when younger members of a big firm have gained some following of their own and see too many others ahead of them or are unhappy with their financial participation, they will split themselves off and take some business with them. The senior partners don't relish the experience. Their egos as well as their pocketbooks are hurt. Yet the cleavage usually occurs in good spirit and without open recriminations. Not so with E.J. and Ross Shumaker. Their mutual disrespect was an open secret.

The day came when I raised with E.J. the question of my Toledo associate and named Ross Shumaker. "I can't control him," said E.J. "That's right," I said, "but I can." E.J.'s proud face remained inscrutable. I know that there was manly love between us, and I had hurt him. He said simply, "That's right, you can." Nothing more. He lived up to his whimsy: "If you don't agree with me, I'm going to agree with you." When I spoke to Ross Shumaker about the engagement, honest man that he was, he said, "E. J. Marshall didn't recommend me, did he?" I replied, "We agreed."

I never had to control Ross Shumaker. He and his associates brought us a wealth of work and wisdom throughout the years of preparation and, finally, during the months of the trial. I never knew how it would have been if E.J. had lived. One day in 1946 I received a long handwritten letter from him—all about the case and how to prepare it and what to look for. Sometime before, as we were driving from Grayling to Toledo, he had said, "Hazard, I give myself only a little time—not enough for the case." Reluctantly I talked with him about his partners and we agreed that Stuart Wall should succeed him—a wise decision. The handwritten letter was a lawyer's masterpiece which I distributed among principals of the legal staff. It was sprinkled with gutty warnings, and the sophisticated George Nebolsine—not given to compliments for others—called it amazingly prescient. Now I was alone.

Attack Is the Better Part of Defense

The rulers, statesmen, generals, and peoples of all times and places can be divided between those who subscribe to my captioned assertion and those who dissent.

The preparation for the defense of an antitrust case and the conduct of the trial have some of the logistic and strategic aspects of war. This truth is worthy of repetition. One point of identity is the very question whether to adopt an aggressive defense or a defensive defense. In our group of 55 lawyers—the total for four major companies and some of their officers and several smaller firms—we had strong proponents for both types of strategy. Fifty-five seem a great many lawyers but not many when the magnitude of the issues is considered. The government was seeking to break up enterprises having aggregate values of at least a billion dollars —1945 dollars. Even a partial victory for the government could have cost our clients tens, perhaps hundreds, of millions. No expense is spared in defending an antitrust case.

The issue of an aggressive versus a defensive defense arose first over the character of the trial brief we would file, the document we must lodge with Judge Kloeb in advance of the trial and in which we would disclose the nature of our defense. Should we all join in one document? One fine lawyer, George D. Welles, said "No!" He would file a separate brief for his client. The others, after weeks of discussion, agreed to a consolidated brief for all the rest of us. I was for a teaching document, by which I meant extensive disclosures concerning the history, technology, and trade practices of the industry, and, especially concerning the epochs in its development. Our problem of exposition was exactly my problem in this book: to tell enough for the purpose but not more than enough.

The government charged that the industry had become concentrated: only two manufacturers of plate glass and only four of window glass; and the government, pointing with alarm to closed glass plants over the Eastern United States, charged that they were casualties of our conspiracy to eliminate competition. Not so, we replied; those closed plants were the casualties of changing technology. But should we disclose in the trial brief how we would prove the changes in technology? Committed to the concept of the aggressive defense, I urged a complete forecast of the revolutionary transition from the hand methods and discontinous processes which had characterized the industry since the time of Louis XIV, and before, to the automatic and continuous technology which emerged in the 1930's. A single unit of plate glass manufacture in 1902 could produce per month 60,000 square feet of product; in 1924, slightly improved, 143,000 square feet. Only seven years later, however, a continuous tank furnace was built that made the earlier pots look like toys; by 1938 it was producing 1,300,000 square feet of plate glass per month. Obviously, the economy would not need as many tank furnaces as pots.

The lawyers for a defensive defense asked me, "Why tell everything in advance? The government has brought the charges and must proceed first with its evidence. Let us wait and see. It will be time enough to tell all when our turn comes to produce evidence." Thus the old issue was joined, as it was between the hesitant McClellan and the militant Grant in the American war between the states. McClellan's inaction in the early days of the war had caused Lincoln to observe, sadly, "If General McClellan doesn't need the army, why doesn't he give it back to me?"

The difference between our hesitant lawyers and our militant lawyers involved a difference of belief about human psychology. A judge's mind is, after all, a human mind, specially trained, it is true, but human. It was my conviction that in a long and complex case the defendants dared not sit back and let weeks of government testimony go by with only the lawyers' routine of cross-examination. The problem would be more complicated than whether witnesses were telling the truth; rather it was what significance to attach to bits and pieces of testimony as they emerged. For that purpose the judge needed a comprehensive knowledge of the industry—and in advance. I kept recalling a story my father, by now deceased, was wont to tell about a justice of the peace — a most ancient, and now trivial, judicial office — who, having heard the plaintiff's case, refused to hear the defendant's observing, "When I hear two sides of a case I tend to become confused."

I thought the rule in Judge Kloeb's court which required a brief in advance of any evidence gave us a good opportunity. The brief was not evidence, but no lawyer of any standing would put into such a brief anything he would be unable to support with substantial evidence. Even so, I complained to myself and to the other lawyers that the conventional lawyer's brief is a drab document, compounded by words, words, words—black print on white paper, bound in white covers, sometimes buff—nothing to reflect the wisdom of the Chinese proverb about the 1,000-word-worth of a single picture. So I proposed pictures—but not photographs, because the magnitude and extent of the fiery furnaces and mile-long machines beggared photography. An artist with an eye for perspective better than the camera's eye and with a sense of color which Eastman with all of its magic could not match — we needed an artist.

Artist's rendition in a brief? Unheard of! Yes, of course, unheard of, but what the text books teach today is always what the good lawyers *did* yesterday. So I argued, and prevailed. We interested Paul Schweinberg, a sensitive Pittsburgh industrial artist, in the problem. In due course we had furnaces in paintings, with their searing flames over molten glass—in flame color and the refractories in their tawny heat; we had pipes and stacks—all the huge parts and processes differentiated by their true colors. We had the great grinders, each electrical unit four stories high, put in its 1,000-foot scale by a single intent workman standing by in a yellow shirt. That was for plate glass.

We had the magic of molten glass, really a liquid, being fished out of a 2,000 degrees tank-furnace and lifted upward as a wide ribbon through rolls to make finished window glass—only 25 feet above the incinerating bath of molten metal. Glass is a non-ferrous metal. There was so much to teach the judge. We did it with words and pictures—and Paul Schweinberg with his brush acted like a lawyer.

We filed the brief in its blue-gray cover — all 213 pages of it, including an index, and full of Schweinberg's paintings, charts in colors, and stacks of glass whose edges, surprisingly to a layman, make an exquisite blue in the pile. We used the stacks instead of charts, and when we needed to show how dependent we were upon our principal customers, the automobile makers, we employed comparative piles of colorful coins which showed our industry to be pigmy beside the giants of the automobile industry who had the resources and the technical skills to make their own glass, as Ford then did in part and now does entirely. There were plenty of words in our document and also plenty of pictures and charts in color, all technically correct. So far as I know, we produced an innovation in brief-making.

When the trial came on in Toledo in 1948, the government had, as a plaintiff always has, the right and duty to go first. Nevertheless, I urged that we employ our right of cross-examination to prove by the government's own witnesses as many of the industrial factors forecast in our brief as possible. Again this strategy was questioned—and honestly—by some of our legal generals, motivated by a conventional, cautious, defensive mood. "Why give our case away?" they asked. "Why take the chance of an unfavorable answer from a hostile witness?" I replied, "Nothing risked, nothing gained. With our teaching brief and many of its statements proved by government witnesses themselves, we will enable the judge, to a considerable extent, to hear both sides of the case at once." It worked out that way. John Cahill, whom we made lead-lawyer on the cross-examination, handled the risky procedures with great skill. Cyrus Anderson checked off for me point after point of our scheduled defense—proved before we ever reached the time for formal defense.

Although John Cahill was principal spokesman, none of the lawyers in any way relinquished his courtroom prerogatives. There were 26 of us every day in the courtroom. The arrangement of counsel tables, while accomplished in less time than at the Vietnam Paris peace talks, was no less critical. I opted for the least conspicuous corner of the room. "The first shall be last." The decision was helpful. Nevertheless, I could be seen and heard when I stood up.

Back at Toledo's Commodore Perry Hotel, where we had an entire floor fitted up as living quarters and offices, other lawyers were at work, a kind of service of supply in a logistical system. We had our own telephone switchboard and our own secretarial staffs. Mine was headed by Essie Ellis who, ten years before, had elected to come from Kansas City with me to Pittsburgh. She was one of four great secretaries in almost fifty years. Herself a good executive, she managed our staff and our extensive filing systems with that sense of personal involvement which always marks secretarial greatness. Any man worthy of a good secretary will humbly admit that life would be awkward without her.

It was no accident that we had, probably, the first tightly integrated defensive procedure in a multi-party antitrust case since the resurgence of antitrust enforcement under Franklin Roosevelt and Thurman Arnold. One of the more successful devices was the daily post-mortem and planning conference. Every lawyer came at 5:00 P.M. to the big conference room in the Commodore Perry Hotel. We assessed our courtroom failures and successes of the day—ruthlessly and quite impersonally. One of the ground rules was that any idea to be employed in court on the next day must emerge in that big rectangular parlor, where we sat in conclave until 6:00 P.M. each court day, the idea there to be appraised by all. The pleasure of watching good minds, highly motivated, dissect a professional concept and then reject it, modify it, or embrace it is great. Our purpose was to avoid ill-considered individual action in the courtroom and we succeeded. The proud ideas of proud lawyers must pass through the dense filter of that high council.

Then came cocktails and dinner—and then the work of the evening and night: interviewing witnesses; preparation of memoranda (no idea is valid until it is reduced to writing); study of the transcription of the day's proceedings; study of the statistics we had been collecting for months. The major tasks had all been parceled out to the office forces and in the evenings the courtroom lawyers must absorb the fruits of their work.

Our staff included not only lawyers but also accountants, statisticians, chartists, publicists, and economists led by Leon Henderson, but recently recuperated from the crushing experience of heading Franklin Roosevelt's World War II Office of Price Administration. One member of our staff was just a plain brilliant thinker, Beardsley Ruml, but of him more later. One member of our staff, a partner of John Cahill, achieved a masterful comprehension of the thousands of documents and myriads of facts, their consistencies, inconsistencies, nuances, risks, and relevancies. The routine for him was to work two-thirds of the night and then sit by John Cahill in the courtroom all day, ready to supply any random fact or document for the cross-examination. Young, lean of body and hard of mind, Fred J. Knauer reminds me in retrospect of the story of Toscanini, who, on an occasion before the 80-minute program rehearsal, was approached by a player with the complaint that his flute would not play E-flat that day. The maestro thought a moment and then said, "You don't have to play E-flat today." The story may be apocryphal, but as the Italian proverb has it, "If not true, it is well invented." We all saw a great future for Fred, but he spent the legal energy of a lifetime on our single case. When it all ended, the means and manner of which I shall now relate, Fred, confronted with another such case, loaded his family into a trailer, quit Wall Street forever, and became a California motel owner, and Candide-like, acquired and cultivated a garden—a man with the great good sense to know that he could not live with his own standards of excellence.

The government tried its case for 12 straight weeks and at the close, the government having done its very best, and we having before the court our brief and our cross-examinations, which were aggressive—not defensive—at the close Judge Kloeb said:

"I rather think that it would do no harm for counsel to discuss their relative positions at some time in the next two or three weeks. I do not think either one of you are (sic) in any condition to knock at the pearly gates and demand admittance without a thorough cleansing and an examination of your consciences. I think that is in order. Knowing that to be the fact, it seems to me that rather than putting the burden on the court and continuing a trial here for another year, that you might get your heads together and settle your differences, settle them just as well as the court could. I merely drop that as an additional suggestion at the close of the plaintiff's case."

What curious language! We sat in the courtroom, stunned, incredulous; but in moments we knew. Judge Kloeb had told the government that it should settle—meaning compromise—its case, and *before* having heard our defense. This pronouncement from the bench was in accordance with trial procedure. A plaintiff must always make out a *prima facie* case, meaning that the plaintiff must have produced enough proof of his allegations that the defendant must then come forward with counter evidence and proof. Judge Kloeb did not say that the government had failed in that regard; what he said, in effect, was that he was not sufficiently moved by the government's case to wish to hear our defense, and that both sides must give enough to settle the case and so relieve him of the burden of further trial. The implication was plain: whoever thwarted the judge's expectation might well have a double burden thereafter.

Curtis Shears, chief of the government's trial lawyers, promptly said, outside the courtroom, that he had no intention of settling the case, but his superior, Herbert A. Bergson, head of the Antitrust Division of the Department of Justice, read the handwriting on the wall with the accuracy of a Daniel. Negotiations for settlement began in Washington in September and lasted until the eve of Truman's spectacular defeat of Dewey.

Now a wholly different type of leadership was needed, both on the government's side and on our side. The axiom that there is no such person as a good lawyer—one must ask good for what—that axiom applied. J. G. Van Cise, a partner of John Cahill, became our spokesman. Jerry was described by John as a walking encyclopedia of antitrust law. More important than that, he, like Anderson, had a deep respect for the doctrines of antitrust and the values of competition; and most important of all, he knew that the government, despite its failure in court, must have some portion of its pound of flesh in the settlement.

The problem with the co-defendants in framing a strategy of settlement was no less acute than it had been in framing a strategy of trial, but for different reasons. The ancient proverb applied:

The devil got sick
And the devil a saint would be;
The devil got well
And the devil of a saint was he.

Some of my colleagues asked, "Why settle? We can win." In any case they had small faith in the government's intention to settle. The whole business would be just a trap to get information from us for use when the trial resumed. Furthermore, in their innermost hearts there was deeply implanted by their clients the conviction that now the enemy was not the government but my client, tycoon of the industry. There was a suspicion that the provisions of settlement might turn out to be more onerous for their clients than for mine. Stuart S. Wall, who had succeeded E.J. as chief of counsel for the second largest member of the industry, offended me by refusing to establish his settlement staff in the old Wardman Park Hotel, where, with that exception, we had as elaborate an assemblage of lawyers, related service, files, clerks, and secretaries as in Toledo for the trial. I believed that we could settle the case, but it would be hard enough without the physical inconvenience of a major party in a separate location. Stuart Wall was a good friend and I never asked him why he added to our burdens. Perhaps he was acting upon his client's insistence and was too good a soldier to say so.

The government's spokesman was Sigmund Timberg, a scholarly lawyer, steeped in antitrust doctrine, and, unlike many government lawyers, sophisticated about the problems and necessities of industry. A *modus operandi* was developed. Jerry Van Cise and Sigmund Timberg agreed from time to time upon the areas for forthcoming settlement discussions. In advance, lawyers for the defendants would caucus alone and take their several positions; then we would all caucus together. Jerry often played the role, quite seriously, of devil's advocate. He knew that we would have to concede more than we would find comfortable. On the other hand, we were hard as nails with him, constantly challenging him to use his knowledge and wits to get what was "right" not just what the government wanted. Occasionally I would emit a resounding "No!" and the caucus would end for that day. One takes considerable risks in the high affairs of industry.

I have often been unpleasant in behalf of a client or a cause. Perhaps it is because a sharp tongue, and brittle tone of voice to match, have been understood as advocacy, that no one, friend or foe, has ever suggested that I apologize. Mary agrees that my mother put it well when she said, "Leland has lots of patience, but when it goes, it goes all at once."

The Great Bourn of all Common Sense: Compromise

For almost two months we worked at compromise. The government gave up its foolishness about reducing each member of the industry to one plant. There was too much offered proof in our brief about the interdependence of technologies among the plants. The government gave up its attempt to compel my client to divest itself of its distribution system, which was a nationwide complex of establishments to bring glass close to the people. Few persons realize why it is that when storms or riots break great glass show windows or vandals wreck their havoc on public school buildings —that the glass replacements can be had promptly. It is because large stocks of glass and the equipment for cutting and installing it are already in the local community, not at some distant factory.

All defendants were dependent upon independent jobbers for that function of local quick service, but my client also *owned* such establishments throughout the United States. The other defendants would have been secretly happy to see us divested of what they thought was a competitive advantage. I was alone on that point; and that was one issue on which I said, "No!"

We prevailed on the two big points, but that was not especially to our credit. The antitrust laws had not gone so far as to preclude a manufacturer from owning more than one plant or from owning establishments for selling its products. Some zealous lawyer in the government services had overreached the law in those demands. The pinch—it was really a bite—came in the incorporation into the settlement—called a "Final Judgment," known also as a "Consent Decree," or "Consent Judgment"—the incorporation of numerous restrictions which were in gray areas of the law. In other words, in order to settle, we resolved many valid legal doubts against ourselves. Take one illustration. We agreed that we would not contract to supply our glass products to any given customer for more than one year at a time. The government's theory of such a restriction was that other suppliers should have access to our customers and should not be barred by a long term contract of ours. Now a long-term supply contract is not illegal in itself. For example, utility companies contract to supply power or fuel for long periods up to 10 to 25 years or more. So we agreed to a restraint which went beyond the law.

My client agreed to increase in the five years following the "Final Judgment" the average number of its so-called factory buyers by 10 per cent over the average number in the preceding five years. It is fundamental in the law that a manufacturer may choose his customers and decide for himself to whom he will sell and to how many. It is otherwise with telephone, utility, railroad, or airline and such companies because they are monopolies of a sort and operate by governmental permission. They may not turn customers away. Not so with a manufacturer of shoes or ships or sealing wax. He may pick and choose his customers in the first instance as he sees it so long as the decision is solely his own. Thus it was that for a time and to a limited extent we gave up an important and unquestionable right.

We ourselves devised some of the restrictions we placed upon ourselves. Jerry Van Cise would come back from his sessions with Sigmund Timberg to report demands to which we could not agree, but then we would ask, "What is the government's problem; what lies back of the demand?" With that question answered we would then let our imagination work toward an honest response but one more temperate than the government's first demand. In the end there were a good fifty of such provisions in the final judgment which made a special code, regardless of general antitrust law, by which our industry must be governed.

The final judgment contained much which was ordinary antitrust law, firmly established by the decided cases, such as provisions against agreement upon prices or exchange of trade information among competitors—what we lawyers call antitrust "boiler plate." The hard fact about the whole final judgment was, however, that with respect to all of its provisions, trite or innovative, the court retained jurisdiction to hear complaints of violation at any time. This meant that without the formalities and delays of a new case the government could on short notice bring us into the same court where the case was tried. If the court found that any officer, or employee, or agent of my client had violated any prohibition of the final judgment, that person could be punished by fine or imprisonment, and the corporation itself could be fined, and heavily. The ancient power of a court of equity to punish for violation of its orders was the Sword of Damocles which would henceforth hang over our heads.

Compliance First, Profits Next

Maurice W. Hibschman had the best sense of what we must give and what we could resist in the settlement negotiations. Just as Anderson sat by my side at the trial, so Hibschman was my mentor in the hard decisions which produced the final judgment. A soft-spoken man, Hibby never said much in a general conference. Often it was not necessary for him to speak because he had briefed me in advance. I learned one thing from watching Hibby. One should always remember the silent one in a conference and find an occasion to speak to him aside. Sometimes he is there as some conferee's aide—there only for show purposes—and in that case a few words will suffice; sometimes he will say in an aside something so important that one wonders why he withheld it from the open meeting. When I have made such finds I have always asked permission to bring them to the attention of the whole company when the conference reconvenes, giving credit to the silent one.

To give credit is not noble; it is good sense. An executive who gives credit will receive from his associates ideas and disclosures which might not otherwise be forthcoming. I never knew why, exactly. There seem to be people with much to contribute but they must be called upon. Years after my rewarding association with Hibby, when I had become a teacher, I noticed that quite frequently a most talkative student—and an interesting talker—would do badly on the examination and an utterly silent student would do well. In any case, to give credit is the mark of a secure and confident executive—one who knows that under his leadership there is credit enough for all.

The insecure executive who gets by—a colloquialism for succeeding without being discovered—is a well-known character in the business world. The Broadway success, "How to Succeed in Business Without Even Trying," is soundly based as are all caricatures—from Quixote to Throttlebottom. There is a story of a highly placed business executive with usual, old mode, clean top desk in the corner of a big office. For years, after-hours office prowlers had noticed that the shallow drawer above the knee-well was always locked. Finally he died and his executor opened the drawer, in which a single sheet of paper was the sole contents: it read, "The debit side is toward the window."

There *is* incompetence in high places in business, and an inept incumbent can stay in office a long time, particularly if the enterprise is large, as Montgomery-Ward was in the days of Sewell Avery. By and large, however, Samuel Johnson's quip to Mrs. Thrale went too far. She had expressed concern about her ability to manage her deceased husband's brewery business. "Be not afeared, Madam," wrote Johnson, "business could not be managed by those who manage it, if it had much difficulty." I had occasion to be proud of my associates among the executives of my client after the Final Judgment became a fact of their lives. Never do men relish the restraints of law which they consider unreasonable —businessmen no more than any other men. Laws in which men believe are not considered restraints. Most men pay their taxes because they believe in organized society, however much they may dissent from its dictates at any given time; but if enough men decide not to pay taxes, then there is not enough enforcement power in government to prevail upon them, as the English Stuarts discovered.

Antitrust laws are in a gray area. Businessmen believe in competition until it gets so acute that profits vanish for everybody. Then there is a tendency to call a halt. "We ought to make dollars instead of tons," is one way distraught competitors put it. Some economists say, "Not at all! The system is one in which competition should be forever the cause of economic death and the invitation to new economic life. Businessmen should compete themselves out of existence so that other businessmen may come into existence. Profits are only transitory between birth and death"—so runs the theoretical economic argument. To businessmen this is sheer nonsense. They spend their lives, the highest and the lowest, in building an institution to last, and the profit is the *sine qua non* of industrial immortality. So long as the competition required by the antitrust laws is a general precept, businessmen are relatively content to leave that to the lawyers, but when the precept is broken down into 29 pages of specific "do's and don'ts," as in the case of our Final Judgment, the trauma becomes acute.

I repeat that I was proud of my business colleagues because of the free hand they gave Anderson and me to promote in the rank and file of the organization the Final Judgment as if it were a new product. We knew that it would be necessary to make deep injections of the new specifics into the corporate body. It is never enough for top executives just to announce a policy. Among thousands of employees, all of whom will be affected in one way or another, there will be many who will reason that the policy is meant for someone else. We needed the equivalent of James Montgomery Flagg's World War I recruiting poster, modified to read, "This Means You."

We prepared a special edition of the Final Judgment in which marginal notations alongside the formal text were so plain that he who ran might read. For example, there was a provision against predatory pricing which read:

The corporate defendants are severally and jointly enjoined and restrained from selling, or causing to be sold, flat glass at any industry level at unreasonably low or discriminatory prices for the purpose of destroying a competitor or suppressing competition in the manufacture or sale of flat glass.

Opposite the paragraph we said: "Don't price in order to destroy." There were 26 such cryptic injunctions, and we made a distribution right down to the newest cub salesman. We were speaking *ex cathedra* in a vernacular and with an authority which sealed the more ponderously stated injunctions of the court.

Furthermore, we prepared a letter of transmittal about the company's compliance program, the burden of which was that a new era had come—a new day calling for new ways. Then, remarkable to relate, the letter included the clinching phrase, "Compliance first, Profits next." Donald C. Burnham, then vice president of the merchandising division, signed the letter. Anderson and I were deeply moved that he would follow our advice in so unequivocal a fashion. Twenty-five years have now elapsed and just now (1973), Anderson has secured a court order terminating the final judgment entirely ten years hence—a first in antitrust history.

One Thing Leads to Another

The establishment in Pittsburgh is Republican, although in 1973 only a few citizens can remember a Republican mayor. The Great Depression broke a long Republican hold on the Commonwealth of Pennsylvania and on the County of Allegheny and its City of Pittsburgh. Nevertheless, a Democrat in Pittsburgh's Duquesne Club, where the establishment has lunch, is as rare as a pearl in an oyster bed and as suspect as a fox in a chicken coop. Occasionally among the presidents and vice presidents of the top 20 corporations headquartered in Pittsburgh there will be an import from some other state, who, by birth or past propinquity, is a Democrat, but too good an executive for his politics to matter. Once I was traveling in the Philippines on an Exchange of Persons program under the auspices of the American State Department. I was lecturing on management problems and, inevitably, on the labor and unionism aspects of industrial administration. An aging tycoon, whose fortune was founded in the early days of William Howard Taft's Philippine administration, sent me an invitation to call on him. The American Embassy at Manila advised me to accept. It developed that he wanted to know whether I was a sound man and had cabled the Mellon Offices in Pittsburgh. The reply, which he showed me, certified that I was all right, and proved it by adding, "Republican"—an affiliation which I have honored as much in the breach as in the observance. Buckley M. Byers, in one of the election years when he was doing his loyal stint as a Republican stalwart, asked me if I would run for mayor of Pittsburgh. I said, "No, there are hopeless causes I can lose with less work."

The settlement of our antitrust case brought me some favorable attention in the Pittsburgh establishment, just as our "Compliance first, Profits next" program did later among the antitrust circles of government and business, when the full sincerity and vigor of that program became known. I saw R. K. Mellon at a board meeting of my client a few days after the settlement, which had occurred on the eve of Thomas E. Dewey's surprising defeat for the American presidency in the 1948 election. He told me how he and his associates had sat gloomily around the offices of the family-holding company, T. Mellon and Sons, on the post-election day, finding nothing to relieve their depression except "what you have done," referring to the settlement of the flat glass antitrust case. The *settlement* of such a case is usually considered a victory in the business world. R. K. Mellon was given to somewhat tangential oral expression, but in context there was never any uncertainty about his thought or meaning. He had reason to feel gratified because one of the famous antitrust cases, tried to the bitter end, involved one of the greatest Mellon companies, Alcoa. A distinguished Pittsburgh lawyer in that case comes to the Duquesne Club to this day on the arm of an attendant, broken, we all have no doubt, by the sense of injustice at Judge Learned Hand's branding Alcoa a monopoly, for which severe penalties were assessed, despite the absence of any wrongdoing. Alcoa had but owned the patents by which it became the sole primary producer of a most useful metal. That was all, but the punishment was for involuntary monopoly. The case had an Oedipus aspect: guilt without sin. The Pittsburgh business community's wonderment at the ways of antitrust deepened, and the settlement in our glass case was considered a substantial achievement. Raymond Pitcairn and Clarence Brown were pleased.

The teaching brief brought me a request to consider the presidency of Carnegie Institute of Technology, now Carnegie-Mellon University. That came about because Elliott Dunlap Smith, Harvard lawyer and Yale educator, was the provost at C.I.T. founded by Andrew Carnegie, and by my time an interesting and seemingly incongruous assemblage of distinguished schools of engineering, drama, music, and architecture, without a liberal arts college. Elliott Smith spead the word on the campus about the teaching brief. He asked me to appear twice before large faculty groups to discuss how the case was handled, which I did, never suspecting that he was preparing to propose me to the trustees to fill the vacancy created by the death of Robert E. Doherty, president of C.I.T.

One day Augustus Oliver, revered Pittsburgh patriarch, came to my office on behalf of the trustees' nominating committee. Would I permit my name to be proposed for the presidency of Carnegie Institute of Technology? Of course I thought about it, but declined. I doubted that I would have the necessarily large financial support of the top Pittsburgh establishment. When one feels that way about an important matter, there is no point in asking, and I did not.

Beardsley Ruml—Talking Thinker

It had been E.J.'s idea that we engage Beardsley Ruml as a consultant in the antitrust case—to signal to the government that we were thinking, not just as advocates but constructively and creatively about the role of a big business company in the American society. At that time there were few men in the United States who would better personify those requirements. He was fresh from his successful institution, as a private citizen, of the pay-as-you-go method of collecting federal income taxes. This 1943 innovation required the cancellation of 1942 income taxes so that payroll deductions and estimated advance payments could be applied to 1943 taxes. The innovation made a huge favorable difference in the cost of financing World War II and the Korean War—the difference between the government's having the money now and having to borrow it at interest until collected a year later.

Obvious—but how would the government ever collect 1942 income taxes? Never, of course. "You simply set the tax clock ahead one year, as in daylight-saving time," said B., the diminutive we affectionately applied to a mentally and physically very big man. The cartoonists, referring to his earlier post as head of social sciences at the University of Chicago, showed him with pointer at the blackboard explaining to an incredulous Congress why nothing in taxes would be lost—in infinite time, of course. The shift from collection of taxes after they have accrued to collection as they accrue, involved a form of cerebration which only a few men and some apes can achieve.

Wolfgang Kohler placed bananas outside an apes' cage and out of reach of the apes' hands except with a straight stick. A baffle, like a bureau drawer with the front against the face of the cage and the rear knocked out, frustrated the ape's natural impulse to rake the fruit inwardly to within range of grasp. Since the baffle did not extend along the entire face of the cage, the solution was first to push the banana away and then move it laterally to a point free of the baffle and then inwardly to the ape. Only a few apes of the highest intelligence (by other tests) had the inspiration to do the unnatural thing first in order to gain the natural end. Such was B. Ruml's quality of insight. The idea was, as with many inventions, obvious as the vacuum cleaner, once conceived. The marvel was that it was sold, as the vernacular goes, to America—probably because in wartime many people are more amenable to intellectual leadership than in peacetime.

B. Ruml, who was the treasurer and later chairman at Macy's, said he got the idea for the pay-as-you-go tax collection plan, not to solve the government's fiscal wartime problems, but to solve the problem of Macy's retiring employees, caught with the necessity of paying income tax on the last year of regular pay out of the first year of lower retirement pay. When he saw the light he was relaxing on the 20th Century Limited from Chicago to New York. He called such relaxation "a state of dispersed attention."

When I encountered him in the mid-1940's, B. Ruml was at the height of his fame. He was, in addition to his offices with Macy's, chairman of the Federal Reserve Bank of New York; director and trustee of public and private institutions; advisor to the Commonwealth of Puerto Rico during the exciting early days of Munos Marin and "Operation Bootstrap." Mostly, however, he was Beardsley Ruml, personage, thinker and talker—always in a comfortable chair. He insisted, and I agree, that there is a direct ratio —one to one—between posterior comfort and effective cerebral activity.

B. Ruml was not modest in his requirements about environ-
mental aids to thought. During the antitrust case we provided a
permanent suite in the Plaza Hotel in New York. He went there
from time to time. Often Leon Henderson, whom he wished as a
companion and economic consultant, would join him. Muzak
Corporation, of which he was a director, supplied music. We lawyers would visit occasionally. B. and Leon read all our documentation. Of course we never came to the time when B. Ruml might
have had the exact idea we needed, because the case was settled,
but one never comes away from such a man empty handed, as
one episode attests.

B. Ruml heard that William Ernest Stephen Turner, a distinguished English scientist and one learned in glass technology, was
in America. Could Ruml and Henderson see Turner? I arranged
the meeting in the Plaza sanctum. Soon, from B's great frame,
dissolved in a great chair, his big face with its enigmatic smile—
from his whole person came the inquiry, "Dr. Turner, in America
we have a doctrine that competition is not only the life of trade
but also the mother of invention. In other words, and stating the
case in reverse, our dogma has it that monopoly is anathema to
technological innovation because the monopolist has no need to
improve his product or reduce his costs or enhance his services.
He can safely say, 'the public be damned.' Now," B. continued,
"the Pilkingtons in England have had a monopoly in glass manufacture for well over a hundred years. Yet that great family company has been highly innovative; much of the glass industry today,
all over the world, pays royalties to Pilkington Brothers on their
patented innovations. How do you account for that fact?"

I was pleased, because the question showed that Ruml had
absorbed some facts about the global glass industry. Dr. Turner
was an elderly man with a neck and head a bit askew as from arth-
ritis. His distorted head position forced the appearance of one who
talks aside, and so gave his response something of the character
of a secret disclosure. "The Pilkingtons," he said, "are Congrega-
tionalists and so are affected with a divine discontent." That ended
that. We all had a drink. However much competition, according
to American antitrust doctrine, might make for innovation, with
the Pilkington monopoly in England it was divine discontent.

B. Ruml brought me onto the Business Committee of National

Planning Association. He had had some health warnings and asked me to take his place as Chairman, which I did and ran it somewhat more efficiently but less creatively than he. B. talked and talked, and very well. He did not write enough. This is not to ignore his important *Tomorrow's Business,* published in 1945, in which he forecast the now more familiar concept of trusteeship in business management—concern for the role of business in the whole of society.

In World War II we had the corporate excess profits tax which took from corporations 82 cents of the top dollars of profits. B. Ruml was aghast that corporations did not rush to form corporate foundations and give the federally permitted 5 per cent of their swollen wartime profits to be used for charitable, educational, and scientific purposes. B. Ruml edited, and National Planning Association published, *The Manual of Corporate Giving,* to which he asked me to contribute the chapter on community chests. He talked and wrote about what he called the "5 per cent," and he challenged business to conceive socially beneficial projects in which 18-cent dollars "could be wisely expended." The "Manual" was a survey of qualified public purposes designed to intrigue business with long range, continuing, intellectual, and financial participation in the public well-being. Yet business had never *given* more than about one per cent of its taxable earnings, and the rate did not substantially increase even when the government would have contributed by way of tax saving 82 cents of every dollar. Even my client was slow about following my advice to form a corporate foundation. Today such foundations are prevalent and some of them have quite imaginative programs. But even yet the rate of corporate giving has not reached even half of the permitted 5 per cent.

In 1959 B. Ruml published *Memo to a College Trustee,* in which he analyzed the financial plight of the small colleges. Those with enrollments of less than 800 students were not viable, he found, and many doses of strong medicine he prescribed, including radical changes in faculty mores. I do not know whether the saying is his, "It is easier to move a graveyard than to change a college curriculum," but he wrote eloquently about such problems.

The Business Committee of National Planning Association always met at the Metropolitan Club in New York. B. continued to attend after I became chairman. We convened at eleven in the morning and I always finished by two. One day as I was getting my hat and coat I turned, and there was B. some feet away watching me with such an expression: whimsical, questioning, envious of my vigor in comparison with his failing strength? I could not tell, but there was affection in his eyes and there must have been in mine. I had encountered a really first-rate mind, and I knew that he had not found me wanting. B. died in 1960 at age 65. Mary and I went to Redding and to the red brick, white portaled church, chaste in the sunshine of an April day. Another friend and mentor had gone away.

Sweet Pickles and Sweet Charity

It was not a mistake for me to take the presidency of the Community Chest of Pittsburgh and Allegheny County in 1949, but it *was* a mistake to take it for a self-imposed period of only one year. Howard Heinz and his son, Henry John Heinz II, my contemporary, had been for many years successively the financial and spiritual angels of social work in Pittsburgh. Jack Heinz, grandson of the founder of "57 Varieties," had succeeded in the third generation to the command of that vast food processing enterprise which the ancestor began by preparing horse radish cultivated on a bit of land in Pittsburgh's suburb, Sharpsburg, for a new type of packaged sale. The grandfather had, with respect to pickles and the other "varieties," that prescience which Carnegie had about steel, Hunt about aluminum, Armstrong about cork, John Pitcairn about glass, and Westinghouse about the necessity for stopping railroad trains dependably with air brakes. Westinghouse also, by his development of alternating electric current, made possible the small household appliances by which 20th Century urbanism lives. They were all Pittsburghers and they founded the industries from which came the artifacts by which the century will be known —tall buildings, picture windows, cans, bottles, and gadgets—as surely as the Greek centuries are known by vases and Venuses. It was an era of ruthless enterprisers—those manipulators of railroad stocks on Wall Street were later called "Robber Barons"; those who lived on Pittsburgh's Penn and Fifth Avenues were men whom Thorstein Veblen would have approved, creators of new methods for new products for material well-being.

Unwittingly they created the need for social work. Carnegie's immigrant steel workers and Heinz' female food processors (a turn of the century photograph shows already an apparent acre of them in luncheon table array) were making the new urbanism. Man's production methods, whether of steel, glass, or horseradish, pickles, or beans, were bringing not only concentrations of people in cities but also the inexorable uncertainties of employment by the hour: to the economist, depressions in the business cycle; to the workers, hardship and hunger and harried minds. Thomas Jefferson's idyllic agrarianism was passing in America and there would be new problems of a kind called *social*.

Among industrialists those who make and sell in tons tend to be concerned with distresses of people less than those who make in tons but package and sell in pounds. This is of course an over-simplification, but it roughly fits my observations. For a rationalization, the seller in tons (trainloads of coal, steel beams, or lumber) deals with only a few people; the seller in pounds (cartons of canned soups; glasses of jelly; tins of corned beef; assortments of men's ties or ladies' dresses) deals with many people. For one thing, there are more sellers in pounds than in tons; therefore competition is keener; therefore there is more awareness among sellers in pounds of the eccentricities of buyers, of the vagaries of ultimate consumers—of their likes, dislikes, irrationalities, and foibles. A housewife has no way of knowing, even if she could see it, whether a two-by-four timber is grade A or a cull, but she reacts sharply to the nature of the cap on a ketchup bottle and to the color, odor, and taste of its contents. A shoe merchant will be aware of more people of little, or less than little, privilege than will an iron merchant. The shoe merchant needs to be liked by more people than the iron merchant; he stands in greater need, to employ modern jargon, of a good image.

In any case, when I took the presidency of Pittsburgh's Community Chest I knew that for many years the second generation Howard Heinz had nurtured social work in Pittsburgh and that the second generation R. B. Mellon, who tended the shop in Pittsburgh during the long years when his brother was away in Washington and London, had always written whatever check Howard Heinz had suggested. But R. B. Mellon had died in 1933 and Howard Heinz a few years later. Meanwhile a new personality,

Frank R. Denton, had entered the Mellon complex, now vast in financial and industrial scope—far and away the greatest Pittsburgh, perhaps American, fortune just as was Carnegie's when H. J. Heinz the Elder was founding his lesser, albeit great, estate.

Man With a Blank Cheque

Frank Denton, son of a distinguished Kansas country banker, was doing a stint in Washington with the U. S. Treasury when in 1929 he came to the attention of Andrew Mellon, who sent him to Pittsburgh ostensibly to look into a problem of some Pittsburgh area banks owned by the Mellons. For four decades he was a powerful figure in the financial world of the city and the nation. Whatever Frank Denton looked into would change. Anyone who encountered him, as I have in the industrial world, would find that he acted, when he first encountered a situation, as if change for change's sake were good. I think that in that regard his driving force was intuitive, not conceptual. So it was that when H. J. Heinz II, who succeeded his father as Pittsburgh's social work sponsor, found Community Chest campaigns regularly failing (when I became president only three campaigns in the past 16 years had succeeded and they were in the World War II years in which charity was inspired by patriotism), and when Jack Heinz found mounting criticism of social work and social workers, he decided to invite the establishment onto the Chest Board. Under Frank Denton's leadership the establishment accepted. They acted on the assumption that there were inefficiencies, at the least, and boondoggling, at the worst, which needed exorcising—all to the end that the goals which had been running at about 5.5 million, and failing, should be reduced. When Frank Denton, Arthur Van Buskirk, and Ben Moreell, of World War II Seabee fame, asked me to head the Chest my first comment was, "I would be too liberal for you." Frank Denton replied, "Maybe we need somebody more liberal."

Mary was doubtful. So were several of my intellectual friends, especially J. Steele Gow, who for years played a significant role in Pittsburgh as head of the Maurice and Laura Falk Foundation. He and Mary, who served on a number of social agency boards, knew what I was to learn, that the social workers of that era were skeptical, not to say paranoid, about the establishment; preoccupied with gaining professional status; obsessed with the conviction that their work was a mystique which no layman should inquire into. Many of them were graduates of the prestigious School of Social Work at the University of Pittsburgh, whose Dean W. J. Newstetter, on whom I called as an early presidential act, said, "I know that much of the social work in Pittsburgh is lousy, but I'm not going to let those fellows in the Duquesne Club tell me so." Frank Denton called Newstetter the "Red Dean" after Inge, the then-thought radical dean at St. Paul's; but the appellation was friendly – almost affectionate. Frank was never vitriolic; he never needed to be. He had a blank cheque for social work ideas from R. K. Mellon—a field which was not of primary interest to Pittsburgh's richest and most powerful citizen and of only tangential interest to Frank.

A Plague on Both Your Houses

I soon lost patience with the social workers and, by the same token, I had problems with the establishment's insensitivity. Few if any among them had read Upton Sinclair's *The Jungle* or John Steinbeck's *The Grapes of Wrath*. Such questions as, "Who (sic) are they feeding?" were asked of Robert P. Lane, a social work executive with impeccable academic qualifications and with clipped speech and banker-like manner. All concerned accepted him, the social workers because of his qualifications and distinguished record; the establishment because of his sober good sense and manners in conformity with theirs. He was my consultant. The question about feeding infuriated the social workers because it showed an antiquated "lady bountiful" concept of welfare.

Yet my ultimate distaste was reserved for a woman I liked intellectually very much. Isabel P. Kennedy was Amazonian in stature and nice of mind, except where her social work empire was involved. Then she became the deadly female of the species, cool and deliberate in action, sure in her knowledge of the intricate mechanisms of the 92 private agencies which, with government agencies, made up the Health and Welfare Federation over which she ruled with a ruthlessness which is possible only under cover of democratic procedures. There were enough committees and mimeograph machines to govern the world. Who knows what the case might have been if Xerox had been available?

Isabel Kennedy's work-world was divided between "we" and "they." They were "those men" of the establishment whose duty, she fervently believed, was not to reason why but to do the fund raising in whatever amount was certified by her Federation as the sum total of the "needs of the agencies." By "those men" she meant Frank Denton and the presidents and vice-presidents of the 20-odd largest corporations in Pittsburgh and Allegheny County—except Jack Heinz. "We" were Isabel Kennedy and a small coterie of women, some of them wealthy and socially prominent, and almost all the social workers of the 92 agencies. There was a gap at mid-century between "we" and "they" which varied in width from skepticism and no-confidence to distrust and contempt—a gap which was as great, ironically, as that which was to divide "the poor" and the professional social workers within less than two decades.

There was an ugly word which was often applied to the relations between social workers and certain laymen, usually board members of the several agencies. The word was "captive," meaning that the board member could be counted upon to support whatever program the staff proposed. It was not uncommon for the staff to present at a board meeting, and not beforehand, a 30, 40, 50 page report, calling for action, and to have a captive member prepared to certify its validity and propose instantaneous action. The rationale was that social work is technical and that while board members should supply bodies for meetings so that procedures and the record would be democratically regular, they should not be more than modestly aggressive about participating in the substance of the planning.

Merchant Prince

Jack Heinz was not a captive, as will be presently apparent. He had held every possible high office in Community Chest and Federation. He was acclaimed nationally as Pittsburgh's young industrialist who cared about social work. He attended the national conventions where social workers, like academicians, engineers, lawyers, doctors, morticians, and beauticians gather to relax, re-create, resolve, and look for better jobs. The academicians with academic candor sardonically call such national gatherings "slave markets."

Jack Heinz always entered any meeting, large or small, with

an air of intense urgency—almost always late. He still does. He comes genetically by a handsome, proud head well carried on fine shoulders. A published picture of grandfather, father, and young Jack shows strong family resemblance and nothing gross in face or body in any of the German generations. He came to social work sponsorship naturally, not only because he was a producer of pre-pared foods in tons, and a merchandiser in pounds, and therefore aware of many people, but also because, in the period after his father's death in 1941, social work was a domain which was his by default.

R. K. Mellon, following a suggestion of *his* father that a man should live and work in the community where he had made his money (a precept which the Carnegies and the Fricks with their New York Fifth Avenue places had not followed), R. K. Mellon was devoting himself to banking, aluminum, oil, carborundum, the Pennsylvania Railroad, and business. He was riding to the hounds at Rolling Rock—working hard in Pittsburgh and playing in the 50-60 mile distant Ligonier Valley. Bernard Shaw said that the idle rich became either neurotic or equestrian. The richest man in Pittsburgh was never idle. He *was,* as long as his health permitted, equestrian—certainly never neurotic. He had no problem in mak-ing up his mind about what was good for Pittsburgh. His mind ran to brick and mortar. He saw a good cause in terms of how it was to be housed or in terms of physical environments such as smoke control or parks, not in terms of humanism such as social work. Although R. K. Mellon was a member of the Board of the Community Chest when I assumed the presidency, it was Frank Denton and Jack Heinz who attended the meetings, even if Jack, perforce, had returned from skiing in Europe.

The Equestrian Mind

I once asked a member of the Rolling Rock Hunt, whose horn and hounds and horses' pounding feet we hear when the fox escape route crosses Peppercorn, "What are the satisfactions to be had from riding to the hounds?" "The open air and the feel of a good horse beneath you," he replied. It is a simplistic world for the equestrian. He is a conservationist vigorously protecting as much of the landscape as possible against the invasions of population and promoters—against any and all invasions except the random incur-sions of the fox in flight. The equestrian mind is attuned to the open air and the feel of a good horse— it *is* equestrian, not sensitive to the neuroses of the masses.

Perhaps I can illuminate this difficult exposition by a reference to Pittsburgh's International Exhibition of Modern Art—an institution which incongruously has graced the community since 1896. I must say more about it in another connection, but just now an episode about equestrianism will help. For some years in the late 1930's and early 1940's an art critic named Royal Cortissoz was invited to the modern art show opening—strange as it may seem— to "pan" the exhibition. On one occasion I heard him speak with some approval of the technical competence in Raphael Soyer's "Bus Passengers," their vapid faces poignant in emptiness. Then Cortissoz said, "But why paint people in a bus when there are people who play polo?" The little world of people on horses was more important than the big world of people in busses – to Cortissoz, and at that time to the Pittsburgh establishment.

The people who came to the socially important opening night of the International liked Cortissoz, who ritualistically and invariably sniffed at the modern art at the International. The best way to authenticate this incredible account is to test credulity even more severely. On one occasion the chairman of the Fine Arts Committee invited the elite of an opening night to the hard-by Golf Club and offered "a drink to get the bad taste out of your mouths." Bus Passengers: the picture was as prescient as Edwin Markham's *Man With a Hoe* had been three decades earlier— prescient of Martin Luther King's Birmingham Boycott to determine who could ride in busses; prescient of the whole ugly challenge to the American establishment to come in the 1960's; prescient of dreary, drab faces turned hateful and harmful—but Cortissoz preferred polo, and the elite in Pittsburgh applauded him— not R. K. Mellon. He usually did not come to the openings of Pittsburgh's International Exhibition of Modern Art.

Dichotomies and Ironies

I have always characterized a good bargain as one which leaves both sides a little unhappy. In mid-century social work in Pittsburgh there were certainly two sides: Isabel Kennedy and Jack Heinz believed social work insufficiently supported by our business leaders, who in turn suspected duplications and inefficiencies in the agencies they were expected to support. The parts of the dichotomy were firmly anchored in the Community Chest (organization of businessmen fund raisers) and the Health and Welfare Federation (organization of social workers). I proposed to consolidate the two institutions, and thus merge the functions of determining total "agency needs" with the function of goal setting. I had a broader and more nebulous purpose: to bring social workers and businessmen together in meaningful association for community well-being.

Isabel used her machine to spread the word at home and abroad that a clique of businessmen in Pittsburgh were striving to take over social work. I did not like the results but I admired her methods. She branded us as the aggressors—absurd as it seemed then that business would want to take over social work.

A committee of eight worthy citizens split 5 to 3 against the consolidation. I was constantly urged by Jack Heinz to effect a settlement. I proposed that consolidation be set aside and that Robert P. Lane become executive director of the Community Chest, a post which had become vacant recently—not without some planning on my part. There were other features of the settlement but the essentials were that the Chest businessmen got a Chest executive of their own kind and Isabel, while winning the consolidation issue, got a thorn in her side in Lane, who could dispute with her from a position of technical competence quite equal to hers. The Board voted overwhelmingly, labor and management, to approve my compromise but Brehon B. Somervell, my comrade in arms in World War I, voted No! because he knew, as I did, that Frank Denton, who was absent in Florida although he knew the importance of the meeting, would not like the settlement. Neither did Isabel Kennedy. She always attended Chest Board meetings ex officio and at adjournment she vowed that she and the social workers would not agree to the settlement. Jack Heinz took a few of us to the Pittsburgh Club which, unlike the Duquesne Club, had been in Pittsburgh from times just after the Indians. There Jack was at his persuasive best and Isabel grudgingly agreed. Hard on all these troubles, her husband died and a few years later she died, not without acute pain. I have always regretted that fortune cast us in roles of ideologic controversy.

My role in the Community Chest episode was not to raise more

money, but to reorganize social work along more efficient lines—
to do with less money. I foolishly allowed myself only one year and
failed—in the short range. In the longer range the second of the
two epilogues I now relate makes an important footnote.

Two Epilogues

There are two epilogues. I might have mentioned Edgar J. Kaufmann earlier. He was chairman of the Chest during the year of
my presidency. Edgar Kaufmann was a Renaissance man. He
would have belonged in that cultural revival which flowered in
Western Europe in the days of Leonardo, Michelangelo, and the
Medici. Dominant figure in Kaufmann's, a Pittsburgh department
store, he was a prime example of the community conscience of a
businessman who sells in pounds.

I saw a good deal of Edgar Kaufmann, first and last—in the
office at the store, an unusual office, unique, a bit stern in decor,
yet, like its occupant, not forbidding. He always talked up to people, his secretary of many years once told me. Curiously, a barber
told me the same thing a few days after Edgar Kaufmann died,
saying "He always made me feel important."

People knew his charm and often were awed by it. His own
mother would come to that office armed with a list of important
matters, but, "After he had kissed me on both cheeks, I forgot my
list and came away with half my questions unasked." Miss Clinton,
the patient secretarial guardian of that half austere office, would
say to Edgar Kaufmann on behalf of a coming visitor, if she
favored the visitor, "Don't frighten him," thus confirming my
long-held conviction that a man's best friend is the other fellow's
secretary.

On the ample board which served as unconventional desk his
hand would lie, palm down, seldom lifted, his eyes bright with
wisdom—a gentle authoritarian, rabbinical in the best Jewish
tradition—always talking *up* to people.

I saw him at Fallingwater, the world-known house by Frank
Lloyd Wright; at Palm Springs, his house where desert sun turned
suddenly to cold mountain shadow; in his hotel apartment in Pittsburgh—often changed· to reflect· his keen understanding of the ·
dynamics of style.

It was in his Pittsburgh apartment that I learned of his tolerance for the artist's vagaries. When the house at Fallingwater was building, an artist and his "little wife" were guests. That was 1936. Times were not good. Edgar Kaufmann had commissioned the artist to do a painting. Nothing came. The artist was guest, not painter. The accountant who drew the checks for the stipend complained, "I think the guy is nuts, claiming he can't get in the proper mood." But Edgar Kaufmann would reply, "He'll come out with a painting some day." Twelve years later the painting did come, a huge canvas delivered by the artist's own hand. It was Peter Blume's "The Rock," and it won first prize in the 1950 Pittsburgh International.

As Edgar Kaufmann was patient with Peter Blume so he was with Pittsburgh. He waited tolerantly for Pittsburgh to grow up. He was not always entirely articulate. But no mind at any conference ever wandered when he spoke, for though he was not always obvious he was never trivial.

The concept of a retractable roof for Pittsburgh's summer opera was Edgar Kaufmann's—a mobile roof structure, open to the stars, closed to inclemency of weather, as the case might be— the idea of a practical and imaginative man, with his feet in the box office and his head in the clouds. The retractable roof was one of his many Pittsburgh benefactions. I gave a year to charity in 1949 and gained the friendship, and now the memory, of a cultured, restless, troubled man.

The second epilogue came 20 years later. Whenever I have undertaken an assignment of a public nature I have always written about the experience—not just in retrospect but as a part of the execution of the assignment. I wrote several pieces to articulate my thinking about community chests and charity in Pittsburgh. Occasionally, in later years, a social work executive would call me or write approvingly about the importance of more consolidations, efficiencies, and economies. Writings never die, particularly if one sees that there are adequate copies for those interested at the time of the original occasion. People remember, or reread the piece when clearing files. Although I had written on many subjects, I had written nothing for publication on welfare and social work since the chapter in Beardsley Ruml's *The Manual of Corporate Giving*. I was pleased, therefore, when I was invited to submit one of three position papers for Governor Nelson Rockefeller's Conference in celebration of the One Hundredth Anniversary of the New York State Board of Social Welfare. The other two papers were: one by Daniel P. Moynihan, later President Nixon's cabinet-level advisor on urban affairs, and one by Eveline M. Burns of Columbia University's social work faculty. I was asked to present a businessman's point of view, and so the following account.

Statistics and Poverty

Change and awareness of change do not necessarily coincide. In the decade of 1960 we had almost continuous prosperity in America and yet it was not until that decade that we became aware of the prevalence and permanence of poverty in our American civilization. The case had been like, to employ an incongruous figure, the inability to see the beauty of clouds with normal eyesight. The forms are dislimned, blurred in the vast canopy of atmosphere, until a dark glass separates the forms from the setting, making them discrete in the whole. So it had been, inversely, with the ugliness of poverty. In our normal American eyesight (Christian ethic) we had not seen the shape of poverty because in our folk-thought poverty should not exist.

True, we had seen in the Great Depression of the 1930's that men could be out of work through no fault of their own. Graduate engineers selling apples on the streets drove that lesson home. But we reasoned that our good system had been set askew by bad men. So we heightened the antitrust crusade against monopolies; we curbed Wall Street with federal controls over financing of enterprise; we insured deposits in banks and savings institutions; we provided unemployment and old age relief with money payments; we gave labor the right to unions of their own choosing, with bargaining power of their own; we equipped the Treasury and the Federal Reserve System with whole batteries of monetary, credit, and fiscal controls; and finally, in the Employment Act of 1946 we declared full employment a national policy and set up the Council of Economic Advisors and a watchdog committee in the Congress to make our dreams come true.

Then after all that, the outlines of an ugly and angry cloud became awesomely clear. Suddenly in the 1960's we saw ourselves as through a glass darkly: crime and violence in our streets; growing, other-worldly ghettos; poverty patches, urban and rural, built as tightly into the national complex as the banalities of suburbia, the luxuries of Florida beaches, the automobile graveyards, the bowls of concrete spaghetti—all so unwanted, like stringy hair, psychodelic drugs, and neurotic guitars.

The ubiquity of extensive poverty pockets in America, so I said to the industrialists at Arden House, threatens our domestic peace and—in a bipolar world of confrontation between capitalism and communism — our international prestige. But the flamboyant phrase, "War on poverty," like the foolish slogan, "abolish poverty," has done much harm by lifting expectations inordinately. We have been led astray by statistical definitions of poverty: earlier in the century a family with less than $1,000 per annum—then as the decades clicked away and inflation rode hard on the heels of technology and affluence—$2,000; $3,500; $4,000; $5,500—such a family was poor. And so it was and so it is. This is relative poverty; by such definition we shall always have it, just as Jesus Christ said. Dollar poverty is like a component in an average; there will always be a low number.

My readers are already ahead of me, and so I can be brief. Statistical poverty cannot be cured. Daniel P. Moynihan proposed at Arden House, and elsewhere, earlier and since, the appealing half-truth "that what it means to be poor is not to have enough money." But there is a haunting, gloomy economic certainty. Payments made by society which do not result in corresponding goods or services make for inflation; hence as prices go up the adequacy of the payments goes down; hence larger payments; more inflation; less adequacy; larger payments—and the dreary spiral winds its futile upward way to what height or what collapse we do not know.

Real poverty can be seen and smelled. It can be touched. Trained eyes and compassionate hearts know it when they see it. Social workers with means tests (statistics) and rule books had failed in considerable measure in the short two decades between my Community Chest experience in Pittsburgh and my attendance at the assembly of businessmen at Arden House. The poor had turned on them saying, "Don't tell us what we need; we know that better than you; just give us the money."

Of course, we will care for society's inevitably non-productive members adequately and economically. Children, who have not yet gained competence, and elders, who have lost it, are the most numerous of the charges. Those who are born defective in mind or body and those who become so later are also a large group. Proponents of the welfare state often say that since these groups are a fixed and unavoidable charge on the community any idea of reducing the cost of welfare, of which they are the major partakers, is a delusion. But that reasoning assumes that because the groups are fixed quantities the per capita cost is also fixed. Social workers make that error—not businessmen.

All costs of non-producing members of society, including the costs of kindergartens, schools, colleges, penitentiaries, hospitals, and old age pensions, are paid by taxes upon the earnings of those who work to produce goods and services. These costs have been escalating by leaps and bounds. Abraham Lincoln's education cost almost nothing. He turned out rather well. The education of the ghetto Negro is very costly, contrary to widespread misinformation, often more costly for blacks than for whites. Yet the distinguished Negro sociologist at Columbia University, Kenneth Clark, says that the blacks are turning out badly.

The retirement of my Boone County, Missouri, grandfather at 50 cost society nothing. There was ample room in the house and the porches were wide, and so he sat for 30 years, room and board provided by wife and children. He would be, today, if in any degree competent, in a home for the aged where some geriatricist would be endeavoring to make his life meaningful at costs per hour higher even than a plumber's rate—otherwise in a nursing home to die. He did die in Boone County without any trouble or cost to the authorities. Sitting between my father and uncle Cad behind the beautiful black horses, in the best buggy, brought out for the mile trip to the Harrisburg cemetery, I wept a little. A gentle voice and hand calmed me, and when I looked there was an ancient smile on the face of my wise and funny uncle. Some seven decades later I can speculate that he was unwittingly named for that Grecian Cadmus, who was not unacquainted with grief. I know more mythology now and can fancy that the enigmatic smile was inherited and was saying then as it had said for centuries, "Death is part of life, why weep?"

A society which can provide work for all of its members who *can* work, men and women, will have lower costs for the necessary keep of its children, defectives, aged, and its environment. This is not only because there would be no able bodied people on relief but also because when all who *can* work are working, the whole social climate is healthier, in the physical sense, and happier in the spiritual sense. When there is work for all, there is more play for all, and hence less illness. I once put it to a very large class when I was a visiting professor at the University of Pennsylvania at Philadelphia, "What America needs is more little theaters and fewer big hospitals." George Taylor told me, years later, that the concept took hold and was still mentioned. I stress the qualitative more than the quantitative. If there were work for all who can work, more families would be intact; hence more children would be corrected by love and affection rather than in juvenile court—at much lower costs per capita. If there were more little theaters more people could escape from themselves and identify with "the general," and thus avoid the hypochondria which keeps the doctors' offices and clinics filled.

I know that it is not a perfect world, that there is no way to cure America or any part of the world in one move. I know also that it is a baffling world. Socialist Sweden usually has full employment and complete social security; almost certain international security —and one of the highest suicide rates of any nation. Mary and I have a life-long friend, a distinguished psychoanalyst, who lives in Stockholm. When Alfred Zanker wrote in *U. S. News and World Report,* April 24, 1967, "The Dilemma in Sweden—A Sad Experience With Social Security," I asked her to comment. She replied, "As to delinquency and particularly drug addiction—life in Sweden is for most people a bore—they have nothing to strive for and they can't wait for anything. . . . The high school students are demanding state salaries. . . . The hospitals are packed and the lack of nurses, maids, and MD's is terrible. . . . Nurses who are married have no help for their children and the taxes are so high that they do not even gain money so they won't work—. . . I have several Med students in analysis and they live in state dormitories—each room with bath and a kitchen and a dining room for each eight. Beautiful buildings. The students write on the walls of the elevators—they leave the kitchen like a pigsty—they destroy everything."

Compare Israel, where also there is no unemployment and there the parallel ends. Populated with refugees from all over the world, by a people whose numbers were reduced in Hitler's gas chambers from a world total of 18 million to 12 million—a people who have never been secure since their brief day in the sun under Saul, David, and Solomon—a people who in Israel today are wrestling from the barren sands and rocks from Dan to Beersheba by science and by work the sustenance of life; in Israel, the suicide rate is less than one-fourth of the rate in Sweden. In Israel, three million people are constantly threatened by sixty million Arabs; they suffer a heritage of insecurity and live in the presence of constant risk—yet they have the will to live. I wrote on the occasion of a visit to Israel in 1963, "Never in Israel will one hear that plaintive sigh, 'I am a Jew.' " In Sweden, the riskless society, my friend affirms that "life in Sweden is for most people a bore." The comparison of the two countries shows how difficult it is to generalize, but it is exactly when the raw data seem to defy organization and analysis that we dig the hardest for the theories which take into account all the facts—theories which can guide us to a wiser use of the power of government. Yet we have not found the theory for the perfectibility of the American economy, although it is the best yet known to man.

The American Penchant for Pious Protest

In the late 1950's there was much talk in corporate circles that businessmen must get into politics in order to offset labor's influence. That was a vague concept. No one supposed that the president of U. S. Steel, or of General Motors, or of IBM would run for political office. Rather, it was an amorphous exhortation to corporate underlings to take a keen and active interest in issues which could be settled at the polls. There were some corporate declarations that middle management could have time out to serve in political posts of intermediate importance without loss of opportunities for promotion within the corporations. But the movement ignored the fact that politics is a profession and that what politicians need is campaign money from those who share their views.

I took the occasion, therefore, to propose the repeal of the pious sounding Federal Corrupt Practices Act of 1925. That Act, coupled with some revisions of the Taft-Hartley Act, precluded campaign contributions of any substantial amount from corporations or from labor unions. These restrictions have been widely subverted and the reporting requirements with respect to contributions are given only token enforcement. The whole business is another evidence of American preference for having *virtue* on the statute books regardless of its absence in real life.

There is in America a widespread lingering folk-thought about business and political corruption which was established in the muckraking days of McClure's Magazine. It is the aftermath of the era in which the Standard Oil Company supposedly had the Ohio legislature in its financial palm and Mark Hanna owned President McKinley. Actually, the scholarship of men such as Herbert D. Croly and Allan Nevins has dispelled these charges, but it is the accusation, not the disproof, which lingers.

My proposition was, and is, that "it takes money to get elected." That is the title which *The Atlantic Monthly* gave my article in February, 1960. Experts estimate expenditures in a presidential campaign at several hundred millions of dollars. My proposal to take off the limits would not create an imbalance of financial support as between corporations and unions. The total resources of unions are two and one-half times those of corporations. At the time I was writing, one per cent of corporate profits, before taxes, averaged approximately 376 million dollars and one per cent of all annual earnings of all union members—then over 18 million— averaged 580 million dollars—roughly the amount of union dues which union leaders can tap for political purposes. The ratios have not substantially changed.

I coupled my proposal for the repeal of campaign contribution restrictions with a demand for greatly increased enforcement of requirements for publicity. I urged, and I still urge, that there should be as much actual disclosure of the unrestricted campaign contributions of corporations and unions as there are disclosures of salaries of corporate and union presidents, the amount of corporate profits, the total of union dues collections (a figure which was then (1960) over 600 million dollars). I argued for a frankness and an openness which was typical of men like Mark Hanna at the turn of the century and which, I think, made for a healthier America than the covert activities which subvert the pious legal protests of our present unenforceable laws.

There is a delusion that political money should come from millions of people in small amounts. This delusion was crushingly dispelled in the second Dwight Eisenhower-Adlai Stevenson campaign. Beardsley Ruml, a Republican, out of great admiration for Adlai Stevenson, undertook the National Chairmanship of a financial campaign to gain contributions in small amounts from the common men and women in America. The campaign was a dismal failure. It was a cruel defeat for Beardsley Ruml. As I have said elsewhere, I saw much of him in those days and I think that his unhappy experience with mass fund-raising for politics accelerated the decline in his health. Certainly the experience fortified my convictions that campaign contributions must come from those who are able to make them and whose convictions can be implemented only by the political process. I predict small results from the new (1972) tax law allowing a federal income deduction up to $100 for husband and wife for political contributions. The Federal Election Campaign Act of 1971 did repeal the Federal Corrupt Practices Act of 1925, but the new law again fails to provide effective enforcement of the publicity provisions.

Undoubtedly institutional expenditures for the campaigns of public office aspirants, for the education and enlightenment of federal and state legislators, and for all of those purposes which we call political are controversial. The institutions most frequently involved are business, labor, and foundations. I insist that the safeguards against the undue influence of money in public life are not to be found in prohibition but in publicity. Prohibition is always evaded. There is no security in that. Publicity would bring the institutional conscience into play. There is a danger in my proposal that the institutional conscience might over-react and the funds properly necessary for carrying on the political process would actually be diminished. I prefer that risk, however, to the certainty of unconscionable violation of unrealistic laws against financial support of political convictions. The brand of political dishonor should be removed from the brow of management and of labor alike. To these institutions the housekeeping of our Western World democracy is committed. True, they do not stand for all the human values. Yet by these institutions life is sustained by that token they should suffer no impediment in the parliament of man.

In 1970 the television industry proposed reduced rates for, or outright contribution of TV time for, national political debates. That would be a big step toward recognition of the fact that it takes money to get elected. However, the problem about free television for political candidates is typical of a democracy: how to confine the free medium to the two candidates, one of whom will surely be elected; how to withhold the free facility from a spate of candidates who insist on making a hopeless race. In a democracy rational solutions are often not possible.

Now (summer 1973) Watergate's disclosures prove the case: prohibition does not work; only the assured, immediate glare of the spotlight will enforce moral sanctions. If Watergate produces only limitations on campaign spending, it will have been to no avail. If limitations are removed but inexorable, instantaneous publicity is assured, nature will take a more honest course.

"Hell with the Lid Off"

James Parton, writing in the *Atlantic Monthly* in 1868, made the phrase about Pittsburgh. Earlier Charles Dickens had written, "It certainly has a quantity of smoke hanging about, and is famous for its iron works." Parton's reference was to the skies aflame when the old Bessemer furnaces "blew off." The term applied to that stage of the process in which compressed air is forced upward through the molten pig iron. The oxygen-induced combustion drives columns of flame high into the night—red, orange, and pale white heat mounting awesomely. The Bessemer process was one of the life-changing inventions of modern times. It is superseded now by newer technologies but it was a break-through in its time to a cheap, dependable material which is still the building block of modern times—steel.

From the air in the nighttime the dark zenith afire and the black earth crawling with flame—such was the weird escutcheon of the erstwhile Andrew Carnegie's Steel City. If Pittsburgh had its pillars of fire by night, it had also its ubiquitous smoke by day. The city sits at river-water level where the Allegheny and the Monongahela join to form the Ohio—and in a pocket in the foothills of the Allegheny Mountains. In this pocket, average annual wind velocity is only about seven miles per hour. Thus, there is a natural entrapment of the ashes, smut, smoke, fumes, gases, smells—all now called pollution—from the steel mills, coal burning locomotives, power plants, and the soft coal dirt of household stoves and furnaces. Older Pittsburghers are wont to remember and proud to forget the days, prolonged into the 1940's, when street lights had to be on at noon-time for dimly glowing landmarks in the darkening smog, and men with spectacles arrived at the Duquesne Club looking like ancient apes with accumulations of aerial muck on the cheekbones beneath the lenses. Some of these blights are gone and I shall now say why.

Death of a Man; End of an Era

It was to the rebuilding of smoke-ridden, decaying Pittsburgh that General Richard King Mellon set his powerful hand after World War II. He had served in both world wars, abroad and at home, and was proud of his decorations and rank—lieutenant general— when he retired from the Army Reserve in 1961. When President Eisenhower came in civilian clothes in 1958 to the bicentennial celebration of Fort Ligonier, R. K. wore his uniform.

Ligonier, some 50 miles easterly of Pittsburgh, is the bucolic metropolis of the Ligonier Valley, named for the fort, which was named for a British Field Marshall who never saw the place. The fort was one of General John Forbes' strongholds on that new road which his sizeable army hacked through the Pennsylvania wilderness to take Fort Duquesne from the French—and to found Pittsburgh. On the slopes, at the heads of the dingles, on the promontories, all within the valley, lives the Pittsburgh industrial and financial establishment—year around for young scions, who can endure the daily automobile commuting, and for the retired; weekends for others. R. K. commuted for many years until his death at 70 in 1970.

R. K. had no serious preference for Stravinsky over Stephen Foster; for Modigliana over Monet; for O'Neil over O'Henry— none—because such men and their ideas were not part of his life. About a good horse, a steeplechase (he supported one of the few in the world) a wildlife preserve, or the trees which he would not cut down, though they over-shaded his Huntland Downs, he was constant as a star—as he was about a park for Pittsburgh's city-center where there had been urban blight or about new buildings for commerce or culture or rapid transit, his last goal for Pittsburgh, all quietly and inexorably pursued to the end. He was no Lorenzo, that prototype of the Renaissance man and prince who wielded temporal power in Florence and wrote lyrics, sonnets, and odes as well; R. K. had a good heart and a clear head and he did not evade either the managerial or the philanthropic responsibilities of vast wealth.

I give this fragment of biography and appraisal, not because I am especially qualified. One of his confidants once said to me, "The poor fellow has no friends." He had a very few trusted business and civic advisors. I was not one of them. We were fellow board members of one corporation; occasionally Mary and I would see R. K. and his wife Constance at a large cocktail party or at a formal reception of theirs. He asked me to lunch alone once—some corporate matter. His confidant was right: he who rules must be quite friendless and alone. R. K. knew how easily advantage could be taken in his name or of his generosity. Once when he was going with a party to shoot in Scotland, he told me, "I might just as well put on that Thomas Cook cap." He was not humorless.

I preface the account of my anomalous role in one of the most widely publicized urban renewals in all the world because one cannot understand its successes and failures without knowing about Pittsburgh's unique power structure. That and the reasons for it I do know — as I know the back of my hand. I must dwell intermittently upon the Mellon role in civic Pittsburgh in order that my readers may finally guess—with me—whether an era ended with his death.

Men and Inertia

There is nothing inherent in society which routinely assures change, much less improvement. The case is not different with the forms of life itself. These principles are understood by modern sociologists and neo-Darwinian biologists. *Social* change comes when a dissonant personality arrives on the scene. What makes him dissonant no one knows. *Biological* change also comes seemingly by accident—some error in usual communication within the cell which produces a deviation from the normal genetic pattern (Mendelian mutation). The new form of life *may* be effective in a particular environment. This is called adaptation, the only correct meaning of the often mistreated phrase, survival of the fittest. The new form may be unsuited genetically for the environment. It dies out. More forms of life in the four billion years of life on earth have died out than have survived.

The human hand is probably a mutation. Oswald Spengler

thought so. It is unique – not so suited for clinging to a crag as the talons of an eagle, but human mountain climbers do cling; not so suited for tearing flesh as the claw of a lion, and yet the human hand can tear flesh. (Witness the scene in any domestic relations court on a Monday morning.) And, in addition to possessing in some measure all the many capabilities of other animal append- ages, the human hand is the only one which can make a circle by joining the tips of the thumb and forefinger or which can construct milady's wrist watch, ever so small and always a little off. The marvel is not that the tiny cosmetic does not keep perfect time but that it exists. Man's accidental hand has made him a successful mutation because the hand can make tools—and here is the point —not only for adapting to environment but also for changing en- vironment—and also to enriching environment. The hand that can tear flesh or make a watch can also sculpt a Venus, construct a Calder, or paint a Picasso.

Whether my sociology and biology are right is not really impor- tant. At first intuitively and then rationally, from my understand- ing of my studies, I have been moved in my work, whether in pri- vate or in public affairs, by the conviction that social inertia (the tendency of people to think and act as they have been thinking and acting) is a necessary object of attack. The *people* will *not* rise up and do the right thing. "They," whoever *they* are in the seats of power, are not necessarily wise or conscientious or responsible. The physical law that a body in rest or in motion will remain so *unless perturbed* applies also to society—to a nation, a state, a county, a city.

R. K. Mellon, through his Allegheny Conference on Commu- nity Development, was a perturbing force against social inertia in Pittsburgh for a quarter of a century following World War II. It was Arthur Van Buskirk, who involved me for a time at the heart of the work of the Conference. He was R. K. Mellon's principal confidant in community affairs in the early years of the Pittsburgh Renaissance. He made me a member of the select Sponsoring Com- mittee and of the small and powerful Executive Committee in 1950; vice-president a year later; first vice-president in 1957. In that seven years I performed the work (perhaps, more accurately, made the speeches) which gave me an individual status independ- ent of the Pittsburgh establishment—one which has kept me active in Pittsburgh; in Pennsylvania; sometimes in wider fields until this day. I became a perturbing force within a perturbing force and in consequence—my impatience was a factor—my friendship with Van was strained. The fact remains however—and I am grateful—that Van at one time called upon me for community work which has enriched my life—and, some say, my community.

In one important respect the Allegheny Conference, from its organization in 1943 to the date of R. K. Mellon's death in 1970, was a method for implementing his aspirations for Pittsburgh and his determinations for the betterment of his native city. Of course R. K. could not declare himself publicly for or against this or that or the other for Pittsburgh. In any case, quite apart from diplomacy and amenities, his whole nature would have rebelled against open, personal leadership. Yet there was no effective leadership but his. Let me explain.

Pittsburgh is a city of immigrants. Such is the case, of course, with any modern city suffering the benefits and the burdens of galloping urbanism, but Pittsburgh—was, is, special, earlier for one reason, later for another. Earlier, at the turn of the Century, it was the steel mills which not only lit the skies by night and clouded the city by day but also drew to Pittsburgh with vortical power the needed manpower. Agents of Carnegie and Frick searched Europe, mostly southern and central Europe, for immigrants to man the mills and the mines. "Carnegie placed a value of $1500 on each adult because in former days an efficient slave sold for this sum," says Stevens in Lorant's *Pittsburgh*. Between 1880 and 1900 Pittsburgh's foreign-born population doubled, the largest components from Slavic and Latin countries. Of course, housing, schools, sanitation, and health and recreation services were inadequate. Upton Sinclair's *The Jungle* might have been written about Pittsburgh rather than Chicago, another vortex for immigrants because of the meat packing industry.

Later, and now, an *elite* immigration has been constantly drawn to Pittsburgh, which justifiably boasts itself the city of corporate headquarters. Steel, alloys, glass, aluminum, coal, oil, chemical engineering, electricals, atomic power, transportation equipment, food (Heinz 57-Varieties), barges and banking—these and other industries have national headquarters in Pittsburgh, which must be manned with executive talent. The corporations headquartered in

Adolph W. Schmidt presiding at a meeting of the Executive Committee of the Allegheny Conference. Alone, on the left, Leland Hazard.

My associates in sweet charity. Left to right: Howard Scarfe, Henry J. Heinz II, Edgar J. Kaufmann, Leland Hazard.

Richard King Mellon made many of his benefactions through the Allegheny Conference on Community Development. Dedication of Mellon Square in the heart of the Golden Triangle. Left to right: Leland Hazard, Mayor David L. Lawrence, Richard King Mellon. *Courtesy of Pittsburgh Sun Telegraph.*

Pittsburgh all have nationwide, some worldwide, manufacturing plants or distribution establishments or business affiliations or all of them. There is, therefore, a perennial in-flow of the very best industrial managers from far-flung industrial provinces—men earlier noticed by aging managements or controlling stockholders and finally tapped for the top. They arrive not by steerage in droves but by sky in executive planes. They are nonetheless immigrants in Pittsburgh. Such men are ambitious, cautious, and as specialized as trapeze artists. They have boundless confidence in their ability to run the business well and are as oblivious to all else as is a billiard ball to the table on which it rolls. My description adds nothing to those of others: Adam Smith or Herbert Joseph Davenport, quoted earlier in this book. I have epitomized the classical descriptions here because of the anomaly that for a quarter of a century the rolls of the executive committee of the Allegheny Conference have been star-studded with names of corporate presidents and chairmen — not by academicians, architects, humanitarians, or even professional planners.

Why? Because Richard King Mellon believed in businessmen and not in many others. An invitation to join the Executive Committee of the Conference, of which R. K. himself was never a member, was considered a command performance; the command was literal because it was almost always addressed to the head of an enterprise in which R. K. or the Mellon Bank has a commanding position.

In the early days of the Conference there were some exceptions to the general practice of appointing only corporate heads to the Conference Executive Committee. Arthur Van Buskirk, my friend and sponsor in Pittsburgh, a lawyer and a director in several important financial and industrial organizations, was not a corporate head. A Republican, he was nonetheless in Pittsburgh and Pennsylvania a liberal. He could live with the New Deal when others of his era spent their time in futile fulmination. When he returned from Washington, where in World War II he served as deputy administrator for Lend Lease, he quit a most promising law career to become a governor of T. Mellon and Sons (the inner sanctum of wealth and power) and R. K.'s spokesman for civic interests. His voice on the executive committee of the Conference was the last word. When he was enthusiastic, the resolutions were affirmative and projects moved. When he said, "W-e-l-l-l, let's think that one over," everyone knew that he was either uncertain himself or uncertain about R. K.'s reaction on the issue. This is not saying that he was merely a messenger—far from it. He was astute and imaginative in an operational way. But he was not an *alter ego* for R. K. and he never pretended to be—nor would he guess in advance what his principal might think. When the early physical revamping of the Golden Triangle, particularly the Point, was hanging in the balance, no prime minister ever employed the sovereign's power more ruthlessly than Van. And when the famed collaboration between Republican R. K. Mellon and Democrat David L. Lawrence, then mayor of Pittsburgh, was forming, Van was a municipal statesman far beyond the reach of any partisan thought or influence. In those days when I would say in my speeches in Boston, St. Louis, Detroit or Dallas "a community must be organized at the level of power" the heads would nod, often sadly, I thought, because no other American city had such an undisputed, individual power center as R. K. Mellon represented in Pittsburgh.

The Point, tip of the Golden Triangle where the two rivers form the Ohio, had long been extolled as a site for a park, covered though it was with the blight of anachronistic railroad sidings and warehouses. In 1835 Philip Nicklen, in a little travel book called, "A Pleasant Peregrination through the Prettiest Parts of Pennsylvania," said of the Point that "Pittsburghers have committed an error in not rescuing from Mammon a triangle of thirty or forty acres . . . an unparalleled position for a park in which to ride or walk." Arthur Van Buskirk took the chairmanship of the Conference Committee for the Park, and held it until his death in 1972. But the Park with the Block House and foundations of Fort Duquesne, now sculptured by Ralph Griswold in greensward, true to original outline, was only Van's stepping stone to Pittsburgh's next renaissance achievement after smoke abatement.

Adjacent to the 36 acres of the park were 23 acres of commercial slums, relieved only by the dignified and graceless front of the Pittsburgh Club to which older Pittsburgh, alphabetically, the Arbuthnots, Dennys, Heinzes, Lockharts, McClintics, Olivers, Scaifes, Thaws—only about one third of the short list—repaired. All that 23 acres was stripped and new office buildings of gleaming steel and glass arose in a setting of grass and pin oaks with fountains, walks, and benches — provisions for idleness which were proof of Pittsburgh's maturation, I said at the time. Van, in R. K.'s name, and in collaboration with staunch Democrat David L. Lawrence, Mayor of Pittsburgh, brought it off.

Of course an urban redevelopment law was passed by the Pennsylvania General Assembly, and that law assured the legal power to acquire and erase the blight. But, to induce the Equitable Life Assurance Society of the United States to begin an investment— then one of the largest of such kind in life insurance investment history—required financial muscle. Van had it and used it. He moved great corporate names around like characters on a chessboard: Westinghouse, Jones and Laughlin, Pittsburgh Plate. They and others must take 20-year leases in the new buildings the Equitable would build in Gateway Plaza, then heralded as the world's finest business address. Hilton was taken to a mountaintop in R. K.'s offices from which Gateway Plaza stood out at the point. "You mean, I can build a hotel there?" "Yes." "Sold," Hilton said.

There were rumblings among the power elite. My principal, Harry Higgins, said "Leland, I have an agreement with the Pennsylvania Railroad that their elevated tracks (an unsightly "overhead" running right down a river front boulevard) into our warehouse will not come down for," I forget how many years. Within a year they were coming down. Harry Higgins found out that he could move glass and paint by truck. Again he was doubtful about a 20-year lease in Gateway Center. We were all right where we were, but one day he walked from the Point to the Duquesne Club and found that it took only one half minute longer than from our then location. Van had told me that Harry Higgins was not cooperating. But he did cooperate as did the whole industrial establishment once the word got around that R. K. was determined to change the physical face of Pittsburgh. Was the Mellon complex not heavily invested in all the corporations involved? Of course so, and Van with smiles and a charismatic voice threw his weight around. Now we have the park and one, perhaps one only, of America's finest business addresses. Van was at his best in those years.

Mayor Lawrence too was at his best in those years and he never ceased being at his best throughout his terms as Mayor of Pittsburgh and then as Governor of Pennsylvania. On the platform at a great Democrat Party rally in Pittsburgh's Syria Mosque, he was

238

stricken and soon died. He was the great pacifier of the Democratic Party in Allegheny County, which was always threatening to split apart in internecine struggles. He did it by persuasion and exhortation. He did it by indefatigable attention to the minutiae of politics: luncheons, dinners, rallies, conferences, official greetings—everything from a pause on the street to shake hands to the reception of presidents of the United States. He was Democratic National Committeeman for Pennsylvania.

I once asked him, "Dave, how do you do it?" He replied, "By being in bed by eleven every night." I could believe it. I often saw him leave a luncheon or banquet table after his part of the program had occurred. Everyone understood. It was not discourtesy but the right of a true public servant. Not that he was a saint. He came up through the grimy processes of petty politics but once in power he graduated to superb municipal statesmanship.

Dave Lawrence took his political life in his hands when he collaborated with the mostly Republican establishment in urban renewal. But he was clever. He always took the credit and R. K. Mellon, who disliked publicity, was happy for him to have it. Actually, either would have been helpless without the other. Mayor Lawrence, powerful as he was politically, could never have imposed smoke control on the Pennsylvania Railroad or upon the giant factories exuding black and yellow smoke from the soft coal of Pittsburgh mammoth coal interests. That took R. K. On the other hand, R. K. could never have secured the ordinances from City Council or the laws from Pennsylvania's General Assembly—all so essential to urban renewal. The two men were a silent partnership, and they almost never saw each other. Arthur Van Buskirk was the intermediary. Once I went to Dave Lawrence to ask an introduction to an official in Washington. He picked up the telephone, got his man, stated my problem; then said, "I will appreciate your taking care of Leland Hazard; he is one of those who have helped me in my (sic) program here in Pittsburgh."

Another man, not out of an executive suite, trusted by R. K. was Wallace Richards. He had a background in journalism: messenger for, and at age 20 art editor for, the *Indianapolis News*. He roved in his early years, a reporter in Europe, theatrical publicity in New York, Europe again, supervisor of Indiana's pavilion of Thomas Hart Benton's murals at the Chicago World's Fair (1933).

Wallace Richards was a Phidian subject for sculpture: a comely head and body such as Michaelangelo attributed to David. On the badminton court I preferred to watch Wally rather than oppose him. Quick as an esoteric fly, he could rescue the bird from an ignoble slump to the floor of the court in so minutely split a second that the eye could not follow. And so he was in the Pittsburgh Renaissance, to which he came by way of Greenbelt, Maryland, one of the New Deal's depression-spawned model planned communities. People wondered how the equestrian, brick and mortar Richard King Mellon could take into his inner sanctum such a visionary. I do not pretend to know why, but the fact was solid. Wallace Richards is said to have conceived the Allegheny Conference. He was its early secretary. Arthur Van Buskirk, financially conservative (Wally always said never think of money first), would pause respectfully when Wally spoke at the Allegheny Conference table. Wally represented an era — my era — when planning was dream-like and practical in the poetic sense. When an unrelieved tension—or perhaps too many cigarettes—struck him down in his early fifties, I mourned a lost spiritual ally. He knew what Yeats knew when he wrote a poem "To a Wealthy Man Who Promised a Second Subscription to the Dublin Municipal Gallery If It Were Proved the *People* Wanted Pictures." Yeats advises his philanthropist to let the people "play at pitch and toss" while you

> Look up in the sun's eye and give
> What the exultant heart calls good
> That some new day may breed the best
> Because you gave, not what they would,
> But the right twigs for an eagle's nest!

Wallace Richard's intensity about Pittsburgh's renewal was all too soon reflected in hypertension in his body. He had launched a system of publicly built and owned parking garages; he had revived the moribund Carnegie Museum and had changed it from little more than a warehouse for a large archaeological and natural history collection, distinguished enough, into brilliant and meaningful displays, which often served to relate the past to the Pittsburgh present. He did not hesitate to depict Pittsburgh's vanishing, yet lingering, grit and grime—subjects which for generations had been taboo. His dramatic exhibits showed causes and suggested cures.

Wally and I were linked in impatience—equally, perhaps imprudently, contemptuous of cautious lethargy. Park Martin, the stable, knowledgeable, competent engineer who was executive director of the Conference, more than once complained to me that, "Wally is capable of talking down to people." But Wally's verve outweighed his imprudence and his inspirations overbalanced his arrogance. Planners have no choice but to be arrogant. They deal in the stuff of dreams and their nightmares are peopled with inert citizens. Would the Athenians have risen up to build the Parthenon, even in ruins one of the world's most beautiful buildings? No! The record shows that it was the mind and will of Pericles which decreed one of man's noblest architectural expressions. Would the Parisians have rebuilt Paris in the mid-nineteenth century? No! It was that misunderstood man, Napoleon III, who willed that Haussmann should make Paris a city not only beautiful but also fit for modern times. Wally knew such facts.

Renaissance or renaissance: Which in Pittsburgh?

The rebuilding of Pittsburgh's Golden Triangle was in full advance. Van was happy. In those days there was a bounce in his step and his energies seemed boundless.

In May, 1951, *The Atlantic Monthly* published a piece (not mine) on the Pittsburgh renaissance, a consequence in part of the low-key but effective public relations program of John Grove. He believed in the Pittsburgh renaissance from the outset and he remains a valued officer of the Conference until this day. The *Atlantic* piece was disturbing. The writer said, "In the minds of some thoughtful Pittsburghers there lurks the suspicion that the work of the Conference has laid too much emphasis on the materialistic side," and added, "There is no question of the truth of this accusation." Van was concerned. Edward Weeks was invited to Pittsburgh to address a small group of which I was one. The first reaction of Conference officials was that there must have been some misunderstanding—something which could be cleared up. Yet a lingering question had been unleashed, "Was the famed Pittsburgh renaissance merely a building boom?" For the record, I was not one of the *Atlantic's* "thoughtful Pittsburghers."

One evening at a cocktail party in the valley, Arthur van Buskirk, his face and whole body slightly vibrating, as was usual when he had set a course, said, "Leland, we have a marvelous plan for the annual Conference dinner." That was an occasion which occurred, still occurs, in mid-fall, at which a report is made to the Conference Sponsors, who have just met within the hour before to elect officers and attend other business. Community leaders, whether or not Sponsors of the Conference, are invited and almost everybody comes—several hundred. The report may be retrospective or prospective.

Van continued in the presence of Mary and several others. "Gwilym Price," then President of Westinghouse Electric Corporation, "will address us on the industrial future of Pittsburgh, and then you will charge us with our cultural responsibilities." The plan, on its face valid enough, was a reflection of the sting in the *Atlantic* article. Furthermore, both Mary and I reacted skeptically. Van's words and manner suggested that I was to play the role of "scold to a community" which he did not really think needed the scolding. I was nevertheless intrigued. I knew much more about the intellectual community than Van did. Mary and I, thanks mostly to Mary, had friendships and associations in the schools, colleges, universities, and in the Pittsburgh community of arts and letters which most of the industrial and financial establishment would have eschewed. I knew that there would be sympathetic ears for what I would say. In any case, it has always been hard for me to resist a big, captive audience. So, when Van pursued the idea and John Grove began to put the program in a more dignified scheme, I accepted.

Mary undertook the research and came up with plenty of invidious material. My thesis was that no community could have a future unrelated to its past. A writer in Harper's magazine (to match the *Atlantic*) had called Pittsburgh, as late as 1930, "on the whole, barbaric." Neville Craig, both first and last important street names, Editor of the *Pittsburgh Gazette,* had said a hundred years earlier: "The fact is, there is not enough of a drama loving population in this city to support a respectable theatre, and we are glad of it. We think it speaks well for the good taste and morality of our inhabitants." Today (1972) there is little and uncertain commercial theatre in Pittsburgh. The community theatre, called *The Playhouse,* has surrendered its "little theatre" character—insufficient patronage and financial support.

The night of the occasion came, September 15, 1952. The setting was the huge marble and gilt foyer to the beautiful Carnegie Music Hall—every table filled, a stellar dias with R. K. Mellon in attendance, as was his wont in those days.

I paid tribute to the smoke clearance and the physical renewals, saying, what is happening in Pittsburgh is frequently called a renaissance; and so it is if the word is spelled with a small "r"; nothing short of a rebirth of spirit and determination could have produced such stupendous rearrangement and reconstruction of the City's physical facilities.

But, I continued, what about renaissance in Pittsburgh if the word is spelled with a capital "R"? For comparison, I suggested, take the role of the scholar in the Renaissance of those three great centuries from the 14th to the 16th; Florence, Milan, Pisa, Venice, Siena, vied with each other for teachers and scholars; poets, painters, philosophers were the intimates of merchant princes who themselves might write poetry without impairing their credit; when rival universities asserted conflicting claims to the services of Soccini, a professor of civil and canon law, the city of Siena prepared for war to defend its claim to the learned man. The incomes of such professors were the envy of prosperous merchants.

Taking the University of Pittsburgh for an invidious comparison, I said that no such wonder exists there. Its building is high, 42 stories of impeccable Gothic; its enrollment is high, 22,000 students; its tuition is low; the salaries of the professors are low. Deficits beset its administration. It is losing good members of its faculty and adequate replacements are difficult to obtain. Such was the case then.

George Westinghouse and William James were contemporaries. What Westinghouse gave to America needs no elaboration. What James gave to America needs some tracer material to identify the origins of those thoughts and convictions which move and mold our lives—the philosophy of the practical. The point is not the validity of James' philosophy, but that for almost 40 years— 1872 to 1910—he thought and wrote from his chair on the Harvard faculty, enjoying an economic and social status which was not inferior to that of his non-academic contemporaries in Boston. If now, decades later, we are moving to an arrangement of rewards and values such that a new airbrake has a better chance to emerge that a new philosophy, the cultural outlook is not good. Then I referred to Conference reaction to the sting about the low estate of culture in Pittsburgh. The Conference, beginning in that methodical and cautious fashion which always characterizes men who work with heavy technology, where mistakes and ill-founded enthusiasm can be so costly, had sponsored an inventory of existing cultural activities in the Pittsburgh area.

The inventory was on the tables as I spoke. Three hundred and fifty-five cultural organizations were listed, their history, activities and present status described. From an Author's Club of Pittsburgh, a Dickens Fellowship, an Organ Player's Club of Pittsburgh, a Society of Sculptors, an African Violet Society of Greater Pittsburgh, a Men's Garden Club, a Homestead Russian Orthodox Male Chorus, the Goose Lookers organized to watch the migration of the Canada Goose, and the Old Westmoreland Rifles devoted to the collecting and shooting of old muzzle-loading rifles and pistols, the Inventory proceeds through the alphabet and through the categories of Art, Ballet and Dance, Drama, Literature, Music, Sculpture, Colleges and Universities, Elementary and Secondary Schools, Cultural Institutions, Garden Clubs, Historical Societies, Leisure Time Groups, and Hobby Clubs, Libraries, Women's Clubs. This was the Conference's proof of culture in Pittsburgh. The audience smiled.

I concluded, Pittsburgh had a poet, Haniel Long. He left some words solid as the blocks of granite in Richardson's distinguished Allegheny County Court House.

"The great man sees how limbs and leaves come out of a tree; he knows . . . the future city lies in the future of its least citizen; its least citizen is bound by tears and blood to its greatest citizen, . . ."
". . . what is a city?
Pittsburghers, what is Pittsburgh? It is the total of the relationships of us who live in Pittsburgh: is nothing else, now and forever."

Then I closed with the doubt that a community could plan for culture as for a park or a building. Culture is not a point of arrival but a receding horizon. There is some ferment in the rise of excellence which transcends optimism or pessimism; hope or fear; even fatalism. Perhaps it is just chance—the only certainty in the universe.

I have come to realize, years after that speech and tens of

thousands of miles of travel, that one of the marvels of the Western World is our belief in the worth of effort, despite chance. Unlike the Muslem or Hindu, who eschews effort because Allah or one of India's 50 million gods (the figure is correct) has predetermined the end, Western man practices trial and error, believing that the travail itself imports the reward.

My speech was heartily received. R. K. Mellon, never given to perfunctory praise, said to me on the spot, "This was a little bit different tonight. Some people had tears in their eyes." The compliment was interestingly anachronistic. One of the American frontier tests of oratory or preaching in the 19th and early 20th centuries was the ability to bring tears to the eyes of the audience. All three newspapers carried front-page and full accounts, and all three promptly published laudatory editorials. It was at once obvious that latent in Pittsburgh was a yearning which Andrew Carnegie earlier had detected. Lorant quotes from Carnegie's letter about Pittsburgh to Gladstone: "It has never been anything but a center of materialism: has never had a fine hall for music, nor a museum, nor an art gallery, nor public library, and yet the result (Carnegie had supplied in the meantime all those facilities) proves that there has been lying dormant the capacity to enjoy all these."

Arthur Van Buskirk had caused the Conference to create a fourth standing committee—one on cultural affairs. It became widely known as Committee No. 4. I was the first chairman. Meanwhile, and perhaps unfortunately for me, I became unjustifiably identified with the whole of the Pittsburgh revival — not just the cultural aspirations of a minority. Invitations to speak in other cities came in, some directly to me: Boston, St. Louis, Dallas. Some requests were referred to me by Van. My "hard copy" produced journalistic convictions of a role for me in the Conference more powerful than the facts would sustain. I was well aware of the awkward situation in which my speech-making had cast me.

In the mid-50's there was a simplistic, almost naive, interest in urban renewal. The concepts were scarcely more sophisticated than programs for clearance of slums, human and commercial. Yet, the foundations were being laid for high-level preoccupation with urbanism, later recognized as a complex of factors not susceptible of cure in one move. For example, not until 1969 did the

Allegheny Conference formally declare that rapid transit had a role in urbanism.

In High Gear

However casually the Conference may have taken Committee No. 4 internally, official and public bodies speedily adopted the committee as the avenue of approach to the Conference for projects considered cultural. Mayor Lawrence had a very able man-Friday, John P. Robin—creative, imaginative, articulate. He wrote the mayor's speeches, but he was more than a speech writer, a person in his own right, whom the mayor moved about in a number of key positions.

In early 1951 Jack Robin was serving as Executive Director of the Urban Redevelopment Authority of Pittsburgh. Mayor Lawrence was the chairman. Such was the high level of rapport in those days between the Democratic and the Republican establishments whenever community betterment was involved. Opponents within the local Democratic Party challenged Dave Lawrence frequently, charging that he was sacrificing party interests to public improvements for which Republicans would get the credit. Dave always faced them down—always won. He became Governor of Pennsylvania on the wings of his philosophy that what is good for the community is good politics. He would often say, "To an ordinary politician like me—it looks thus and so." He was far from an ordinary politician.

Jack Robin wrote me when I was chairman of Committee No. 4 about a program under state and federal laws to clear an area of 105 acres of slum and blight (1951). This episode provides an insight into the then admirable methods of the Conference. The federal law subsidized a renewal project by reimbursing an urban redevelopment authority for any deficit in the cost of slums or blighted area acquisition remaining after the cleared land had been sold to redevelopers. The Conference in such a project would take the lead through its lawyers and other agencies in working out the details—immensely complicated. In the case in question private philanthropy, city, county, state, and federal funds would be commingled to erect at the heart of the former slum area a civic arena to house summer light opera, sports events, circuses, sunrise prayer meetings, Billy Graham, hockey, Jehovah's Witnesses, and every good or great event which could attract 14,000 people or any substantial portion of that number.

In all such projects, after all the major details had been settled and the political and Conference leaders considered a project architecturally, financially, and politically feasible, then a high level assemblage of Pittsburgh's industrial and financial leaders would be convened, often at the Duquesne Club, to make the announcement—sometimes to raise additional funds or sometimes just to test establishment sentiment. On this occasion, as on others, I was to make the announcement. I found myself by that time developing a tendency to whimsy and to analogies to classical times and circumstances. The architects for the proposed arena had been instructed to produce a world's first, particularly a vast dome which would open to the stars for summer light opera. Edgar Kaufmann had given the first million toward the 22 million dollar project and ultimately he gave another million to provide the controversial opening and closing dome. The show could go on—rain or stars. When the dome first opened at the dedication years later, there were tears—the sight was so majestically beautiful.*

The Romans had in their Pantheon something of the sort. Theirs was a vast circular structure with a great aperture in its dome always open to the heavens; so that, as the Romans thought, their gods could enter. They gave their Pantheon a spiritual quality, according to their lights.

Our marvel, I said, the first of its kind in the world, will replace a slum where men and women now live in misery and degradation; and its opening to the heavens may be closed against inclemency, thanks to Westinghouse, Steinmetz, and Edison.

How little we understood in those days that there was more to a slum than met the eye! It was said by John Grove and Jack Robin that the removal of the people, mostly Negroes, was accomplished smoothly and with consideration, but all of that was long before our "hot summers." Today, one of the redevelopments in the arena area is Alcoa's Washington Plaza, a good apartment building for top and middle management executives, including

---

*The great domed structure has become largely a sports arena. The Civic (Summer) Light Opera is housed in a gorgeously refurbished motion picture house named Heinz Hall—a monument to that family of many benefactions. This hall is also the home of Pittsburgh's world famous symphony orchestra.

Negroes, but the residents are concerned about violence from a Negro ghetto community hard by.

In High Gear: Educational Television

Three women and one man and a penchant for lost causes involved me in educational television, now some 20 years ago. I say lost causes, because in the postwar flush of victory, an America, short of so many material things, had come to identify television with cosmetics, gasolines, automobiles, and cleaning agents. Television was a business, a good business, and a proper business. But it was not content to be just that. It was putting in juxtaposition for merit by osmosis such dissonant program elements as soap and Shakespeare; shaving creams and Socrates; Christmas cards and Christmas carols; vitamins and virtues—such a reaching of the material for support from the spiritual that what should be the clean hard lines of our culture were being blurred. Indeed, such was the zeal of the advertising agencies that frequently one could not be sure whether the soap was to gain luster from Shakespeare or vice versa. And I have not even mentioned the absence—utter absence—on commercial television of any alternative for children to the clatter of anachronistic hooves in the video violence of the Westerns. Even so I might have pacified myself with a letter to the editor, except for three women and one man.

It was not that I objected then, or that I object now, to culture on commercial television, if the offering is sufficiently disassociated from the advertised product. Much excellence is made available on the profit-making channels. But in any case, I had a second point. I believed then, as I do now, that intellectual minorities, for whom advertising agencies dare not care at all, should have their fair share of television. Such minorities in all ages have made the critical difference. They have ever been the leaven of society. And they cling always to a precarious position—threatened with what de Tocqueville called the tyranny of the majority.

And the three women: Leonore Elkus, a tough-minded intellectual, convinced me of the cultural need; Carolyn Patterson, one of those stalwart public school principals we all gratefully remember, convinced me of the educational importance of the new medium— the first wholly new medium since printing 500 years before; Dorothy Daniel, journalist and radio personality, whose husband,

Royal, Editor then of Pittsburgh's *Sun-Telegraph,* had married her and then fired her from that newspaper's staff, convinced me that she could put together the initial programming, and she did— these were the women. The man was Mayor David L. Lawrence, who had used his influence in the fight at the national level to reserve television channels, some 12 per cent of all of them, for non-commercial educational broadcasting. He had appointed a committee of educators and others to activate Pittsburgh's Channel 13, assigned by the Federal Communications Commission for community television, provided the community would raise the money.

Now Pittsburgh is not exactly a matriarchal community, as I have said, and a mayor, even such a distinguished one as David L. Lawrence, was after all only a mayor. Three women and a politician were not enough for so new and suspect a community venture as non-commercial television. They knew that; and I knew it.

We must look to the Conference for a blessing from those unofficial city fathers who sat on the Executive Committee. I proposed to the Conference that the activation of Channel 13 be approved in principle. There was opposition. Who would manage the station, what influences, subversive, Communist, Democratic, or otherwise objectionable, might gain control? Westinghouse Broadcasting Company presented a plan for shared time if the valuable Channel 13 were assigned to it for commercial purposes. There were faces black with feeling about the Conference board. It was not fun.

After weeks of tension there came the crucial day of a special meeting of the Executive Committee of the Conference on July 14, 1952. Park Martin, the influential Executive Director, made a report affirming the feasibility of community television. Doubts persisted, those of Arthur Van Buskirk not the least. But no one from Westinghouse was present, apparently by design. I had called Gwilym Price, then head of Westinghouse: "Bill, do you say I should abandon my efforts for educational television in Pittsburgh?" The reply: "No, Leland, I don't." In those brief words WQED received its first big contribution. Westinghouse, if its shared-time plan—utterly inadequate for educational television, of course—had been approved, would have had Channel 13 for nothing. Ultimately Westinghouse paid over 10 millions for Channel 2, then owned by DuMont; gave to WQED the tower which it had built in anticipation of getting 13; and has been a good and generous friend ever after.

Then came the Conference resolution, an uncertain blessing. But it was more a blessing than a curse, and that was all I hoped for. Thus the world's first community educational television station was approved in principle. It remained only to raise a half million dollars for the physical facilities and some uncertain amount for operations.

Those around town who were knowledgeable about television laughed at us. Suppose we did raise the half million for capital requirements. Where would we get the million dollars every year to pay the operating costs? We did not think it would be as much as a million per annum. But we did not know. We were like children, believing that something we wanted so much would somehow come.

Adolph Schmidt, then President of the A. W. Mellon Educational and Charitable Trust, gave us $50,000 for seed money—money we could spend for just exploring ways and means to realize our dreams. Dorothy Daniel opened an office in the Civic Building and began writing letters and issuing statements asserting that Pittsburgh would have educational television. How she knew it, I shall never know. I did not know. Later she told me *she* did not know it.

One day Robert B. Hudson came to the A. W. Mellon Educational and Charitable Trust and to me and said that the Fund for Adult Education, under a grant from the Ford Foundation, would give WQED $150,000 if we could raise matching amounts locally. In those great tomes where saints set down marks to record the good deeds of men and foundations and heavenly hosts sing praises, the Ford Foundation shall be called blessed for ETV; and so will the A. W. Mellon Educational and Charitable Trust for its next $100,000; and so also a foundation the reader will not have heard of, the Arbuckle-Jamison Foundation.

One day George Roth Craig, one of those salt-of-the-earth lawyers, told me that he was a Trustee of the Arbuckle-Jamison Foundation and that a little more than $100,000 remained in that Fund. Arbuckle, a name charged with memories for me, the name of a coffee of whole beans packed in beautiful chocolate brown bags.

Still afraid of some dogs and some older boys, I often traveled the block to Mr. Rene's store where in exchange for 15¢ he would send me back with a pound of the beans to be ground by me in an old fashioned hand mill. And now we were to get some of Mother's money back for Pittsburgh's ETV. We did—$100,000— thanks to George Craig for that and much more of aid and comfort during the intervening years.

Pittsburgh Plate Glass Company owned a valuable property hard by the campus of the University of Pittsburgh. It was to be given to the University and I asked Harry Higgins to earmark it for our ETV embryonic station. He agreed and Chancellor Rufus Fitzgerald honored the request.

Now we had money and properties of more than a half million dollars. Could we get on the air? There were endless technical questions. Buying equipment for a broadcasting station is not like selecting furniture for a living room. Even that is often not easy. Western Pennsylvania's terrain is bad for television. There were difficult choices. Suppose we made the wrong decisions and wasted some of our precious money. In all of this, John T. Ryan, Jr., himself a distinguished engineer, was a tower of strength. He and his organization, Mine Safety Appliances Company, saw us through. The great day came when we had a successful test pattern on the air.

Dorothy Daniel thought up the name. Quod erat demonstrandum—that which was to be demonstrated—WQED. She rode the circuits of women's clubs, the PTA's, the school systems. In those days the corporations would not look at us. Educational television—what's that? Finally Dorothy got together about $120,000, for the greater part in two-dollar donations—upwards to 60,000 people in Pittsburgh wanted Educational Television.

WQED took to the air on April 1, 1954. Frieda B. Hennock was in the studio. She was a woman more deadly than any of her male colleagues on the Federal Communications Commission. A lawyer, she had fought with skill, cunning, and utter conviction to get set aside for non-commercial television 12 per cent of television channels for ETV—some 242 out of 2,000. This was a monumental achievement, because, unlike printing presses, there is only so much television. If anyone who had the inclination could own a television station and broadcast, there would be bedlam. Every set owner knows that government separates the channels and that there are only a few to each community. Television, the most powerful of all communications media—because it appeals simultaneously to the eye and the ear and instantaneously upon the event —is the first unique development in communications since Gutenberg. But suppose his press and all others since had been controlled by advertisers. The pages of the printed Bible which bears Gutenberg's name would have been interspersed with appeals to use this or that medieval nostrum, or money-back guarantees from alchemists if their secrets did not change lead into gold or restore the prowess of spent Don Juans. Frieda Hennock had conducted a preventive rescue operation and we in Pittsburgh were the first community to reward her successful efforts.

There is a delusion, I said in the November 1955 *Atlantic,* that all television must be entertaining—as if all I.Q.'s from 65 to 165 could be entertained alike and as if all books should be written in the mode of Elinor Glyn or Mickey Spillane. (Later it would be Roth's *Portnoy's Complaint.*) This delusion is a heritage from the movies and from the radio, which fell almost wholly to commercialism. But a necessity for popular appeal is no more inherent in television as a means of communication than in the human vocal cords or the hand that writes.

There were, and are, other delusions: that education is not entertaining—as if the classes of the great teachers have not always been crowded, even by those who had no plan about learning beyond the desire to qualify for the university club back home. Dr. Frank Baxter, a contemporary in 1955, had responded almost mournfully to the suggestion that his regular classroom instruction in Shakespearean plays be put on television. He and CBS were equally astounded that the audience quickly reached 400,000.

Another delusion was, and is, that every television audience must be large—as if an Arthur Miller play could attract at any one performance as large an audience as a World Series baseball game. This sprang, springs, from the natural desire of the advertiser. When he talks about his product, he wants the world to listen. Why not? But it does not necessarily follow that there should be no television programs at all except those which attract the masses.

There was, is, the delusion that educational television must compete with commercial television and will therefore fail, because where would the money come from for another Ed Murrow (now it would be Eric Sevareid)? And there was, is, the delusion that charitably supported television should not, if it could, compete with commercial television. One Pittsburgher, a power in the financial world, said in 1955, "I am against it because it is not commercial." This naiveté made me realize how highly the ideological reflexes to television were already conditioned—as if the medium belonged exclusively to business. Even good friends of the movement faltered on this point. They complained of the lack of realism of the Federal Communications Commission in barring all advertising from educational television. They speculated about schemes for consolidation between education and commercial stations—only to learn that the very hours which are needed by God are also needed by Mammon. I asked, "Why should television be considered the exclusive property of the bazaar?"

There was the delusion that commercial television with its public service time would provide ample opportunity for cultural offerings if only the educators have the wit to grasp the nettle. But at what hours and for how long? There would be no point to offering courses by television at hours when millworkers are on shift, when housewives are in the kitchen, when teenagers are in the sandlots —no point to beginning what cannot be finished. Of this I was sure. I watched the screen at all hours and in many places—and I knew. As an advertiser I would have been no better myself; I would get my product as commingled as possible with the emotional and intellectual appeal of some eternal truth or beauty. In my crusade I viewed with alarm and struck with sarcasm. The following personal concoction, I said, was no exaggeration of a daily television screen:

Lady Macbeth:
Here's the smell of the blood still:
all the perfumes of Arabia will not
sweeten this little hand.
Gentlewoman:
'Tis strange indeed, the lady's blind,
It's not perfume she needs to find;
But Acme Flakes within the pan
Will do the job and also scan.

Then in speaking I would shift to sonorous sobriety. "I know that sound thinking and enduring emotions are not induced by a bedlam of irrelevancies. And I believe that television, which appeals simultaneously to the eye and to the ear, and instantaneously upon the event, has potential for men's minds not less critical than that of atomic energy for their bodies."

There is the delusion, my argument continued, that people will not give money for what they can get free. But they will; they have done so already in Pittsburgh, St. Louis, Chicago, and other cities and communities. Churches are free; a person could pray for a long time without suffering ostracism as a free rider. But enough people give money to keep the churches going, not as a purchase of service but from a conviction of the worth of organized religion. The case has been the same with hospitals, colleges, and social work. Voluntaryism in cultural affairs is an American way which is not defunct. Indeed, it is a positive principle—a bulwark against statism.

In Pittsburgh a majority of our television board had discouraged the idea of an all-out appeal for legislative financial support. Admittedly we knew that the legislature would turn us down, but over and above that we knew the importance of developing local community standards for this new cultural medium. Poor but proud we remained. This is not to say, we asserted, that municipal and state grants-in-aid are not to be sought, once the soundness of the local controls has been proved the hard way. The decentralization of decision-making power is as essential for educational television as for education itself, for health and welfare, and for business. Only by these means can the force of community television remain dynamic—free of bureaucracy.

Now that we were on the air, soon followed in 1954 by other pioneer community stations, Boston, San Francisco, Chicago, what would we do with our air time? In some respects we did a more imaginative job in those very first years than we have done since. We knew that one-half the students who entered American high schools did not stay to graduate, and so we opened a High School of the Air. In collaboration with local and state school authorities we offered by television systematic courses in algebra, English, American history, and other subjects. We had enrollments in the hundreds. The fee was $5.00 a semester. Of those who took the official examination, 71 per cent passed and obtained their high school diplomas. We ran a school for drop-outs.

In the same vein, knowing that 10 per cent of high school students fail in some subject each year and that it is extremely costly to the public school systems for them to make up the failure in already overloaded classrooms, again in collaboration with the school systems, WQED began an experiment in make-up work. Here was a case in which we programmed one hour and a half per day, five days a week, at prime time, for only 323 people, the number of high school student enrollees. Out of that number, 265 took the state prescribed examination and 78 per cent passed. We had proved the point. At that time over 8,000 high school students in our area were failing in one or more subjects each year. We estimated that television could cure these failures at less than 10 per cent of the cost of any other method. Thus, we said, these less apt young students would be able to keep pace with their fellows and at the same time get off the taxpayer's bounty.

With a grant from the Ford Foundation, we carried out an experiment in total teaching by television. Fifth grade arithmetic, reading, and French were taught in nine demonstration schools. The young students whose parents consented viewed television screens in the classrooms but saw and heard a teacher who stood, not in the classroom, but in our studio. For the first time in all history the same sights and sounds of teaching which reach the child in the classroom could reach the mother at home. Thus a breach which occurs as the child has experiences foreign to the mother would be ameliorated.

We predicted lower costs of education for taxpayers; keeping educational pace with the population explosion; multiplication of the influence of great teachers; more economic design of school housing; at long last, more effective adult education. With respect to the last item, Dorothy Daniel would say, "People will not come out to settlement houses and other public places to expose their lack of education. They do not wish to publicly admit the need." Dorothy was an earthy person; she would say, "Adults want to get their education in secret and without putting on a clean shirt."

Don and Art, two inspired teachers of polytechnics, started on a basement floor with a sawbuck and the simplest tools and moved to quite sophisticated wood and metal working. Their "Shop Talk" provided systematic utilitarian aid to home making in an economy of prohibitive costs for small jobs.

Margaret Bourke-White put me on a stool at the WQED studios and said, "Talk to me, Mr. Hazard." I did.

Arthur Van Buskirk.

King Friday the Thirteenth, Mister Rogers, and Queen Sara with Prince Tuesday.

Fred and Joanne Rogers with their two sons.

At a birthday party for Martha Graham. At the right, John F. White, President of National Educational Television and former General Manager of WQED, when he gambled our entire treasury of $35,000 to produce Martha Graham's "A Dancer's World".

In Martha Graham's studio in New York, Mary watches a rehearsal for "A Dancer's World".

Mary becomes a Distinguished Daughter of
Pennsylvania, 1973.

Unfolding the banner on a windy day for Pittsburgh's Three Rivers
Arts Festival, 1964. Left to right: Mary, Adolph W. Schmidt, and
Maria Conderman. *Courtesy, Pittsburgh Post Gazette.*

Steel sculpture by Anders P. Anderson constructed on the site of
Three Rivers Arts Festival, June 1974, and then erected at Peppercorn
by the sculptor.

Edwin Peterson, the University of Pittsburgh's nationally known teacher of creative writing, reduced on our screen the mysteries of good writing to their honest, unpretentious simplicities. Ben Spock, in those days confining himself to his profession and not so distempered about Vietnam, presided for months over an informal, unrehearsed panel of mothers learning with their viewers, case by case, the attitudes and techniques which make childhood—and adulthood—flower.

Our real triumph was the "Children's Corner." Dorothy Daniel had told me that she had a program which was of professional quality which could go on our air immediately we opened. Daniel S. Tiger, a puppet on the fingers of the inspired Fred Rogers, was president of "The Tame Tiger Torganization." He was a humanitarian tiger, with a scratchy, minuscule voice. There were other characters in the Children's Corner: X the owl, King Friday the 13th, and others. There were songs by Fred Rogers, rendered by the puppets. We had no idea what the audience was. We knew we were getting letters from mothers, saying, "Thanks for baby-sitting."

Dorothy Daniel and Fred Rogers decided to have an open-house for Daniel S. Tiger, expecting some hundreds of children, but the queue was blocks long and even Dorothy's ingenuity was acutely tested to supply refreshments.

Fred Rogers' show is today the oldest continuous show for children on the North American continent. For awhile he took it to NBC but commercialism was not for him. For awhile he took it to CBC in Canada, only to return to his native heath. Today the modern version of the Children's Corner is Mister Rogers' Neighborhood, viewed by millions of American children—and produced at WQED. Fred Rogers, a master of divinity, a psychologist, a humanitarian, the first Presbyterian minister ever to be ordained without having served a church pastorate, is a unique person himself. His programs express to children the Christian concept of the worth of the individual. He says to his young audience—everyday, "You make each day a special day by just your being you. There is only one person in the whole world like you and I like you just the way you are." No person so precious and so powerful as Fred Rogers could ever have survived on commercial television.

We cannot claim, now more than a decade later, successes in

education comparable to those in children's programming. The figures on instructional ETV are impressive. Television *is* used in thousands of classrooms, but it is used for enrichment; it is not used at the heart of the curriculum. It is not used to save costs of education. It is not used to enhance the influence of the great teachers. It has been arrested in its progress—I believe temporarily—by two factors: first, the innate conservatism of educationists with the dogma that one teacher is as good as another; that none must be rewarded for excellence; that the inspired or the aimless, helpless, hopeless must be treated alike, and, above all else, that, for example, no classroom teacher must be embarrassed by a television teacher whose French pronunciation, just for an example, is correct.

The second factor in delayed ETV utilization in the schools has been the Vietnam War. What *was* a teacher shortage in the fifties was more than cured by draft avoiders—men who went into teaching from no motive other than to escape the draft. Such men have been easy targets for the cocktail party organizing methods of old-line unions, whose field among hod carriers—just to pick an illustration—has been restricted by automation and who are looking for new sources of dues. The surpluses left over from hod carriers' and other craft treasuries have been used for social blandishments which have given great impetus to unionization of teachers.

Unfortunately, there is always some degree of justification for untoward sociological developments. Ironically, it is because the public intuitively knows that education is too costly, and therefore will not pay for the old methods, that unions are able to make a *prima facie* case for unionization of teachers. The point is that education needs to be subjected to modern technology and modern techniques, of which television is one, not only to improve its quality but also to reduce its costs. That will come, but there has been an interruption in the process.

Although Pittsburgh in chronological order was first on the air in educational television, the movement was national. With Ford Foundation funds, National Educational Television and Radio Center was established. I was a member of the early board of directors—from 1954 to 1962. After an unfortunate start, I had secured a general manager for our Pittsburgh WQED, John F.

White, who came to us from his position as director of development for Western Reserve University. He was a promoter, an
impresario, a cultured and cultivated man, and he gave our station a great leap forward. For example, with our scarce dollars,
we invested, on his advice—a really great gamble—$35,000 in a
program to record Martha Graham's teaching, dancing, and phil-
osophical greatness. The Dancer's World was a great success. It
received worldwide acclaim.

I had to struggle with Norman Cousins, of all people, to make
John F. White president of NET. Norman's candidate was an
educator. I was myself disillusioned by educators. My wife, Mary,
had told me, early in the game, "Leland, the educators will let
you down." She was right. My experiences with educators in ETV
showed me that they had but one purpose: to make sure that the
new medium did not have an important impact upon established
educationism. Of course, a generalization like this also makes
the exceptions stand out, such as our own Carolyn Patterson or
Kenneth A. Oberholtzer, superintendent of Denver schools, a colleague on the NET Board.

And so Jack White became the second president of NET, and
on the national scene achieved the prominence and the distinction and a place in American culture for the National Educational
Television movement which he helped us to achieve in Pittsburgh.

Today, there are 237 educational (now called public) television
stations. The original 242 stations have all but been taken up by
the several communities to which they have been assigned. The
total budget of these stations is now upwards of $150 million. Dis-
tinguished commissions have considered educational television.
The Carnegie Commission was the first to recommend federal
governmental annual support. That support is coming in relatively small amounts—only $35 (1971) million at present.

My original philosophy that local communities should establish standards before governmental support entered the field has
had plenty of time to work. There is now a profession of ETV
personnel who will protect its standards as lawyers, doctors, engineers, and others protect the standards of their professions. I am
not now fearful of governmental support, although a recent conference in New Orleans, called by National Citizens Committee
for Public Television, under the chairmanship of Thomas P. F.

Hoving, gave me the occasion to issue a declaration of independence. The committee, under tightly managed leadership, proposed to adopt a resolution to the effect that educational television would fail and would be lost to our American community unless governmental support were forthcoming. I declared from the floor that, "You can abolish the presidency, dissolve the Congress, eradicate the Supreme Court of the United States, and take the dome off the Capitol Building, but WQED in Pittsburgh will go forward." Of course there was applause, but a fellow conference member in a seat nearby turned to me and in a low voice said, bitterly, "We don't all have a Dick Mellon in our communities." It is true that after the early skeptical days, R. K. Mellon's foundation has given handsome financial support to WQED.

My arrogance at New Orleans was not without foundation. In the upwards of 20 years since our ETV beginnings, much had changed. ETV had gained powerful friends, both in the nation and in the city of its first community station. The board of NET had come to look like a blue-ribbon list of financial, industrial, and social elite. The Pittsburgh Board of WQED has been greatly enlarged from its original nine and was perhaps more widely representative than the national board. By the late 1960's the annual fund-raising campaigns at WQED began to succeed after 10 years of constant failures. Today it has become as much a tradition for leading industrialists to accept the chairmanship of the WQED fund-raising campaign as in the case of the United Fund.

When I responded to an award for my local and national contributions to educational television, made by the National Association of Educational Broadcasters at its annual convention in Washington, D.C., in November, 1965, I said "I would be strictly conventional if I told you that I accept this award not so much as a tribute to me as a tribute to those loyal and indefatigable men and women who worked with me in the movement. But I pass that convention and accept the award as it is granted because there were many times when I was very much alone." Almost before I could get out the word, "alone," the huge audience burst into applause. There were many there who had also been alone.

The day came when I was not alone. Arthur Van Buskirk began saying to me, "I watch WQED regularly." True, we had encountered a number of financial crises. We had had some bad management after Jack White went to NET, but then George Ketchum, head of one of the largest public relations agencies in the world, acted as a personnel searcher and brought from the State of Maine, Donald V. Taverner—to teach Pittsburghers how English is spoken in Maine and to bring with him a flood of salt-water stories and a fine fiscal and financial sense, not to mention aptitude for fund raising which has made budget construction a quite manageable annual exercise.

We were still in the old house which was originally donated. The studio was in a reconstructed ballroom which at one time the Order of Masons had added to the old grey stone front. Our growing staff was hampered in the inadequate nooks and crannies of the old place. Again, at just the critical moment, the Ford Foundation offered a program to all ETV stations as an inducement to improve physical facilities. Our portion of the total program would be two million dollars, but we must match the two million. Influenced in our favor by Arthur Van Buskirk and by his younger associate, Joseph D. Hughes, a former colleague of mine, the Richard King Mellon Foundation made a two million dollar grant, but we must raise another million or thereabouts from the Pittsburgh corporations and foundations.* This we did under the leadership of William P. Stevens, chairman of Jones and Laughlin Steel Corporation. Thus we had 5 million dollars for a new building.

A former executive vice president of Alcoa, M. M. Anderson, headed a building committee which selected Paul Schweikher, then head of the architectural department at Carnegie-Mellon University, to design our new temple. The building is in concrete— unique, startling at first, functionally effective. I suspect, not that it would make any difference to Paul Schweikher, that Frank Lloyd Wright would approve. We could not locate the building on the original site. That would have been architectually feasible and the executive committee of the board of trustees of the University of Pittsburgh, under the leadership of Gwilym Price, would

---

*The reader may wonder why R. K. Mellon would support WQED so handsomely when one of his principal financial executives was so opposed. The answer is simple. R. K. divided his affairs roughly between business and civic interests. He looked to different advisers for the two interests.

have given us the property. But that man who, years before, had said that he was against educational television because it is not commercial, had power enough to overrule the decision.

So we turned to Carnegie-Mellon University. H. Guyford Stever, its president, looked with careful favor upon our request for valuable land on the campus of that institution, growing in excellence and enhanced in potential by the addition of the Mellon name to that of Carnegie. The national distinction of the Carnegie-Mellon School of Drama made a closer association with WQED one of cultural significance, although, as from the first day of our concept, WQED will be autonomous.

In High Gear: A Fatal Wreck

A public mention of Franz Kline's Leda, an abstract square in four loose, wide-brush black strokes on a background of gray, as I remember the painting, brought me in touch with G. David Thompson, one of the great mid-century collector-dealers of modern paintings and sculpture, known among dealers in London and Paris years before the art circles in Pittsburgh became aware of him. He owned Leda, unbeknown to me—a fact smoked out by an aggressive news reporter. Thus began an association, the memory of which I prize to this day and which involved me in a disaster—for me and for Pittsburgh.

The facts and circumstances leading up to the denouement in which Pittsburgh lost a world-famous collection of late 19th and early 20th century art were in the making over some 30 years. G. David Thompson, an engineer educated at Pittsburgh's Carnegie Institute of Technology, was as enigmatic as the great ones in the art world often are. All one need do is look at the Barnes collection of Renoir and Cézanne in Philadelphia to know how gauche and gluttonous a collector can be. Yet Barnes was probably a collector in the true sense of the word—in the sense that he bought and bought and kept and kept and made preparations for the preservation of his collection. G. David Thompson, on the other hand, turned over several collections, any one of which would have been distinguished. He told me that he once owned all of John Kane, the genre Pittsburgh painter—a house painter by trade, who painted fewer than a hundred pictures, not all of them good, but any one of which commands high prices in the great American museums. At another time, he owned Blythe, another genre painter — humorist, satirist. Thompson himself boasted that his great collection of the greatest names cost him nothing despite its ultimate value in the millions. He traded his provincial beginnings into ownerships of unmistakable greatness.

The relationship between Gordon B. Washburn, the sensitive, articulate, knowledgeable director of Pittsburgh's Carnegie Institute's Museum of Art, 1950-1962, and Dave Thompson is as interesting to me in retrospect as is Thompson himself. To Washburn and his charming wife, Ruth, Dave Thompson was a breath of fresh air in Pittsburgh, almost bucolic in its lack of artistic sophistication. Washburn knew that Thompson could be as tough as nails, at his best, crafty; at his worst, sneaky, deceptive, brutal—if an art acquisition were involved. Gordon Washburn knew also that Dave Thompson, while regarding art with the evil eye of a pawnbroker, knew art as the highest poetry; that Dave had an insatiable thirst for new wonders and new delights in art, ever adventuring joyfully in pursuit of freshly talented artists and their unfolding works. Gordon Washburn has described for me with what bursts of excitement Dave Thompson would make the discovery of a powerful new creator, saying that such discoveries were his greatest pleasure in life and his greatest concern as a man. Gordon Washburn has told me that Thompson's eye was as sharp as an eagle's in the viewing of art, yet that eagle eye functioned only after long study and contemplation—not impulsively. Dave Thompson often said to me, in showing a new picture for the first time, "I had to study that one a long time before I decided to hang it." He was as sternly fastidious about hanging a picture he owned as a poet about a word for a couplet.

Thompson had a modest financial base in a small steel business in Pittsburgh — ancillary to the basic industry. What is small is always relative. At one time he had a stock brokerage business and also an antique shop—evidences of proclivity for dealership. He several times told me with a chuckle, how he had read the fine print in a securities issue and had exacted his pound of flesh from some members of the really big Pittsburgh financial establishment. That seemed right to him — a lonely underdog, mildly paranoid and more than a little sadistic. It left him with the contempt of the establishment.

Gordon Washburn made every effort to obtain for Pittsburgh the Thompson collection. It would have been, at that time, the only claim to great distinction for the institution's collection. Gordon Washburn knew how magnificent Thompson's collection was: Rodin to Lipchitz; Monet to Jackson Pollock. The Picassos, Klees, and Giacomettis alone came to be worth millions. Dave Thompson had famous pieces of the great modern names, except Matisse. Would Thompson give them to Pittsburgh? It was Gordon Washburn's duty to try.

Mary and I were traveling rather widely in the 1950's: for business, for public purposes, and for personal pleasure. We had our own small collection, and we always visited galleries. As soon as we said "Pittsburgh" in a gallery the dealer would ask, "Do you know G. David Thompson?" We did. One woman dealer said, "Oh, I wish I had never seen him. One year he was my best customer and it was the only year in thirty when I lost money. At the end of a year he had my pictures and I had a loss." Ruth Washburn reports seeing him in Paris hammer down the price of a now famous painting by Giacometti (Portrait of the Artist as a Young Man), asserting to the artist that he wanted to give it to the Pittsburgh Museum. Dave himself would turn even my stomach with his account of how he waited a half day in Paris for the all-but-starving Soulage to come madly to sell something for anything to the great man.

Dave was generous to a fault—in small things: dinner parties in Paris, New York, or Pittsburgh; presents. But if a painting or sculpture was his goal he would take a widow's mite. "I got a call one day from a woman who said she had a large painting of George Washington. I would look at anything," said Dave. "As soon as I saw the painting, I knew it was no good," he continued, "but I asked how much?" Three hundred dollars was the price and G. David asked if she had anything else. " 'Only a little painting upstairs'," was the reply. The little painting turned out to be a David Blythe — famous Pennsylvania genre painter, as I have previously mentioned. Dave said, "I will take the Washington if you throw in the little painting. I paid her the $300 for the George Washington, and took the Blythe under my arm, saying I would send for the big Washington. She is still waiting for me to send for it," he ended his tale of triumph.

Dave Thompson kept his shifting collections almost a secret. Gordon Washburn, years before he came to Pittsburgh as our art museum director, thought that he had an appointment to see what Thompson had in the mid-1930's, Kanes and Blythes and such paintings. Ruth and Gordon traveled to Pittsburgh, but at the door of the modest house which Dave Thompson then occupied they were gruffly turned away. Years later Dave Thompson said that he did not remember the episode. Then, some years still later, he told Washburn that he had indeed discovered the correspondence which demonstrated that the appointment had been made. Gordon said to me recently, "I thought that was in his favor." Ultimately, Dave Thompson had a larger house, a suburban home called Stone's Throw, to which he added galleries for the display of his paintings and sculptures. There were names to make one's mouth water: Klee, Giacometti, Léger, Fautrier, Burri, Dubuffet, Stael, Picasso. These are the names he himself selected in an introduction to "One Hundred Paintings From the G. David Thompson Collection"— catalogue of the 1961 exhibition at the Guggenheim Museum in New York. He regularly kept on exhibition at Stone's Throw 200 works out of the shifting hundreds of his collection. One was all but abashed by the walls of awesome color. Outside the grounds were sculpture gardens of Calder, Arp, Maillol. But for two decades he all but lived alone with these treasures.

G. David Thompson had a bizarre analogy for expressing his phobia about any disclosure of his modern masterpieces. He would say to me, more than once, apropos his belated decision to invite in a few Pittsburghers, "Leland, you know I would as soon show my wife as my pictures." I did not guess then nor do I now guess what Dr. Freud would have made of that. Even Mary, for whom he had the affectionate respect which most of the important men in our lives have always shown, suffered from Dave's ambivalence. He had promised Mary and one other of the more active members of the prestigious Women's Committee of the Museum of Art, a showing of his collection for which handsome admissions would be charged to raise funds for the Committee. But Dave, at the last minute, claimed that he had only promised to show *slides* of his pictures on a screen. "You know, Leland," said Mary, "I am not stupid. We could not both have been that wrong."

Of course, the plans for the occasion had to be cancelled.

Dave Thompson could command the assembly in Pittsburgh of any museum directors in America his whimsy might suggest to him. They all knew what he had. There are few secrets among art dealers and museum directors. Every museum head lives for the day when some owner, moved by what random provocation, will give a priceless work or a whole collection to his museum. Strange things happen, the most unlikely. No museum director will look even the most unlikely gift horse in the mouth.

Dave Thompson embarked in the mid-1950's upon some kind of campaign to expose himself and his collection to a limited outside world. His detractors would cite cases in which he, having over-bought a given artist, would make moves to enhance the market value of that artist. But I shall never know what was his objective. If I did know, the story might be less interesting. For example, one among many, he said to me, "Leland, I am going to have a kind of cultural weekend and I want you to help me." Then the plan unfolded. The great-name directors from Boston, New York, Philadelphia, St. Louis would be his guests. His collection would be displayed. There would be dinners and luncheons and some 20 people in all. Mary and I were to come, and on one occasion I was to address the great men on the role of art in civilization or some such subject—I have forgotten what. Furthermore, Dave Thompson was real in a visceral sense, as most people are not.

A person with a collection such as Dave Thompson's will be lionized, not only by the professionals but also by the lay devotees of art. Some of the directors of New York's Museum of Modern Art began to notice Dave and his wife, Helene, at least in a social way. Particularly, Blanchette, wife of John D. Rockefeller III, took notice of him. He was able to bring Blanchette to Pittsburgh for an address to the Women's Committee, a significant adjunct to our Carnegie Institute's Museum of Art. On another occasion he induced John D. III to come to Pittsburgh as my guest for a WQED luncheon—on the theory that the visit would help New York's Lincoln Center, then in the fund-raising stage. On still another occasion Dave Thompson brought David Rockefeller and his wife, Margaret, to Pittsburgh. I must preside at a "cultural" luncheon, he told me, and introduce all the speakers; also say something on my own. At the luncheon I raised the question: which comes first, art or science? Afterward Jonas Salk said, "Leland, of course you are right; art *does* come first." I had quoted William Blake, "What is now proved, was first imagin'd."

Gradually the Pittsburgh social establishment began to realize that Dave Thompson was coming out of his shell and, ominously, was thinking about a disposition of his collection. No longer young, and with some health warnings, he was still a comely man—fine, well-knit body and a good, perhaps classic in the Roman sense, head. Giacometti when painting his portrait had said, "You pretty," so Dave told me.

Rachel Hunt, wife of Roy, of the original vast aluminum fortune — she and Roy were Mr. and Mrs. Culture and they went to everything. Rachel invited Dave Thompson to dinner, usually a command performance because, although the Hunts were modest financial supporters of Pittsburgh institutions, everyone always hoped for something big. Dave told me what he replied, "Rachel, you could have invited me to dinner anytime during the past 30 years. It is too late now." What social pains, fancied or real, the man must have suffered! Actually, for most of the 30 years Rachel Hunt could not possibly have known of Dave Thompson.

The recognition which Dave Thompson desperately wanted, and did not know how to accept graciously, came in bits and pieces. Gordon Washburn made him a member of the jury one year for the Pittsburgh International. Dave told me himself how arrogantly he behaved toward his colleagues. He became a trustee of the Museum of Modern Art in New York City. One cannot do better than that in the art world of America. He told me himself how he opposed his judgment to that of the majority on the committee for the selection of new acquisitions. He was voluble but not always articulate. Yet he loved talk. He would ask me to tell him why Mary and I had bought a Vasarely. In 1958 he noted a piece I wrote for the *Pittsburgh Post-Gazette,* reporting on Fifty Years of Modern Art, a remarkable exhibit at the Brussels World's Fair. I had named Poliakoff with Picasso and Matisse as three any one of whom no man would ever regret owning. Dave was so surprised that I would name Poliakoff with the other two that he gave me a Poliakoff saying simply, "It's a tough picture." If I had ever said to him—and I never did—in the work of all those three artists, and some others, of course, "It is the Gestalt of hard lines and firm curves, static only to seem to move, which gives the paintings a mystery no less subtle than that of the famous face and smile in the Louvre"— if I had said that, he would have snorted, only to say days later, "Leland, you might be right." His passions were far too amorphous to permit a ready acceptance of a formulation so neat as mine. He had only his "magnificent eye," or, as Gordon Washburn said later, modifying his earlier judgment, his "magnificent ear," to symbolize his skill as a sharp listener and trader rather than his virtue as a connoisseur.

The Thompson collection brought me a civic failure the seeds of which had been planted on Christmas Day in the *Pittsburgh Post-Gazette* in the year 1953. The question had been asked by the newspaper of several civic leaders: "What would you do—if it were within your power—for Pittsburgh in 1954?" The instructions from the editor were to nominate "five things we should do during 1954." Among the five, I said that Pittsburgh should plan for an art museum and begin that plan in 1954; that what we have in the ancient pile on Forbes Street (this was a reference to that part of Andrew Carnegie's Carnegie Institute which housed the then Department of Fine Arts) is not an art museum either in name or in fact. I pointed out that the name was Department of Fine Arts of Carnegie Institute—just a department of something else. I said that the fact is that the collection contains no Titian nor, except for some English portraits, anything great of the 500 years between Titian and Speicher. I charged that this is as if the Carnegie Library had no Boccaccio, Shakespeare, Milton, or Tennyson. I said that what we have in art is Gordon Washburn, an excellent director, with no museum; that in Pittsburgh money has never been provided for serious collecting of art; that the standards of the past cannot be shown in Pittsburgh because we do not have the models; that we borrow from poor Europe some contemporary paintings for the periodic International and look at the Exhibit briefly with no background for comparison. I urged that a new art museum, liberated from the shades of Carnegie, should become part of the new development where the Civic Arena was to be located—there the art museum to have a life and destiny of its own.

I had read my piece to Arthur Van Buskirk before releasing it to the *Pittsburgh Post-Gazette*. He had made a few suggestions which I had accepted, but he had not touched that part which seared the cultural establishment to the quick. I knew there was nothing of much consequence in the big galleries of the Department of Fine Arts; I knew it not only because of my own admittedly limited but nevertheless useful knowledge of the great collections of the world, but also because of Gordon Washburn and, importantly and embarrassingly to me, I knew it from business associates who came from Europe. In those days I was seeing both in Europe and in the United States a considerable number of European industrialists. Such men are more classicly educated than are American businessmen. When they would visit my company and me in our city of Pittsburgh, some of them would ask about our art museums. More than once I had the awkward experience of seeing one of these industrialists gallop through the rooms of the permanent exhibit, obviously finding nothing to arrest his attention.

I knew also that the administration of the museum was commingled with that of the Carnegie Library, the Carnegie Institute of Technology, the Carnegie Museum of Natural History. I knew that the president of Carnegie Institute with multiple responsibilities had a difficult job. He was a scion of the establishment, James M. Bovard, who served from 1948 to 1960, an elegant gentleman, who was properly preoccupied with getting the money for a new roof and a new power plant for Andrew Carnegie's monumental structure. After Wallace Richards there was a tendency in the small group surrounding Richard King Mellon to appoint to civic and cultural posts members of the intimate industrial complex serving in some capacity or other some segment of the Mellon empire. I had no criticism of this. It was natural that trusted managers should be assigned to administer philanthropic benevolences. The fact was, however, that conscientious and cautious Jim Bovard (during his administration the housekeeping in the Institute was perfect) had an almost Communist-like fear of what might be considered subversive art. Once, even after the art committee of the Board of Trustees of Carnegie Institute had authorized Gordon Washburn to include a Picasso in an International, President Bovard directed him not to do it—incredible, but Washburn affirms the episode.

Furthermore, in the Christmas Day piece, I had deeply offended

Roy A. Hunt, who was chairman of the art committee from 1946 to 1962. Now and then he would be reported in the newspapers as knowing what he liked in art, but from then on the delineation of his taste was negative: he simply did not like the contemporary paintings which appeared in Pittsburgh's world famous Internationals. I must hasten to say that Gordon Washburn appeared to have a nearly free hand in the selection of the paintings and sculptures; yet he must suffer at each Pittsburgh International the slings and arrows of outrageous fortune, for after the demise of Andrew W. Mellon there was no powerful leader in Pittsburgh who cared about art. It is said that Andrew's son, Paul, once stated that the Pittsburgh community did not justify a distinguished collection of art. I report this as pure rumor. Someone will correct me if I am wrong. Of course, I do not agree that Pittsburgh, or any other city, is unworthy of a good art museum. It is the function of leadership to lead—in industry, business, politics, art. What people are given an opportunity to experience they will come to appreciate and enjoy. Nothing justifies leadership unless it will lead. No community is utterly unregenerate.

I had offended in the Christmas Day piece a small segment of the Pittsburgh social establishment—those who thought they knew and thought they cared about art in Pittsburgh. Actually the record shows that they did not know, however much they may have thought they cared. I knew the record at the time; and later it was completely confirmed in a 1958 Pittsburgh Bicentennial International, in which there was a retrospective show of pieces which had been at some time exhibited in a Pittsburgh International since its founding in 1896, over 60 years earlier. The total value of the pieces exhibited in the retrospective show as of 1958 was $3,400,000. The total price for which all of those pieces could have been bought over the years as of the date of their first exhibition in a Pittsburgh International was approximately $375,000. In other words, Homer Saint-Gaudens, son of the famous Augustus, American sculptor, and the Fine Arts Committee could have bought all of the 95 pieces as of the date of their first exhibition in Pittsburgh at a bargain of ten cents on the dollar. Where was the committee? And what were they thinking? And how could Homer Saint-Gaudens have been so wrong? Some of the pieces are spectacular, as the following list shows. The default was not

utter. Two of the pieces—2 out of 95—which have so greatly increased in value were indeed added to the Carnegie Institute
collection.

Original Value	Artist	Title of Painting	Estimated Value Today
$ 5,000.00	EDGAR DEGAS	"The Rehearsal Room"	$ 75,000.00
	Lent by the Metropolitan Museum of Art		
5,000.00	JAMES A. McNEILL WHISTLER	"Sarasate"	30,000.00
	Carnegie Institute Collection		
5,000.00	WINSLOW HOMER	"The Wreck"	80,000.00
	Carnegie Institute Collection		
650.00	ALFRED SISLEY	"Village on the Shore of the Marne"	100,000.00
	Carnegie Institute Collection		
25,000.00	CLAUDE MONET	"La Seine à Lavacour"	80,000.00
	Lent by Dallas Museum of Fine Arts		
5,000.00	PIERRE AUGUSTE RENOIR	"Portrait of a Girl Sewing"	100,000.00
	Lent by Paul Rosenberg & Co., New York City		
10,000.00	GEORGE W. BELLOWS	"Elinor, Jean and Anna"	60,000.00
	Lent by Albright Art Gallery, Buffalo		
5,850.00	PABLO PICASSO	"Figures in Pink"	150,000.00
	Lent by The Cleveland Museum of Art		
7,840.00	RAOUL DUFY	"L'artiste et son module dans l'atelier du Havre"	80,000.00
	Lent by Collection Bernheim-Jeune, Paris		
8,000.00 (First Prize)	GEORGES BRAQUE	"The Yellow Cloth"	125,000.00
1,255.00	WASSILY KANDINSKY	"Blue World, No. 602"	60,000.00
Lent by Collection The Solomon R. Guggenheim Museum, New York City			

During the period in which Pittsburgh was permitting priceless
art to slip through its fingers, Chicago was buying; Cleveland was
buying; Toledo, Ohio, was buying. Fine collections of the art of

the turn of the century and of the first decades of the twentieth century were growing elsewhere, but not to Pittsburgh. I knew these facts; and they were in my mind when I wrote the Christmas Day piece in 1953. Gordon Washburn told me that Roy and Rachel Hunt had said it ruined their holiday. I was sorry for that; but, after all, I did not set the day when the *Post-Gazette* would publish my piece nor had I asked that it be published. Of course I had encountered an American folkway — resentment of any criticism.

I was not asked to leave Pittsburgh as deTocqueville and Beaumont had been, more than a century earlier, invited to leave America because of their criticism of America. The worst that happened to me was that John O'Conner, Jr., an associate director of the Department of Fine Arts, Carnegie Institute, privately called me "an upstart." Otherwise the silence was eloquent—no voice raised to challenge me, to say that I was wrong or had overlooked this or that, to assert that the collection was in fact good, or at least important. One could almost hear in the silence the voice again of Neville Craig praising Pittsburgh for not caring enough about its art museum to defend it, as he had praised the City's inhabitants 100 years earlier for their disinterest in theatre.

I had made a poor preparation for influencing the Pittsburgh establishment to notice favorably the remarkable G. David Thompson collection. Nevertheless, my speeches and my writings had given me a kind of standing, even though the silent establishment was turning cool to my impatience. It became more and more apparent that Pittsburgh was on the verge of losing the G. David Thompson collection. I collaborated with Adolph Schmidt, who was then president of the Allegheny Conference but not always a power in his own right, and with H. J. Heinz II, who was financially potent but not always able to stand up in a confrontation against the Mellon establishment. Nevertheless, the three of us offered a plan for a temporary housing of the Thompson collection. Dave Thompson had said that he would never give it to the Carnegie Museum as it was then constituted. We were unwilling to undertake to try to reconstitute it but we thought that funds could be raised for temporary housing which would tide us over the decision.

Our formal effort was laid before a meeting of the executive committee of the Allegheny Conference, the 162nd meeting, held on June 17, 1957. Jack Heinz was late as usual, but he urged that the consideration of the proposal be held up until he could get there. He did arrive. We did present a plan for temporary housing of the Thompson collection. It was opposed by Arthur Van Buskirk and, understandably, by Jim Bovard; and this time those who had supported me in the educational television project of more than five years earlier were silent: George Lockhart, who had been a tower of strength on the earlier occasion; likewise Bill Snyder and Jack Ryan sat silent. A. W. Schmidt, Schmitty we called him—(he was later Ambassador to Canada) and Jack Heinz and I did what we could. Finally, Arthur Van Buskirk called upon Bill Snyder, saying, "Well, Bill, you are one of our leaders, what do you think?" and he made a curious statement, saying, "Well, I think we have a pretty good reputation. We ought to be careful not to impair it." In this awkward phrasing there emerged the establishment's resentment of G. David Thompson, a man who had once read the fine print and had cost the great ones some money. They did not "trust him." How could *he* have a collection of art worthy of the community's efforts?

That June, 1957, meeting was filled with vigorous discussion about the Thompson collection and the absence of any real distinction in the Carnegie Museum galleries. At that meeting Pittsburgh lost the Thompson collection, and yet there is not a word of the discussion or action in the official minutes of the meeting. At one point Park Martin said in an aside to me, "If your proposal fails, that will be the end of Committee No. 4." It failed, and today there is no committee of the Conference with a mandate such as my committee possessed. Yet, so far as the minutes of the meeting are concerned, the Thompson matter was never considered.

It was, and is, a folkway of the Mellon establishment that the procedures of community decision-making should not be disclosed. Copies of minutes of the meetings of the Conference Executive Committee are sent to the editors of the principal newspapers in Pittsburgh—in confidence, "off the record." Why off the record? The minutes are as bland and bloodless as a turnip stew, however vital the decision may have been. To this day scholars in the social sciences, especially in the new science (art?) of community planning, will come to me seeking information from behind the iron curtain of unrevealing records: what were the factors and the considerations which resulted in the decision—any decision? Sometimes I can elucidate; sometimes I can only say, if I elect to say it, "The powers that be wanted it that way."

I must say right now that I do not hold with participatory democracy as it is offered in song, dance, and disordered invasions of meetings of school boards, corporation boards, and other institutional assemblies—circa 1970. I do not believe that the poor are the only competent analysts of the cause and cure of their plight; nor do I believe that the uneducated are the best curriculum designers for their education. I do believe in expertness and in leadership, but I do believe that there should be forthright and informative explanations at the time of the decision and a record which is meaningful for posterity. Certainly those conditions were lacking in the Thompson affair.

I did not resign from the Conference after the Thompson debacle. Why? I am not quite clear. Actually, I might have resigned earlier when Van passed me up for the presidency. It would make a kind of sense to say that I was stubbornly waiting for the day, which came ultimately, when Van would ask me to ask George Lockhart not to nominate me again for a vice-presidency. Yet I cannot honestly ascribe to myself that low motive. My causes transcended my pride—that is the best I can say in retrospect, because, as I look at the cold record, I can see that my colleagues must have wondered about my insensitivity. But I had visions: metropolitanism and modern transit for our community, among others. I had been early in my speeches and articles about the growth of urbanism and the incongruous decline in the quality of cities. I was at least 10 years ahead of the now common and general concern about the automobile as the be-all and end-all of public mobility. I was in almost continuous demand for speaking on these subjects and other causes considered lost by more lethargic citizens. I was too euphoric about my life and times to notice what particular official role, if any, was assigned to me. If all this sounds miserably pious, I am the first to know it, but it is the best I can make out of the record already disclosed and now to be continued.

When I told G. David Thompson of the rout of our campaign to infiltrate his collection into the consciousness of Pittsburgh, he just grunted. He had known what I was proposing but I had no specific permission from him. I was quite willing to take that chance. If I could have had an approval in principle from the Conference, then the bargaining with G. David could have started.

Fifteen months passed, during which there were more occasions at Stone's Throw—typically, members of the Women's Committee of the Museum and their husbands on a Sunday at four. There would be cocktails and then the tour in two parts, one led by Gordon Washburn and one by Dave. On one occasion he was interested in Ben Kopman and had me read a most sensitive piece by a friendly critic of Kopman. There was applause. Of course I came away with a Kopman, "Man With a Bottle." There would be guessing games (how many pieces in the collection) and prizes. Judge Henry X. O'Brien and his wife, Rosemary, were always there—perhaps the only intimates of Dave and Helene. Yet only a few Pittsburghers ever saw the Thompson collection. Lorant, in his pictorial history of Pittsburgh, shows scenes from the important collections of Mr. and Mrs. Charles J. Rosenbloom and Mr. and Mrs. H. J. Heinz, II, and then complains, "Another large collection of modern paintings is gathered together by the eccentric steelman G. David Thompson . . . Mr. Thompson, for reasons only fathomed by him, will not allow local photographers to memorialize his collection." Lorant consulted me a number of times during the 10 years in which he and the establishment agonized over his good but unbalanced book. He never consulted me about Dave Thompson, who had, I could have told Lorant, a far different concept of how to memorialize his collection.

One day in early March, 1959, Dave Thompson called me to say he was sending me a copy of a letter to his lawyer, Walter T. McGough, authorizing him to offer the Thompson collection for preservation in Pittsburgh. Dave showed me all the correspondence as it developed but he never asked my advice, nor did I offer it. The letter to McGough, dated March 7, 1959, deplored "the billions available to science for use in perfecting ever deadlier methods to destroy mankind and the anthills in which he lives." McGough, executing his lawyer's mandate, wrote the A.W. Mellon Educational and Charitable Trust (Andrew Mellon's original foundation for Pittsburgh beneficences) offering, "anonymously", Stone's Throw and its collection as a center "designed to advance the community's interest in the humanities." McGough's letter said that the "Center" could be an addition to Carnegie Institute or otherwise. The letter said that there were no restrictions on disposition of the collection except that it should be exhibited for one year in its entirety.

McGough's letter conveyed Thompson's estimate that the property and collection were worth 5-6 million dollars and suggested an appraisal. Then came the conditions: there must be an endowment of not less in value than the appraised value of the collection to maintain the "Center," and "one-third of the income (must) be placed at the disposal of the donors of the collection." Furthermore, an amount equal to the endowment must be raised for a "nucleus for housing the activities of the proposed Center."

The trustees did consider the offer—some of them viewed the collection, according to A.W. Schmidt's letter of May 15, 1959, to McGough. Schmidt, President of the Foundation, called the offer munificent but the trustees declined it, pointing out that the Foundation had a policy of conserving assets for Pittsburgh projects already launched over the years; making reference to the National Gallery in Washington, founded with A.W. Mellon charitable funds and his magnificent collection of classical art; and mentioning that the Trust had committed funds for three more Pittsburgh Internationals—through 1967. (The Trust has continued to support the Internationals.)

There can be no doubt that the Thompson offer was legally binding. If accepted, the benefits to Pittsburgh would have been great. It developed that his collection, the portions he later sold and the portion in his estate, aggregated in value 10 to 12 million dollars. In the years which have elapsed since his offer the values of his works of painting and sculpture have very greatly increased.

Of course he went about his philanthropy in a very awkward fashion. The reservation of one-third the income from the endowment was interpreted as an offer to sell. He told me afterward that he intended to use the money to fill in some gaps in the collection. He should have said so in his offer. In any case, the whole matter should have been handled by intermediaries—not by a letter prepared by a lawyer, even a good one like McGough. Yet the hard fact remains that he did make a valid offer and if it had been accepted he would have been bound to deliver his truly great collection. There was another hard fact that if the Thompson offer had been accepted, stringent though its conditions may have been, the transaction would have been culturally beneficial for Pittsburgh and profitable in terms of increased community wealth.

It was unfair, in one sense, for Thompson to put the whole responsibility on the A.W. Mellon Educational and Charitable Trust—a charity declining in its assets and much less able to undertake a major program such as Thompson proposed than would have been the foundations of Paul Mellon, son of Andrew, or of R. K. Mellon or of Sarah Mellon Scaife, son and daughter of R. B. Mellon. On the other hand, the A.W. Mellon original foundation had supported for many years the Pittsburgh International, originally, beginning in 1896, an annual, then a biennial, and for the past decade a triennial. It was reasonable for Thompson to assume that a foundation which had so well supported contemporary art would be interested in developing a plan to assure the Thompson collection for Pittsburgh. It was usual practice among the several Mellon foundations when a large project, as in the University of Pittsburgh Medical School or in any of the universities, was involved to collaborate among themselves and to pool sizable contributions. Of course, some bargaining with Thompson would have been required, but that necessity is not unusual with substantial donors. I must conclude that there was simply no will in the Mellon establishment to deal with Dave Thompson or to be associated with him in an artistic movement—ironically the very thing which he inordinately desired. It would have been an ultimate triumph for him, by his standards, if his offer had been the occasion for the Mellons and the Mellon establishment in Pittsburgh to raise funds in substantially twice the amount of the value of his collection to house and endow the fruits of his "magnificent eye." The elements of a Greek tragedy were present.

Dave began spending summer vacations in Northeast Harbor, Maine, in the area where the Rockefellers have establishments. He urged Mary and me to be his guests at Asticou Inn. I could do my writing there, he urged. Our engagements never permitted us to accept. Ultimately Dave built a house in the midst of the Rockefeller preserves—according to plans by Paul Schweikher, a house fitted atop a vast rock rising sheer from the water. It was a great and good house and, of course, an agony to both owner and architect in the building. There in that house he was stricken. A wrong medical diagnosis kept him in Maine too long. He died in Pittsburgh in anguish as cruel as his life had been passionate. But he had lived long enough to make a controversial and conditional offer of his collection to A.W. Mellon's original foundation, to have his proposal rejected; then to sell the heart of his collection to European collectors or dealers (97 Klees are now in Berne, Switzerland; others in the German state of Westphalia)—in short to send back to Europe the treasures he had brought from there.

It has been suggested that his proposal was never in good faith and that he gambled that it would not be accepted. Yet it was in writing, prepared by a partner in Pittsburgh's very old and largest law firm. I saw the proposal in advance. I thought it was legally valid and binding. It never occurred to me that the Pittsburgh philanthropic establishment would not bargain with Dave about the conditions. In any case, I should have tried to intervene. Adolph Schmidt and I were good friends and thought alike about art and culture. I should have tried.

Dave Thompson did make some contributions to the Carnegie Museum of Art. He was making these contributions over a number of years well prior to the rejection of his offer. It used to be said that he gave to the Museum pieces which he thought might have value in the next generation of moderns. They very well may become important.

Of course, Dave Thompson was a trader with a mild paranoia and a compensating megalomania. Of course, he was eccentric, as Lorant said, and difficult, not to say cruel, as the Washburns found. But none of that had anything to do with the significance of his collection. If Adolph Schmidt could have brought himself to open negotiations, if in the end he could have produced that impossible day when either R. K. Mellon or Paul Mellon would have invited Dave Thompson into the inner sanctum and had said, "Dave, you have made a generous proposal; there are some things about it that we would like to discuss with you;" well, Dave Thompson would have melted like butter in the sun. But there are limits beyond which even philanthropists will not go. They do weary of good works, and why not?

Alfred M. Hunt, elder son of Roy, said an interesting thing to me at one stage of the critical period in which Dave was making up his mind. Alfred said, "Leland, I wonder if Dave Thompson couldn't be persuaded to wait awhile. You know," said Alfred, "things will not always be as they are now." I am sure that Alfred could not have brought his father to say, "Dave, let's talk about your proposal." After the heart of the collection had been sold, Alfred Hunt was instrumental in causing Alcoa, one of the more humanistic of American corporations, to purchase some remnants of the Thompson collection. Even they were exhibited at Carnegie Museum, and Alcoa sent that show on tour throughout the United States, considering the cost a good investment in public relations.

It is important to note (1970) that Sarah Mellon Scaife, beginning with the year 1960 until her death in 1965, and members of her family, both before and after her death, have given important works to the Museum. The names are great names: Bonnard, Boudin, Cezanne, Corot, Gauguin, Goya, Hals, Hassam, Matisse, Monet, Munch, Pissarro, Renoir, Signac, Sisley, Toulouse-Lautrec, Valadon, Vuillard. Included in the Scaife benefactions is a Vannucci, "St. Augustine with Members of the Confraternity of Perugia." Most of these and other gifts were made during the ten-year administration (1962-1971) of James H. Beal as chairman of the Fine Arts Committee of the Museum of Art. He and his wife, Rebecca, are native Pittsburghers, a distinction in this city of swift moving changes in commercial and industrial people. Beal is a second generation lawyer in one of the city's most prestigious law firms and his wife is author of *Jacob Eichholtz, 1776-1842; Portrait Painter of Pennsylvania,* published by Historical Society of Pennsylvania, Philadelphia (1969). Mr. and Mrs. Beal have themselves made important contributions to the Museum of Art.

Sarah Mellon Scaife authorized her representative, James M. Bovard, to bid an amount close to the top for "Aristotle Contemplating the Bust of Homer," the Rembrandt which New York's Metropolitan Museum acquired for $2,300,000. Sarah Scaife's son, Richard, with Scaife funds, is now guiding what will be a magnificent building addition to Carnegie Institute, exclusively for the Museum of Art. But the G. David Thompson collection is lost to Pittsburgh forever.

Never in One Basket

While the Thompson affair destroyed forever Pittsburgh's chances to retain a great collection of paintings and sculptures, nevertheless it did not destroy me. That overemphasis on my role in the Pittsburgh Renaissance, occasioned entirely by my writings and speeches, had brought me several and diverse opportunities. One came in late 1954. A letter from Harold E. Howland of the State Department's International Cultural and Educational Exchange Service proposed that I go for 10 weeks to Formosa, the Phillippines, Australia, Singapore, and Malaya, to speak about problems of management and problems of community redevelopment.

In that era, the early 1950's, the United States was spending some 20 million dollars a year for the lend-leasing and reverse lend-leasing of people. For example, in the fiscal year 1954 almost six thousand persons were involved—students, teachers, lecturers, research scholars, foreign leaders, and specialists. Nearly four thousand people from other countries were guests of the United States, coming here to study, teach, do research, gain practical experience, and observe American life in cities and towns in all of our 48 states. Americans in about half that number were sent abroad. Russia was trying a similar program. My project involved more than 40,000 miles of overseas and foreign air travel and 40 principal speaking engagements, all on a rather tight schedule. The program was not at a high diplomatic level, but I found myself exposed in vital situations in which my cue invariably was simply to say what I knew about the subject based on my American experience and to answer questions.

In the hot, moist air of the Philippines and Malaya I often went without coat or tie, and in the Philippines I adopted for social occasions the Filipino Barong Tagalog—a shirt of sheer material, ramie or piña cloth, worn outside the trousers with the collar open for "black tie" and buttoned for "tails". The shirt had white or gray embroidery on the front and sleeves and the undershirt must have quarter sleeves. The Filipinos were strict about that. One would have been put out of a first-class restaurant or club for appearing in one of these sheer garments without quarter sleeves on the undershirt as readily as he still would be excluded from the Palm Court in the Plaza Hotel in New York if he appeared without a jacket. (Who knows how long any convention can survive?) Of course, I was indebted to Mary for insisting that I replace the American jacket with this sensible Filipino garment, popularized by President Magsaysay. She liked the embroidery and the Filipino men liked me for wearing it. This custom of wearing the shirt outside the trousers had a Spanish origin. Those conquerors had imposed a mark of inferiority upon the Filipinos by requiring that the shirt be worn with the tails outside. President Magsaysay made a virtue of this former colonial insult, and to a very good effect. The garment is practical; it is cooler outside the trousers than inside.

An exchange person does not always know in advance what his schedule will be. The United States Information Service would inform me on arrival, and sometimes the information was a bit sketchy. My first appointment in Manila was listed as a luncheon with some "labor leaders." At the luncheon I found the joint committee of the Philippine Congress, the Department of Labor, and the Industrial Court all assembled, with the Secretary of Labor presiding—about 100 people.

There was at that time in the Philippines a considerable amount of residual paternalism in Filipino labor relations. Nevertheless, I spoke out on the importance of strong unions, saying that weak unions are often irresponsible. The industrializing society of the Philippines was encountering unionism (1954). Filipino management was reacting normally in support of weak manageable unions. Of course I was attacked by conservative congressmen, but stood my ground. The next day the Secretary of Labor asked that I come to see him—only for him to say to me, "You just kept smiling, and saying weak unions no good."

They baited me, particularly the reporters, "What advice have you for us, Mr. Hazard?" I would reply, "I have no advice; I am a lawyer; I know that people don't like advice and they usually don't take advice—even good advice—even when they pay for it." Then I would continue to say that I had come to talk about some of our problems in America and how we try to solve them, and "if your problems are similar to ours, then perhaps our solutions may be useful to you." At one point, near Cebu in the Philippines, top management was installing for the first time an executive job-evaluation plan and things were hot with the heat which always attends the rearrangement and redefinition of executive functions. I instantly saw that my cue at this meeting of some 40 high-level supervisors was to listen while they worked off their aggressions, somewhat modified, of course, by my presence.

Of course one wonders what was the value of all of that program of the United States Information Service. Since the time of my trip the offices of some agencies have been attacked, in some cases, destroyed. Esteem and respect for the United States has declined. In 1955 I found the people in the Service alert, hard-working, and competent. They were not living plush lives; their offices were usually in rented buildings of local design and construction; their transportation, the lowly jeep. I felt at the time, and I have had no reason to change by reason of my experiences abroad subsequently, that the people of U.S.I.S. were as dedicated, in their way, as were our early missionaries. One can only hope that the result of the effort is to be more efficacious than was that of the missionaries. I noted on this fairly extensive trip—in the heart of the far Asian scene of earlier missionary activity—that the only visible vestiges of all of that missionary effort of the late 19th and early 20th centuries, the only visible monuments were some good hospitals—perhaps sufficient in themselves to have justified all of the expenditure, the dedication, and the stress and strain of that, I think, misplaced Christian evangelism.

The brooding question then was, as it is now, "What do you think about communism?" in Malaya or Singapore or Bangkok—out there. The answer I gave then, and I think the answer is still valid, was that millions of Asians are neutral. In America, in our comfortable prosperity, communism is as unclean as the hair of some of the members of the SDS who espoused it in the 1960's. But contempt for communism was not the attitude in Southeast Asia. One had to be there to get the feel of the Asian masses.

I tried to convey that feeling in a published article in October, 1956. I asked my readers to imagine themselves as little farmers on the edge of the jungle in Malaya; or perhaps Chinese shop-keepers in Singapore, shop fronts open to the hot, humid streets, little stocks of roots or herbs or fruits or tins exposed to the dust or quickly covered with tattered canvas for protection from sudden rain; cooking, heating, and sleeping all done there—no drive to a cool suburb at the end of the day's work. There are millions of such Asians. They are there today. America tells them about democracy and freedom and about the evils of communism, and they listen. It all sounds all right, but the men have wives and kids and little businesses or little farms; they are not accustomed to voting;

nothing in their experience is as clean-cut as the difference between a Republican and a Democrat in America, however unclean that difference may be in America. They have heard more bullets than they have seen ballots.

In many Asian languages, the word for "government" is "conqueror." They have known nothing except authority from outside, no rule indigenous to the culture. I saw in the late 1950's, and I have no reason to change my conclusions, that the domino theory has nothing to do with ideology; it has simply to do with power. Who is going to make the rules tomorrow? All that the little merchant wishes to know, all that the little farmer wants to know, all that they can hope to know is: who has the authority? By whose grace do I hold my life and sustenance? If I can find out who he is, I am for him. And when one understands this homespun fact about most of Asia, then one gains some concept of the unrealism which moved four American presidents: Eisenhower, Kennedy, Johnson, and Nixon—moved them to talk in terms of freedom and democracy—for South Vietnam, for Southeast Asia.

The program of the United States Information Service, although standard in some respects—a library, documentary films, a place for meetings and discussion—necessarily varied, still varies, from place to place. The program counts for its success not only upon the formal meetings but also upon informal exchanges and continuing relationships. In Kuala Lumpur my wife and I were invited to a meeting of the Arts Council. The host for the occasion was one of the last of British representatives in Malaya. The dinner was served almost as a ballet, the waiters numbering as many as the 20 guests, making graceful entrances and exits *(ancien régime)*. After dinner I was asked to speak on how money is raised for the arts in the United States. In the Far East philanthropy is almost unknown as a major institution for support for public activities. I spoke about how we in the United States divide up the cards and beg the money from each other for the arts. I said also that the arts will always be relatively poor, no less in the United States than elsewhere.

> Seven wealthy towns contend
> For Homer, dead,
> Through which the living Homer
> Beg'd his bread.

In Australia (1955) there was scarcely a hotel at which the service was equal to that of a second or third rate hotel in the United States or in Europe. We arrived at Melbourne in very hot weather with an accumulation of laundry. In the nondescript room Mary saw a one-day laundry sign, only to be told by the maid, "Oh, we don't have that service anymore; too many people wanted to use it." I always frankly mentioned the bad hotels in small business groups and among those with whom I was invited to discuss management problems. Hotels are notably at the heart of management problems. Some months after my return I had a cablegram asking that I arrange appointments for an Australian builder with American hotel architects and managers. When the representative of the contracting firm arrived, I found that he had not known that we had in the United States a famous school at Cornell which devoted itself exclusively to the techniques of hotel management.

In the days of the 1950's there was the same uncertainty about how to oppose the American system to communism which exists today. Some said then, as they do now, that we should oppose communism with capital investments, technology and engineering, with hydroelectric projects and electrification of the villages. Probably we lost Egypt because of our mistake in withdrawing American support of the Aswan Dam. This was a bad decision, occasioned by the irascibility of the then Secretary of State John Foster Dulles, a fateful mistake as the Mideast crisis (1972) attests. In extenuation of Dulles I can testify from my own experiences in Egypt that the Arabs must have given Dulles abundant provocation. Perhaps Kissinger may correct Dulles' mistakes (1974).

Some said in the 1950's, as they do now, that we should do it with labor relations; and so embassies have labor attachés, and in some places there are projects to teach American concepts of labor-management relations. Some said in the 1950's, as they do now, that we should do it with health services, as so many frustrated missionaries concluded many years ago. Some said we must talk more about freedom and not so much about democracy; and some said that we should build roads so that the Filipinos, for example, or the Malayans could move about and trade with each other. Others said that we should frame our foreign trade policies to buy more products from the undeveloped countries and thus remove the ever present dollar shortages. (That concept has been implemented and has shown that the American dollar can be hurt by too much global philanthropy.)

Now the incongruous confrontation in Vietnam and the Nixon visits to Peking and Moscow (1971-1972) outmode all those hopeful methodologies of the mid-century. It takes sterner stuff than cultural outposts to keep bipolarism viable.

I did have one good, hard, solid piece of evidence from Formosa that the trip was worthwhile. The capital, Taipei, lies in the north of the island. In the south is Kaohsiung, an important port and industrial city. The trip from Taipei to Kaohsiung is overnight on a rather famous Formosan train, which was charming in a way. Chinese people are an average size smaller than the American people. The berths were tight but there were *berths* and we could try to sleep. The roadbed was not perfect; the ride was not smooth. We arrived, shaken and not refreshed at hot Kaohsiung, to be received by a sensitive U.S.I.S. executive, Harold McConeghey. He took me to speak at a Rotary Club luncheon. My audience, although all seats were filled, was a scant 25. I was feeling queasy. As any traveler in the Far East knows, it is a classical Chinese custom to make sounds while eating—just as the belch after eating is a courtesy to the host. At our luncheon there were little slices of yellow watermelon, and the sucking sounds did not add to the stability of my stomach.

When I was introduced I still had a question. Should I just mouth some pleasantries or should I tell the story of the Pittsburgh development, particularly the rather technical story of how, through the use of authorities, we had put together private, federal, state, county, city, local funds to accomplish projects which otherwise could not be funded by any one particular entity? Fortune was with me. I told the story just as I had told it in Detroit, St. Louis, and Boston to more sophisticated audiences, so I thought, and left the scene without great applause.

Within the year the U.S.I.S. had its reward and I had my lesson. Chinese-speaking Harold McConeghey wrote me that "the city officials of Kaohsiung, the directors of the industrial water system, and the Chinese Navy had created an area-wide water authority . . . to rationalize and greatly improve water service to the Navy, industry, and the city of Kaohsiung." He added, "It was the continuing interest in the idea of an 'authority' which you introduced when you spoke before the Rotary Club at Kaohsiung that led to this development." I shudder to remember how close I came, after a bad night on the train and the Eastern custom of noisy eating, I shudder to remember how close I came to talking down to that little audience.

America's Essential Goodness

In all the miles of travel, in the cold halls on Formosa, in the hot halls of the Philippines and of Malaya, in the halls of Australia—both hot and cold—for there is much latitude from north to south of that continent, in the offices, in the clubs, in the homes, at the cocktail parties in Singapore—no one ever asked me what is essentially good about America. Their questions invariably had to do with the assumed American success, usually pronounced "suckcess." They wanted "how-do-you-do-it" answers: How do you prevent a strike? How do you settle one? How much should a minimum wage be? How do you organize a community chest? How do you train management? How do you get production? How do you do *it*?

At the Chinese feasts and Taiwanese luncheons on Formosa, where Mary and I minimized consumption of shark's fins and hundred-year-old eggs, black and pickled, by insisting on using chopsticks; on the conference porches of the U. S. Information Centers in the Philippines, open to the hot, dusty streets of Davao or Iloilo or Cebu; in the radio interviews in Manila or Sydney or Brisbane; among the newsmen who usually met Mary and me at the airports or came at inconvenient hours to the hotel rooms to interview me; at the round table of directors of the Chamber of Manufacturers in Melbourne; in the Australian clubs, as antique and as sophisticated as those about Wall Street; in Singapore, where an Indian feature writer, black and intelligent, came three times to the Raffles Hotel to perfect his story on American training within industry; in Malaya, at Kuala Lumpur, where there came, strangely, just at midnight, on the broad porches of the British residency an equatorial breeze—the questions were always not why America does what she does, but *what* she does.

I could have concluded superficially from experiences in the Orient that our ways are being extensively adopted. In Taipei, at the Rotary Club, Formosans were being taught by an Americanized Chinese executive secretary to adopt the first-name banter which is usual among Rotarians in America. At Iloilo the Jaycees had brought to the luncheon a child who was being cured of tetanus by a Filipino woman doctor with costly serums purchased with monies raised by the Jaycees. In Cebu, an aggressive Filipino had just organized some 3,000 country newspapers into an association pretty much in the American style. The editor distributed to his association my 1,000-word capsule on "Free Enterprise," and it was published replete with American-like journalistic spreads. All of this the Russians called American "Cultural Aggression."

I discovered something about the American image abroad on the Asian trip that one might have discovered on paper, that is, out of official records if enough research were devoted to the project. Abroad, on the scene, it is readily apparent that the so-called American aid programs reflect the pluralism at home—reflect our technical and fragmented approach to our own problems rather than a spiritually whole conviction. It is not easy to say what I am trying to say. Of the pluralistic American pressure groups, each is convinced that it has the only sensible approach to the problems of underdeveloped countries. (I have never had any patience with euphemistic terms, abroad or at home, such as developing for underdeveloped or underprivileged for poor, or black for Negro, or Hebrew for Jew.) I observed the struggle among all of these techniques in the Far East; and within a decade, when I spent some time in India, I observed it again—the fragmented nature of our programs. The image of America was one of techniques, of technologies, of methodologies, almost one of magic. The question was, "What is America's mystique?" Never—"What is essentially good about America?"

I thought hard on this question which was never asked of me and I came hesitatingly to an answer. America has compassion; our colonists built the tradition of neighborliness, else the wilderness would have consigned us to oblivion; our covered wagons broke the trails to the West, and sickness, childbirth, thirst, hunger, and death were assuaged by kind, rough hands. The full story of how people helped each other in our great depression has not yet been told; our troops went to Korea and added social work for Korean children to the *Manual of Arms;* so, also, in the Indochina

War, the record of compassion has been obscured by the publicized reports of atrocities.

I had come to this concept of American compassion versus American methodologies by the close of my Far-Eastern tour and expressed it at an Annual Brotherhood dinner of the National Conference of Christians and Jews in Pittsburgh in April of 1955. It seemed vague, even to me, but John F. Kennedy went further than any other American statesman in all of American history in giving some practical application of the American urge to compassion. In the International Peace Corps there was something new in methodology—not the hard, uncompromising assurance of this expert or that expert in this method or that method of saving a continent in a series of neatly designed moves, not that, but just a globally-organized program of people to do what they could do, or learn to do, some place in the world for someone else.

I have always had difficulty in becoming a complete partisan for any president or an out-and-out critic. I know that the Peace Corps has been as controversial as J.F.K. himself, but I think it has implemented what seems to me the great genius of the American people—compassion. I know that Peter F. Drucker, in the *Age of Discontinuity*, charges that students who join the Peace Corps do so to avoid decision-making at home. I am, myself, sometimes a bit disturbed when a very able student of mine decides not to go into American business but to try his hand for a time in the Peace Corps. Yet I see the Peace Corps as the most tangible proof that America, despite all of her hard-nosed efficiency, is compassionate.

No One Else To Do It

By September, 1956, Mary and I had lived in Pittsburgh for 18 years. I held a responsible position as General Counsel, Vice President, and Director of my company. I had built a sizable law department, manned with people only one of whom ever disappointed me; I knew how to delegate, both in my private corporate work and in my public work There was never a time when I could not leave the city or the country if the invitation or the occasion interested me. Mary and I traveled a great deal. The *Pittsburgh Post-Gazette* invariably published my observations upon the foreign scene, European or elsewhere.

I had many invitations to head this or that, but I knew my limitations after the experiences on the Allegheny Conference. I had the power of rhetoric, but only limited power otherwise. I could call up anybody in Pittsburgh and ask for an appointment and get it; I can still do that today. I could have a respectful hearing; I could often be effective, but not invariably. I think I must have been a little bit baffling to the establishment. If I undertook an assignment, particularly one which I thought no one else would undertake, then I pulled all the stops and said what I thought and did what seemed necessary.

An occasion arose, known as the Pittsburgh Assembly of the Aaronsburg Story. There was to be a great meeting on Friday, September 28, 1956, and I was to address the meeting. The movement gained its name from a little village of Aaronsburg near the geographical center of Pennsylvania, where, in 1949, 50,000 people had gathered to honor the memory of the Jew, Aaron Levy, who in 1786 had given land and money for a church house and subsequently a pewter communion service to its Lutheran congregation. These acts would seem scarcely sufficient in themselves to merit historical treatment, but a Jew's benevolence to a faith not his own had captured the imagination of some American leaders and had inspired the Pittsburgh Assembly of the Aaronsburg Story which was to be a first in a proposed series of such meetings. I accepted the assignment.

It was a stellar audience of liberals, but the 400 people who filled the ballroom of the William Penn Hotel were not my real audience. I knew that. The real audience would be the readers of Pittsburgh's newspapers.

I said that white, Protestant Americans north of the Rio Grande river are a minority on our globe of 2-7/10 billion people (how rapidly the number has become 3 billion and more)—a decided minority, outnumbered 40 to 1 by black, brown, and yellow people. But we of the white faces are the dominant majority in America.

Truly, I asserted, it is easier for a camel to pass through the eye of a needle than for the dominant majority to gain *infeeling* with the excluded minority. "How does a Catholic who aspires to the presidency feel? (J. F. K. had not yet been elected President.) How does Roland Hayes, for whom the stormiest applause is reserved for the dialectical Negro spirituals, not for the beautifully articulated French and German songs, how does he feel? How does a Jewish community leader and benefactor feel when he enters, never but by invitation, one of our clubs, membership in which is an indicium of acceptability?" I did not mention the Duquesne Club, but everybody knew what club I was talking about. (In 1969 two corporate vice-presidents, a long-time Pittsburgh philanthropist, and the Chancellor of the University of Pittsburgh were admitted simultaneously, thus ending an unwritten rule which had been breached only once, unwittingly, in favor of an Episcopalian Jew.) "Is it possible that no Negro musician is qualified for a chair in the Pittsburgh Symphony?" (There are now two or three Negroes in the orchestra, one of whom is Patricia Prattis, an accomplished pianist, daughter of a former editor of the Negro newspaper, *Pittsburgh Courier.)* Is it possible that there is only one Negro educator qualified to be a Pittsburgh public school principal?" (There are now several.)

Within 10 years of that speech the hot winds of black power were blowing; the clenched fists of black defiance were raised; riots were disrupting our cities. I had raised the question on the Aaronsburg occasion. "Will there be time?" and the ensuing decade answered my question. There was not time! In closing I had said, "The awful question remains. Is the pendulum to swing now in a long alternate phase? Is history to reverse itself when the power shifts from our white Christian hands to those whose gods are as strange to us as we have made our white faces anathema to them?"

Everyone knew that I was not endearing myself to the conservatives of Pittsburgh. David Glick, one of Pittsburgh's most revered Jews, came forward and said to me, "Leland, if they put you out of the Duquesne Club for that speech I will get you into my club."

"And Gladly Teach"

By 1958 I would be eligible for retirement. I could elect, however, to remain active for an additional 3 years. I had long been inveighing against an arbitrary retirement age, yet I favored for the upper echelons of executives a change of jobs—I sometimes called it a shifting of gears—at age 65. In the mid-1950's, some three or four years ahead of age 65, I began thinking and talking with a few friends about a second career. George Taylor was one of them. We were seeing each other rather often in those days. In Washington, we frequently met at the Hay-Adams House. One day, in a pleasant parlor overlooking the park, with the White House in view, I opened the conversation in which we discussed various alternatives: full-time writing, teaching, governmental service. My own inclination was toward teaching; my writings and publications would be helpful. George Taylor was a good nondirective counsellor. He let me talk myself into a decision, simply saying at the end, "Leland, I think you have chalk in your blood."

In Pittsburgh the big streetcar university was, is, the University of Pittsburgh—over 20,000 students. Along side—campuses all but adjoining, divided only by one of Pittsburgh's gulches, known as "Panther Hollow"— was Carnegie Institute of Technology (now Carnegie-Mellon University). Andrew Carnegie's trade school had become by my time a complex of a good engineering school, a superior school of drama, an excellent school of architecture, a good school of fine arts, music, and painting—but mediocre in humanities. In the mid-1950's, William Larimer Mellon established at Carnegie Institute of Technology the Graduate School of Industrial Administration. George Leland Bach was the first dean of that school. He was a lithe man with an ascetic face—by all accounts of his pupils, a great teacher. He was a product of Grinnell and Chicago University's Graduate School of Business, a conservative by academic standards, a liberal by the standards of the national industrial establishment, but he made sense to our Pittsburgh industrial community. He appointed me a full professor of industrial administration and law, and I assumed the duties in late 1958.

The school, under the leadership of Bach and the early influence of Elliott Dunlap Smith, an early proponent at Yale of scientism in industrial management, was committed to the discovery of the fundamentals of the science of business, if indeed business is a science. The school's most distinguished academician in this field, Herbert A. Simon, is a true Renaissance scholar, distinguished as economist, sociologist, and political scientist. Herb Simon, with a face as sensitive as the face of Einstein, is one of the innovative thinkers of our times. Once in a big seminar, when he was talking about learning capacities of a computer, a fellow academician said to him, "Why do you study this material?" and his reply was, "Because I want to know how man thinks and I learn that from how a programmed computer behaves." One of his many citations credits him with employing computer science to revitalize the ancient and central problem of cognition in psychology. In 1967 he was elected to the coveted membership in the National Academy of Science. At the time of the School's tenth anniversary we held a symposium called, "Management and the Corporation: 1980." There were a dozen participants of national and international prominence. Barbara Ward (Lady Jackson) was seated next to me and Herb Simon was across the semicircle. "He has the face of a fanatic," Barbara Ward said to me. Before I could reply the television lights came on, but I thought silently that a few such men in all time have changed the course of human thought and action.

What a joke that the editorial comments would credit me with some leaven of practicality to the School! As a matter of fact, I did not wish to teach business management; I did not wish to teach law; I was interested in teaching humanities to business students. My most successful course turned out to be one called "Ideas and the Changing Environment." I employed ten ideas: the idea of man, deity, law, empire, change, government, freedom, chance, progress, and market. My materials were, for the most part, novels and historical novels; a few examples: Thomas Mann's *The Tables of the Law;* Thornton Wilder's *The Ides of March;* Charles Reade's *The Cloister and the Hearth;* Amy Kelly's *Eleanor of Aquitaine.* I employed Sophocles' *The Oedipus Cycle.* Possibly Antigone was my most useful character because she was the dissonant one in her revolt against the state (Creon), a prototype of our contemporary youth. The course stood up—an impracticality in a curriculum of science and applied science.

I taught some more practical courses: antitrust law, labor law, law as cultural material, but humanities for businessmen made my principal contribution to the curriculum. Even in the school's program for advanced managers—those who are brought in each year for a nine-weeks' refresher; even the no-nonsense vice-presidents and the horny-handed plant managers who came to that course stood still while we compared the characters of Moses, Oedipus, Julius Caesar, William the Conqueror, and the English Harold with respect to introversion, extroversion, effectiveness, and our 20th century standards of success. I often told my students, "This is the only useless course in the curriculum but the faculty has made it a requirement." That, during my tenure, was indeed the fact. The curriculum had been altered to make two semesters, one in the ancient and medieval world and one in the changing developments of America from colonial times to the Great Depression —the faculty had made these courses a requirement.

In truth I did not think that my course, Ideals and the Changing Environment, was useless, and my students, both the candidates for the master's degree and the mature executives, knew as much. I believe in the subjective hunch in business management, just as I recognize the role it has played in art, medicine, philosophy—in the development of society itself. All the great leaps forward in the growth of civilization occurred long before the scientific laboratory and the controlled experiment. Fire, agriculture, navigation, irrigation, the formation of the family, of the clan, of the tribe, of the larger community—all of these developments by which society, such as it is, hangs together today—occurred without benefit of research reports or the findings of royal or presidential commissions. I repeat that I am a Faustian man and a respecter of the scientific method. It is simply that where science is not ready to take over the job, the subjective judgment, the hunch, is all we have.

I believe that the hunch can be qualitatively developed by intellectual and emotional experiences. I believe that the love of a wife, the love of a poem, of a novel, of a symphony; I believe that a knowledge of the past, experiences in the discovery of identities as between and among apparently different periods in history— in short, I believe that a rich life of the mind and of the emotions make for improvement in the quality of subjective judgments in any area of life, in business not the least. To have felt, more than once, a choking in the throat and the forming of tears in the eyes at some exquisite passage of writing; to suddenly burst into uncontrollable laughter at some extravagant absurdity, pregnant with wisdom—enough of such long-forgotten experiences are the qualitative stuff on which the superior hunch is founded. Prove it? Of course, I cannot!

I suppose the fact that I taught Ideas and the Changing Environment for over 12 years in a school which rejects many more applicants for the master's degree than it accepts—a really tough lot of Young Turks—I suppose that fact is significant. Students who pay a high tuition or are bright enough to receive scholarships will not tolerate a waste of their time.

I was encouraged throughout most of the twelve years by Dean Bach's successor, Richard M. Cyert, and also by a colleague on the faculty, Allan H. Meltzer, an economist, who is learned in monetary and fiscal matters—and a Renaissance man who is a great teacher. They were stout in their support of the use of materials such as I have described as having a proper role in business education. The editors in a *Harvard Business Review* issue urged a spread of the humanities elements in the curricula of business schools. Dean Cyert told me the other day that such a spread had occurred. During one semester I was invited, at George Taylor's suggestion, to teach the course as a visiting professor at the Wharton School of Business at the University of Pennsylvania. The Dean and faculty at Wharton urged me to continue the course as a visiting professor, and I would have been glad to do that for a few years, but an invitation to spend an extended period as a management consultant in India precluded that plan. That was in 1962-1964.

In 1970 I said to Dean Cyert that I should not go on-and-on teaching in our Graduate School of Industrial Administration at Carnegie-Mellon. Although I had passed all established ages for retirement, the trustees had approved my annual appointments. Dean Cyert (now president of Carnegie-Mellon) said that I might well be right about my decision but added, "We want you to maintain an office and have a secretary here in our school. We would like you to be around. If you care to teach a course now and then, we shall be glad to have you do that." In 1971 Mary and I went to India for a sixth time where I updated my earlier experiences in that baffling land. I had earlier written two articles for the *Atlantic*: "Mahatma Gandhi Was Wrong" (July, 1964); and "Strong Medicine for India" (December, 1965). India is the victim of anachronistic bureaucracy. We went also for the first time, to Yugoslavia, where I studied the unique experiment of worker-management in industry—decentralization of decision making in that special communistic land. I am now (1972) teaching at Carnegie-Mellon University a small course on alternative models of society employing socialist India, in the grip of bureaucratic planning, and communist Yugoslavia, decentralized to the point of anarchy, as cases in point. I shall repeat the theme in the fall of 1972 using Sweden and Poland as models.

Lost Causes

I might well have done a better job of teaching if I had devoted myself exclusively to that work. I elected otherwise. My company continued me as a consultant and as a member of the Board of Directors. For seven years following the beginning of my teaching in 1959, I maintained an office on the corporate premises and all of the trappings of my earlier official status. I served on company management committees, such as the Appropriations and Policy Committee and the Tax Committee and continued as a director until age 72—the age limit for that position.

Some of my most gratifying business experiences occurred during that seven years. I had initiated important overseas corporate activities which came to fruition during that period. I participated in major litigation involving the United States Internal Revenue Service. We won the case (1971). This victory was even more gratifying than the antitrust case. I had literally made the facts in my advice to my client. Thus I was a principal witness as well as a consultant to the lawyers in the case.

In fact, the School approved my extracurricular activities. They helped to perpetuate the student's realization that even though I taught Greek plays I was in fact a manager. Furthermore, the School approved my espousal of ostensibly lost public causes because, almost invariably, I wrote about those causes, and my writings were published or, in any case, my speeches were prominently reported, so that the community-conscious student (a growing note in academia) knew that I was a public figure and, what may have been more important, frequently controversial.

My method of taking up a lost cause was almost casual. An invitation to speak would come—usually the request would include the statement that "anything you wish to speak about will be all right." Then, if my views on a matter of public concern were firm and the forum and timing seemed right, I would seize the opportunity. I never accepted an invitation to speak on just anything. A request came from James H. Rogers, father of Fred Rogers, creator of the original and now nationally successful children's program, Mister Rogers' Neighborhood. Would I address the Latrobe Chamber of Commerce on its big annual dinner to celebrate business-industry-education day? Latrobe is an old community of sizeable industry, about an hour's drive from Pittsburgh. It lies within the boundaries of Pittsburgh's commercial and cultural hegemony.

I had long watched the fragmentation of what I called real communities—the prevalence, for example, of the 129 little boroughs, townships, and other forms of mini-municipalities, "snuggling up to Pittsburgh for economic sustenance like little pigs at the teats of an old sow." Down to the moment, metropolitanism is, in the Pittsburgh area, a lost cause. It is pretty much a lost cause everywhere. The reason is entirely human and entirely understandable, but fragmentation is nonetheless a jeopardy to the viability of an urban region. There is a nostalgic pride of people whose grandfathers and fathers lived in an identified area. The area may have originally been prescribed by cowpaths or Indian trails or a brook —all now utterly irrelevant in an automobile, airplane, and television age, in which the old boundaries are as anachronistic for government as they are helpless and futile against a cyclone, pollution, or the depredations of a crime syndicate.

When the Latrobe invitation came I was ready to make another frontal assault—this time on provincialism and immobility in our Western Pennsylvania community. This is not to say that I accepted the assignment, or any other speech-making assignment, lightly. I continued to do my own research and writing, always with Mary's stout help. The making of a major address would take a good week of computable time out of my life and, of course, a non-computable amount of unconscious and subconscious activity, awake or sleeping. The Latrobe speech forecast my basic argumentation about urbanism, metropolitanism, and immobility; and, as it turned out, set for me a scope of activity for the next several years—activities which have left one goal, rapid transit for Pittsburgh, hanging in precarious balance down to the moment.

At Latrobe I knew that the word "metropolitanism" in Western Pennsylvania was an ugly word, so I used it, charging that ancient mini-political jurisdictions were the disease of our times. Indeed, the crises of both central city and suburbia mount so rapidly that what is bad about our presently highly-fragmented political economy will soon yield and what is good will find its cooperative place in a new functional metropolitanism. Some models are to be found, in Toronto, for example, where the Ontario provincial legislature forced consolidation of multiple municipalities in the Toronto area in order to effect rapid transit developments.

I paid my disrespects to suburbia, saying that people had been fleeing the central cities in pursuit of a vague notion about country life, often finding there only the worst of both city and country life. I quoted Ernest Van Den Hagg in the *American Scholar* for Autumn, 1959. His was only one of many eloquent voices deploring the conformity of suburbia, the de-individualization, the absence of spontaneity, the monotony of people of about the same age and income all getting up in the same houses, feeding, catching trains, returning, drinking cocktails, sleeping, and starting all over again. Van Den Hagg concluded that "Attempts to relieve the deadly boredom that oozes through the suburbs—by drinking, adultery, and nervous breakdowns—are usually unsuccessful."

There is the persistent delusion that the bucolic life is virtuous and the city life evil. Cain, after God put the curse upon him for the slaying of Abel, founded a city only because the curse condemned to infertility any land that Cain might till. But we have moved from the primordial societies, such as Cain's, in which it took 90 farmers to maintain themselves and one non-farmer, to recent times in which in America one farmer maintains himself and upwards of 30 other people. Technology has driven us to a non-agrarian society, but the cultural lag has saddled us with the unconscious delusion that the cities are not really the best way of life. To adjust our cities to their new role in the life of mankind is the greatest challenge of the 20th century.

Yet all excellence—literally almost all excellence—is to be found only in our cities, ancient and modern. There can never be more than a few great art galleries, museums of natural history, theaters, symphonies in any one metropolitan area. The stuff of excellence is limited. Fine conservatories, old trees, noble churches and cathedrals, gracious architecture, placid parks, comprehensive libraries, original manuscripts, rare books—of all of these, the central city has the greatest treasuries. There are not enough Picassos, prolific as that artist has been, to put even one in each shopping center.

The suburbs cannot afford even a full line of merchandise. Ask any central city department store manager if his branches in suburbia carry as many choices as his downtown store. If he is a friend of yours, he will say, "No." Herein lies one cause of the cultural blight of suburbia. (I often call the suburbs "cultural slums.") The choices are limited. Limited choices make for mediocrity and banality. Good tastes, good manners, sophistication are achieved from opportunities to make choices, selections, and rejections.

The flights from the city have involved mixed motives: desires to escape Negroes and school and housing integration; to escape city taxes; to raise dahlias and radishes and have better views of sunsets; to find better schools. There have been massive migrations from the city civilizations fomented by policies of the Federal Housing Administration and the Veterans Administration with rules, regulations, and mortgage guarantees which encouraged speculative builders to tumble housing units about the peripheries of our cities, to fall where they would like dice on a gambling table, miserably unplanned and architecturally unblessed, bought by pathetic young people unwarned that a real estate development is not necessarily a community. In 1963 there was little popular use of the word *ecology,* either in its biological or sociological sense. The real estate developer could function without regard to established transit corridors, with the assurance that, however remotely and absurdly he located his development, the automobile and gasoline lobbies, at local, state, and national levels, would assure roads and highways to his erstwhile cornfield.

Suburbia has drained off from our cities into cultural wildernesses the more economically competent citizens. Left are those who cannot flee the city—maintenance workers, policemen, utility operators, minority groups (Negroes, principally), and, of course, some professionals who must be close to their places of work, and praise be, enough city lovers, like Mary and me, to fight back. In general, however, the less affluent have been left to bear the burdens of maintenance of the central city and to be the tax-overburdened custodians of the central city's excellences.

I need not prolong the elaborations of these views. In a short few years they have become common in daily and periodical journalism. In 1963, it is now difficult to believe, these alarms had to be fished out of the works of a relatively small coterie of community planners and critics. Lewis Mumford, Jane Jacobs, Doxiadis, just for examples.

Two solutions are eloquently implicit in the facts. Metropoli-

Members of the Board of the Port Authority of Allegheny County: At the table, left to right: C. E. Palmer, Richard McL. Hillman, William L. Henry (Chairman), Senator Robert D. Fleming. Standing, left to right: Hal C. Davis, Frederick J. Close, Leland Hazard, Judge Loran L. Lewis, C. D. Palmer, K. Leroy Irvis (Representative, State Legislature of Pennsylvania).

Pittsburgh Renaissance in progress, 1969. The two bridges in the foreground have been removed and a jet of water 150 feet high arises from the very point. *Courtesy of Carnegie Library of Pittsburgh.*

tanism would enlarge the political boundaries of the central city to include what I have called, and continue to call, the real community—the community which is made by the radio and television —not by creeks, gulches, foothills, the random boundaries of nature, and the fortuitous circumstances of past cultures. Even without metropolitanism, the one single predominant factor which could make the modern real community effective would be rapid transit to keep God's great open spaces in vital association with God's great closed spaces. The automobile has become a deterrent to metropolitanism because it uses space out of all proportion to the mobility it provides. This was heresy a few years ago. It is not yet orthodoxy, but it is rapidly becoming so.

Very little research on facilities for mass and rapid transportation has been done during the past 50 years. Our cities, states, and federal governments had been busy building streets, roads, and expressways for motorized private passenger vehicles and trucks—and at the same time smothering railroads and tramways with taxation and regulation. The automobile has been the opium of the people. Now we know that it drugs us physically as well as spiritually. In consequence, the technologies of mass and rapid transportation have fallen far behind.

There are conditions that all-out research on facilities for mass and rapid transportation must satisfy. From suburbia to the central city and throughout the metropolitan complex, the service must be so inviting, regular, dependable, frequent, cheap, and comfortable that the people will forego the private vehicle for the public method. Within the central city itself there must be a separation of the pedestrian from his natural enemy, the private automobilist. This means that most of the private vehicles must be stopped before they enter the heart of the central city. Within the city proper there must be ramps, escalators, underpasses, and overpasses. Pedestrians must be free to move easily and comfortably apart from the lethal motor. There should be more taxicabs. They should be better designed and better maintained. They should not be so heavily taxed. So far as design is concerned, London cabs have long been a model into which a non-contortionist can enter with some degree of ease and grace. There must be gondola-type busses, such as a world's fair provides, easy for a man or woman with a baby in one arm and packages in the other to enter or leave, and they must move day and night about the retail and entertainment sections of the city. Big truck deliveries must be confined to hours other than the daytime rush periods.

At Latrobe I urged again that we continue to study the economies of free public transit. I said that the necessarily vast arrangements of transit facilities would require funds beyond the capacity even of metropolitan governments, that the federal government must establish standards of excellence in transit which would be conditions precedent to the required huge grants for the financing.

If all of this and much more seems to the reader something which he has heard before, let him try to recall when he first began to hear it in loud tones—only in quite recent times, he will find. One proof that I was a voice crying in the wilderness was the action of the *Pittsburgh Press,* which asked for permission to publish my Latrobe speech, 29 typewritten pages, triple space, in full, provided the *Press* could have an exclusive. Fortunately, I had marked the manuscript "copyright" and was able to satisfy the condition. The piece was published in full with a big spread. What is now respected but not yet predominate thinking was news as recently as 1963.

Works in Progress

An appointment to the Board of Directors of the Port Authority of Allegheny County has given much stress and strain to my advancing years. The Port Authority had been moribund for a number of years but was beginning to stir under the leadership of a new chairman, Judge Loran L. Lewis, a confidant and political associate of William D. McClelland, chairman of Allegheny County's governing body. McClelland was a former University of Pittsburgh football player of local repute under the famous coach, Jock Sutherland. He was a dentist and former Allegheny County coroner, an office which often leads on to political fortune in our community. Doc McClelland, although of the same Democratic party, was a political foe of David L. Lawrence and no friend of the Mellon establishment. His political strength lay not in the elements of our community which understood urbanism and metropolitanism, but rather precisely in those mini-municipalities against which I have often inveighed. When Loran Lewis brought to me Doc McClelland's invitation to become a board member of the Port Authority, he said, "We think we need the kind of thinking which you exhibited in your Latrobe speech."

After warning Loran Lewis, who I assumed would warn McClelland, that any solution of transit problems in Allegheny County would cost millions of dollars, I accepted. Loran Lewis' reaction to my "millions" was, "Oh, yes, I think we might have to spend as much as a hundred million dollars." In fact, the cost will be several times a hundred million. It turned out that, as chairman of the Rapid Transit Committee for the Port Authority, I went at times too fast to suit Loran Lewis, but on all of the major moves which have advanced rapid transit in Allegheny County, Commissioner McClelland supported me. Perhaps Doc McClelland's greatest contribution to rapid transit was the appointment of Frederick J. Close, Chairman of Alcoa, to our Port Authority Board. A magnificent salesman, Fritz Close was a prime mover for us in Washington.

The appointment to the Port Authority, which came within 60 days of the Latrobe speech, gave me the basis I needed for pushing rapid transit as the functional handmaiden of political metropolitanism. When I came to the Port Authority Board it was struggling with a worthy program to acquire some 33 privately-owned bus lines with wheezing equipment as archaic and inadequate as Pennsylvania's 1873 Constitution. These acquisitions were reasonable enough beginnings but they really had nothing to do with rapid transit. A bus is not rapid transit. It is mass transit in the sense that it will carry some thirty times the average number of persons carried by the private automobile, and therefore per square foot of space or per unit of atmospheric pollution it is better than the private automobile. But it is not rapid transit for the reason that the bus commingled with private automobiles and trucks can be no more rapid than the whole assortment of the low-powered, high-powered, underloaded, overloaded, flat-tired, dead-engined vehicles in the longitudinal complex. And when some youth (circa 1965) decides to share his driving responsibilities with a willowy female plastered to his right side, the whole community mass transit is subject to utterly unpredictable erotic vagaries.

I put the question: "More automobiles in the central city or more graceful urbanism?" Nine square feet are required for a human being per step of locomotion. In a traffic jam, the same human being in an automobile requires roughly 150 square feet. Yet, it is precisely in the central city where mobility and space are at a premium. Rapid transit on exclusive rights-of-way will eliminate, drastically minimize, the random movements by which we try to get from here to there in the private automobile or even in busses.

As to the economies, a rapid transit installation involves a cost of upwards of a billion dollars for a medium-size community like Pittsburgh, but the investment will pay off. Maintenance and operation costs of a modern efficient transportation system, including the debt service, will be less than will be the costs of policing, patrolling, parking, traffic courts, hauling away to hospitals and morgues the maimed and the dead from automobile accidents, coroner's inquests—the costs of the whole frustrating attempt to put our motorized camels through the eye of the municipal needle. The whole concept of trade-offs in community accounting was, still is, new. A huge job of education is still in progress.

I hammered away under speech captions, such as:
- The Challenge of Urban Obsolescence
- Mass Transit—A New Dimension For An Old Community
- The Central City—Island of Excellence—The Role of Rapid Transit
- Inertia and Our Cities
- Transportation and the Metropolis
- Technology and the Wheels of the Mind
- Technological Challenges for Urban Policy
- Inertia and Urbanism
- Transportation Strangulation
- New Movements by New Methods
- Pennsylvania Transportation: How To Catch Up With the Indians
- The Intermodality Aspect of Transportation
- Pennsylvania: To Go or Not To Go
- Transportation for Progress
- Transportation: The Importance of the Whole
- Society and Transit: 2000—A Serious Fantasy

The Westinghouse Electric Corporation has developed in our Pittsburgh area a new technology for transit—not new in the sense that it is patented or exclusive to Westinghouse but rather in the sense that it is a new combination of conventional components. Transit vehicles, running on exclusive rights of way, at ground level or underground or elevated, are computer-controlled. The vehicles are unmanned. The system is one of horizontal elevators running, of course, on fixed, exclusive rights of way.

The entire story of the development of civilization and of the ever-increasing comfort of mankind is the story of the replacement of manpower with the machine. For example, if we were still dependent upon the handmaking of shoes, then most of the world's population would be unshod—too large a proportion of the total manpower of the world would be required for shoemaking. The hand methods would be so inefficient and costly that the non-shoemakers of the world would not be able to purchase the product.

In the great cities of the world, whether American or European, the cost of transit vehicle operators varies from 90 percent to over 100 percent of the total receipts of the fare-box. This means that there is nothing left out of fare-box receipts for maintenance, for replacements, or extensions, expansions, or new types of equipment. In industry this condition is constantly corrected by the installation of new machines—labor-saving machinery. Technology can stand anything but manpower. John L. Lewis understood this; he never resisted the introduction of automation in coal mines. He *did* demand that those who retained jobs have their fair share of the savings of automation.

The development of public acceptance of fully-automated, non-manned transit, computer controlled, will be more complicated than John Lewis' acceptance of automation in coal mines. Although the records are eloquent on the fact that surface transit accidents are in large part the consequence of human failures, nevertheless there is a strong tendency on the part of human beings to trust other human beings rather than machines with their safety. However, there are encouraging signs to the contrary. People accepted automated elevators quite readily, even in buildings preponderantly used for medical services, where a very high percentage of elevator passengers are in some way physically impaired or psychologically timid.

Rapid transit came into the consciousness of the officials of Pittsburgh and Allegheny County almost as a shock. The City Planning Commission had no plans for rapid transit; the County

Planning Commission had no plans for a rapid transit. Under the guidance of the Allegheny Conference, which had no plans for rapid transit, smoke had been cleared away, parks had been created, new buildings had been put up, but transit had been out of mind—incredible but true.

It was the industrial community, stimulated by the Westinghouse developments, which at long last organized a First International Transportation Conference, to be held in February, 1966. The theme of the Conference was that Pittsburgh had a great deal of technical competence in transit hardware, and certainly that was true. Pittsburgh was the home of George Westinghouse's airbrake, which revolutionized railroading, and now a Westinghouse Company had come up with a whole new transit system. Steel, aluminum, glass, forgings, car manufacture in nearby Butler, there were dozens of makers of transportation components. The purpose of the First International Transportation Conference was to tell that to the world. Bennett Chapple and Frederick J. Close, of U. S. Steel and Alcoa, respectively, were the moderators — heavy metal and light metal sharing the honors.

Ten days before the scheduled date for the Conference, Bennett Chapple came to see me. "Leland," he said, "my face is red. We had expected to get the President of the United States to deliver the keynote address at our Conference. Apparently, we are not going to get him. Perhaps, for one reason, because I was an ardent supporter, as you know, of Barry Goldwater." I said nothing. Bennett Chapple continued, "I come here with my hat in my hand. Will you be second choice to the President and deliver the keynote address?" "Why not?" I replied. "Why should I be proud when transit is involved, and, in any case, who should complain about being second choice to the President?"

The Conference was attended by some 1300 registrants. There was a heavy snowstorm and a vast traffic jam on the day the delegates arrived, but the three-day Conference began substantially on time. R. K. Mellon was sitting at the head table because it was at that Conference that he would establish with a substantial grant a transportation research institute at Carnegie Institute of Technology, now Carnegie-Mellon University.

For my keynote address I had only to put together during the ten days, quite short notice, it is true, what I had been saying in the three years since my appointment to the Port Authority, always updating, always changing, always adding emphasis here and effecting de-emphasis there.

James P. Romualdi, active head of the new Transportation Research Institute, became my trusted technical advisor in all of my transit activities. The association has been a rewarding one. Transportation Research Institute publishes a series of research reports. In Number 4 my articles and speeches on transit, skillfully edited by Denton Beal, were published under the caption, *Leland Hazard on Transportation.*

In my collected transit writings I urged interim measures such as truck deliveries at night. I justified the practicality of the idea, pointing out the absurdity and waste of a 40-ton monster blocking a whole lane of a principal street to deliver a lady's dress—a motorized, belching bull in our municipal china closet.

More than once in the essays I explained computer-controlled transit trains. I was pleased that my engineer-editors treated my explanations respectfully. Romualdi noted that I want people to see their surroundings as they travel, that I wish transit to be a participation in the environment. I *did* think for a moment about lining the walls of subways with Titians and Picassos, but, of course, rejected the idea. There is no substitute for the amenities of above-ground transit environment.

As to costs, I often mentioned the fact that we move human waste at the taxpayer's expense; why not living human bodies? The open sewers of the past century were no more noxious and lethal than the auto-polluted air and the immobilized humanity of this century.

One consequence of my keynote transit address was my appointment as chairman of Governor Shafer's Committee for Transportation. He had made a campaign promise to consolidate the State's fragmented transit jurisdictions into one department of transportation. My blue ribbon committee, supported with $700,000 in research funds from the Commonwealth and private foundations, produced a wealth of basic transportation data and a design for a Department of Transportation. Governor Shafer's administration, because of acute partisanship in the legislature and internecine conflict within the Governor's own Republican Party, was not a happy one. Yet we put through a model law on a Department of Transportation for Pennsylvania. Curiously, Shafer's appointments to the key posts in the new department were all experienced in highways—not in rapid transit. He did not know, and, in his final general frustrations, would not ask, what a wealth of transportation skills exist. However that may be, we have the department and the structure is there for another governor some day yet to come to man more properly.

Transit, like war, is heady business. Once the subject is up, everyone knows just how it should be accomplished. Transit is dirty politics; it is not only the vicious competition among suppliers, and particularly between conventionalists and innovators in transit technology, but also that ineffable social devil, inertia. Furthermore, in our case we suffer the current misfortune of a nihilist mayor, riding the contemporary waves of taxpayers' revolts and citizen distempers. The grand days of the 1950's when Mayor Lawrence and R. K. Mellon never thought of politics when something big for the city was up—those days are gone. Now the establishment must fight for the opportunity to improve the community, and even the Allegheny Conference is timid.

William Henry, a highly placed officer of Gulf Oil Corporation, became chairman of our Port Authority. His acceptance of such a post was proof that the traditional gasoline-concrete-automobile lobby was relaxing its grip. Times *do* change.

In the End

Autobiographies often end on a note of frustration or in a philosophic vein about the importance of the journey rather than the arrival. I cannot pretend such objectivity. My failures would leave me inconsolable if I had not gained some successes, if a few friends and Mary had not approved me.

I do not think my public works have been unselfish. I needed to do them. I don't like an untidy society any more than a dirty street or a traffic jam. Compulsion drives me to attack sloth and banality. Despite all warnings and my own better judgment, I do take myself seriously—and pay some sort of price for that.

I do believe that to live is to function. Justice O. W. Holmes said it and his life proved it. I do believe also in the converse—not to function is to die—sometimes literally, always spiritually. I do not object to death but I cringe in craven fear at the thought of incapacity. Competence is maintained by performance. I *do* that I may continue to do so. Is it as simple as that? Perhaps the memory of the sight of my Boone County, Missouri, grandfather who sat useless for 30 years until eighty-one—I shudder.

I do not think I have changed, or improved, or gained wisdom in a long lifetime. I am impatient unless patience is necessary to an end; arrogant unless humility serves a purpose; weak and afraid until a cause makes me bold. I conceal my lack of affection for more than a few people by a love of mankind: contempt for the individual; concern for all.

There is a story that Robert E. Lee, asked by a fearful farm wife whether she should plant her garden just back of the weakening Confederate line, said, "Plant your seeds, madam, there is reward in the doing." He must have been right unless humanity has been deceived cruelly by the fates.

Index